£25.00

# Understanding Markets

By the same authors

An Introduction to Monetary Economics (Longman, 1985)
Government and the Economy (Longman, 1987)

Understanding Markets

An Introduction to the Theory, Institutions and Practice of Markets

Keith Bain
Senior Lecturer in Applied Economics
North East London Polytechnic

Peter Howells
Principal Lecturer in Applied Economics
North East London Polytechnic

HARVESTER · WHEATSHEAF
NEW YORK LONDON TORONTO SYDNEY TOKYO

First published 1988 by
Harvester · Wheatsheaf
66 Wood Lane End, Hemel Hempstead,
Hertfordshire HP2 4RG
A Division of
Simon & Schuster International Group

© 1988 Keith Bain and Peter Howells

All rights reserved. No part of this publication may be reproduced, stored in a retrieval system, or transmitted in any form, or by any means, electronic, mechanical, photocopying, recording or otherwise, without the prior permission, in writing, from the publisher.

Printed and bound in Great Britain by
Billing & Sons Ltd, Worcester

British Library Cataloguing in Publication Data

Bain, K (Keith), *1942–*
Understanding markets: an introduction
to the theory, institutions and practice
of markets.
1. Economics. Markets
I. Title II. Howells, P.G.A. (Peter G A)
1947–
338.5

ISBN 0–7450–0382–6

1 2 3 4 5 92 91 90 89 88

Contents

List of Figures	viii
List of Tables	ix
Author's Preface	xi
Acknowledgements	xiii

1	Characteristics of Modern Markets		1
	1.1	The nature of modern markets	2
	1.2	Demand and supply	11
	1.3	Prices and market clearing	16
	1.4	People and markets	23
2	Consumers in Product Markets		27
	2.1	Changes leading to shifts in demand curve	28
	2.2	A summary of influences on demand	38
	2.3	Some alternative notions	40
	2.4	Regulation of consumer markets	45
	2.5	The fairness of consumer markets	49
	2.6	The problem with government regulation	51
3	Firms in Product Markets		54
	3.1	Competition in Product Markets	54
	3.2	Product markets in practice	62
	3.3	Firms and their objectives	64
	3.4	Rivalry and competition	67
	3.5	Choice and strategies—firms in practice	67
	3.6	Small firms and failure	72
	3.7	Government intervention	73
4	The Labour Market		77
	4.1	The demand for labour	78
	4.2	The supply of labour	86

	4.3	Unemployment and the role of search	90
	4.4	The net advantages approach to wage differentials	91
	4.5	Price adjusting labour markets and the real world	93
	4.6	Distinctive features of labour markets	93
	4.7	A quantity adjusting labour market	103
5	The Markets for Money and Bills		106
	5.1	Characteristics	106
	5.2	The supply of money	112
	5.3	The demand for money	118
	5.4	Money market equilibrium	121
	5.5	Some difficulties	123
	5.6	The importance of flows	125
	5.7	The supply of bills	129
	5.8	The demand for bills	130
	5.9	The discount market	131
6	The Market for Bonds		145
	6.1	Characteristics	145
	6.2	The supply of bonds	150
	6.3	The demand for bonds	152
	6.4	The trading of bonds	160
7	Equities		165
	7.1	Characteristics	165
	7.2	The supply of equities	169
	7.3	The demand for equities	171
	7.4	The behaviour of share prices	175
	7.5	The buying and selling of equities	187
8	Foreign Exchange Markets		190
	8.1	Expressions of exchange rates	193
	8.2	The demand for and supply of foreign currencies	197
	8.3	Government intervention in foreign exchange markets	201
	8.4	Foreign exchange assets	206
	8.5	Market clearing and exchange rate systems	213
9	Commodity Markets		219
	9.1	The demand for and supply of commodities	219
	9.2	Commodity market problems	222
	9.3	Attempts to control supply	226

9.4	The protection of agriculture	230
9.5	International commodity prices	240
9.6	Futures markets in commodities	245

Index 250

List of Figures

1.1	Demand and supply	12
1.2	A fix-price market	17
1.3	Excess demand	22
2.1	An increase in demand	40
2.2	Veblen effects	42
2.3	Taxation and social costs	47
2.4	The effect of regulation on price	52
3.1	A supply response to an increase in demand	55
3.2	Demand for blood cell counters	57
4.1	A backward-bending labour supply curve	88
4.2	Demand for and supply of labour	89
4.3	A fix-price labour market	99
5.1	Money market equilibrium	112
5.2	The discount market and bank lending	132
6.1	The supply of bonds	150
6.2	The market for bonds	153
6.3	The term structure of interest rates	159
7.1	The market for equities	169
8.1	Demand for and supply of dollars	191
8.2	A fix-price foreign exchange market	214
9.1	A fall in demand	220
9.2	An increase in supply	222
9.3	An unstable equilibrium	224
9.4	A reduction in supply	227
9.5	A buffer stock scheme	229
9.6	The effect of subsidies	231
9.7	Consumer surplus	233
9.8	A variable levy	235

List of Tables

2.1	Effects of Changes on Demand	39
5.1	Relationships among Monetary Aggregates and their components	108
5.2	Banks' balance sheet (1)	114
5.3	Banks' balance sheet (2)	115
5.4	Banks' balance sheet (3)	116
5.5	Money Supply: Targets and Outturns	124
6.1	The effect of maturity on price variability of bonds	149
6.2	Government Bond Sales and PSBR 1980–86 (£m)	151
6.3	Selected Stock Exchange Transactions, July 1987	160
8.1	Pound Spot—Forward Against the Pound	192
8.2	Other Currencies	194
8.3	Sterling Index	196
9.1	Commodities Prices	246

Authors' Preface

This book shows students how markets work. 'How markets work' here means how they work in practice and therefore we have had to look at particular markets, and to include a certain amount of institutional detail. The book is intended as a response to the needs of what we think is a large number of undergraduate students. These are students who have come to economics as intending non-specialists, in Business Studies, in Sociology or in Accounting or Finance, for example. Their interests are in particular markets first, the markets for labour or for financial assets or for products, and in economic theory only second. However, the book is also intended to stimulate those students of economics as a major discipline who were attracted to it by its apparent promise to say something about the world they observe for themselves and through the media. Anyone who chose to study economics because he hoped to understand the *Financial Times* will, we hope, find this book rewarding.

The choice of markets is not uncontroversial. We were guided by what experience suggested to us students were generally interested in. However, being utterly faithful to this principle would have produced a very long book and so we included a second, which was that a market had also to demonstrate the operation of some general economic principle which would not otherwise appear. Thus the market for products introduces the usual framework of price, income, taste and substitutes, the labour market introduces income and substitution effects, while the markets for bonds and equities in particular demonstrate the importance of expectations.

In choosing to discuss markets as they work in practice we have, inevitably, set ourselves another theme.

This is that markets do not generally function as outlined in conventional economic theory. This might not matter, except to economic theory, were it not for the fact that the merits of the market system have been heavily promoted by politicians and administrators in recent years *as if* they yielded the benefits listed in the text books. Unfortunately people *do* take the decisions whose consequences become apparent only over time, they take them on poor information, in markets dominated by a few major participants, in markets subject to extensive regulation, where it is quantity rather than price which adjusts, where stocks dominate flows, and where the market power of individuals is predetermined by non-market allocations of wealth, income and privilege.

K. Bain
P.G.A. Howells
December 1987

Acknowledgements

We are grateful to the following for their permission to use copyright material:

The publishers of the *Financial Times* for tables 8.1, 8.2, 8.3, 9.1, and for material in case studies 5.1, 5.2, 5.3;
Her Majesty's Stationery Office for figures contained in tables 6.2 and 6.3;
The Royal Economic Society for the quotation from J.M. Keynes, *General Theory* in chapter 7;
The Bank of England for material incorporated in table 5.1 and figure 6.3.

We wish also to thank Peter Johns of Harvester · Wheatsheaf for his help and suggestions at many points in the preparation of this book.

1 Characteristics of Modern Markets

Markets are simply arrangements to allow one thing to be exchanged for another. The image most people have of a market involves the sale of a good directly for money as in a street market. But such transactions make up only a small proportion of total market activity. Far more sales are made in large retail stores, by wholesalers, or through brokers. Exchanges can be arranged by mail, telephone, telex or computer link. Buyer and seller often do not meet face to face.

We can talk of markets for virtually anything—for cornflakes, videos, holidays in Spain, textile machinery, stocks and shares, government bonds... Many markets, however, have much in common. After all, the arrangements for selling pins are very similar to those for selling needles. For many purposes it is sufficient to group markets into those for products, assets, and labour.

Where it is helpful, these aggregate markets can be subdivided. For example, we may divide products into goods and services or into tradables (exports and import-competing goods) and non-tradables. Asset markets may be divided into those for capital assets (such as machinery and buildings which may themselves be used in production) and for assets which are principally a way of holding wealth. The latter, in turn, include both real assets such as paintings, diamonds, and rare stamps, and financial assets such as bonds, equities, pension entitlements, or money itself. Alternatively, we may concentrate on important groups of products or assets. In this book, for instance, we pay particular attention to markets for equities, foreign exchange and commodities.

Markets may be classified as wholesale or retail, depending on whether or not the purchaser is the final user. They may also be classified by geographical area. Labour economics deals with local and regional labour markets. For internationally traded goods and services we talk of the world market.

1.1 THE NATURE OF MODERN MARKETS

1.1.1 Contracts

Transactions such as the purchase of tomatoes in a street market are a misleading guide to the nature of modern markets.

To begin with, products are often not exchanged directly for money. Consider some possible transactions. When people buy consumer durables (washing machines, videos, etc.), they may pay for them in instalments, or use credit cards and then repay the credit card company over an extended period. The vast majority of people who buy houses only come to own them after making mortgage payments for twenty or more years. Most workers are paid in arrears—usually at the end of a week or month. People sell dollars 'forward'. That is, they agree to sell dollars in perhaps thirty or ninety days time. A person selling dollars forward will not usually have them at the time the agreement is made. There are many examples especially in the financial world of people selling things they do not yet own. In international commodity markets it was possible in October 1987 to buy November 1988 potatoes, March 1989 cocoa and other products yet to be grown. Many market transactions, then, involve an exchange not of goods for money now but of contracts to pay, to deliver, or to work at some time in the future. This strongly influences the nature of modern markets.

1.1.2 Lack of knowledge

The street market is misleading also because it suggests that people can easily judge the quality of what is being sold and compare the prices being charged by different sellers. Often neither of these things is true. Many products are technically complex. Their performance and reliability must be taken on trust. Sometimes a product comes with a promised after-sale service whose quality cannot be known in advance.

The sheer number of types of many products makes it impossible for consumers to be fully informed about all of them. Videos, for example, are produced by several companies with each one offering a variety of models. The price of any one model may differ from one shop to another.

To make things even more difficult, people can't know what is going to happen to prices in the future; and there is a constant flow of new models, sometimes little changed from older ones. The prospect of future changes in product quality or price is especially important since many market decisions concern not just what or from whom to buy, but also whether to buy now or later.

1.1.3 The importance of time

Time is crucial for both sellers and buyers. Sellers must store unsold stocks of goods and storage may be expensive. They may have to order goods for future sale a long time in advance. For example, a Christmas card company needs to design cards for Christmas in the summer and autumn of the previous year, before it even knows how its cards for the coming Christmas will sell. Decisions about future orders will influence the speed at which the existing stock has to be sold.

Buyers would usually be able to make wiser purchases if only they had more time. Consider the hurried choices of travellers from railway book stalls. Or people who, because of shortage of time, buy all their groceries at one shop, although they know that many of the goods are likely to be cheaper elsewhere.

1.1.4 The range of motives

The motives of buyers and sellers vary widely. Tomatoes bought in a street market will be eaten soon after. Some purchases, however, are of goods which will be used for a time and then re-sold. Only a small proportion of car buyers intend to drive the car they buy until it falls apart. Potential re-sale value of a product can, therefore, be very important. In financial markets especially, an asset may be bought solely to be re-sold later.

Sellers may sell at a loss in order to break into a market or to prevent others from entering one. Or they may sell cheaply because they need to meet debts which are due for payment.

1.1.5 Property rights

There used to be a saying: 'possession is nine points of the law'. Someone buying tomatoes to eat in the next few days will not worry much about the legal right of the trader to sell them. However, people purchasing goods which won't be delivered for some time or which are to be consumed only slowly or not at all will be very interested in the question of legal rights to sell.

Equally, producers will be very concerned to retain the sole right to sell their product. This is not as easy as it may seem since products often contain designs or ideas which can be copied by others. Brand names or distinctive labels can be copied. Technological advance has made imitation of many products much easier. Audio and video tapes and computer software are pirated; books are photocopied and records borrowed and taped. All such activities undermine the operation of markets. Governments introduce patent and copyright laws to try to prevent them, but such laws are difficult to enforce. And it is very hard to obtain international agreement on these issues.

The important general point is that if markets are to operate in an orderly fashion and people are to be fairly rewarded by them for their efforts, some form of regulation is necessary. There are other reasons for regulating markets, but here we have the most basic- the need to establish clear and enforceable rights of ownership.

1.1.6 Public and private goods

If clear property rights must be established before a market can operate effectively, we have another problem to deal with. Consider what is meant by private ownership of something.

A person who buys a product expects that other people cannot also own it. If one person buys and eats a hamburger, it is perfectly obvious that other people cannot eat the same hamburger. Hamburgers, and most other things, are private goods. Consumption of them is competitive—if you own them, someone else can't.

But there are some goods and services where this does not apply. Suppose the light from a street lamp allows you to avoid a large hole in the footpath. You have benefited from the light, but this has not reduced the amount of light available to other people. Consumption is not competitive. What, then, if street lamps were not provided by local councils but had to be provided through a market? Although you benefit from the light, you may be unwilling to pay towards the cost of erecting the lamp, because you realise that people who do not pay (free riders) will still benefit from it. But if everybody thinks in the same way, the market will not provide the product although the community really wants it.

It follows that a market is only likely to work properly if people who do not pay for a product can be excluded from benefiting from it. And there are some products, like the light from street lamps where this is impossible. These are known as public goods. There are not many examples of pure public goods, but some of them are important, including national defence. How many others can you think of?

It is generally accepted that markets cannot operate for public goods. They must be provided and paid for collectively, with everyone being compelled to contribute through taxation. It is worth noting that once a public good is provided, it is there for all people, even those who do not benefit. In other words, people cannot, as individuals, reject them. A street lamp exists for blind people too, even though for them it is just another obstacle. People who are opposed to Trident missiles are defended or endangered by them to exactly the same extent as people who are in favour of them.

1.1.7 Social costs and government intervention

Most private goods have an element of public goods, in the sense that both the production and the consumption of them impose costs on or give benefits to people other than those who buy or sell them: even the sale of hamburgers leads to litter in the streets. These are known as externalities or as social costs and social benefits. The best examples on the production side are the environmental ones—power stations which cause acid rain, nuclear plants which dump waste into oceans, or aeroplanes which make a lot of noise in taking off and landing. On the consumption side, as well as the litter from fast food shops, there are the accidents caused by drunken drivers, the irritation and health damage to others produced by smokers, and many others. These are all examples of social costs. Can you think of examples of social benefits arising from either production or consumption?

The existence of externalities may provide a reason for government intervention in markets—to ensure that the prices at which products are bought and sold reflect the full costs and benefits to the society of their production and consumption, not just the costs and benefits to the sellers and buyers.

However, Ronald Coase, an American economist, suggested that social costs only arise in market economies because property rights are not adequately defined. Let us take an example to explain what he meant. Consider the case of a firm which dumps chemical waste into a river estuary with the result that people who eat fish caught nearby suffer from mercury poisoning. According to Coase the market could find a solution to this problem if only the right to make use of the estuary was clearly defined.

The government could give the firm the right to use the estuary as it wished. Then, if people wanted to eat mercury-free fish, they would need to buy this right from the company. The market would establish a price for the right which would depend on how strongly each group wanted it. Alternatively, the legal right could be given to the community. Then if the firm wished to dump its waste into the river it would need to buy the right from the people. Again a market price would be established. Once the property right had been granted, no government intervention would be required. We could be said to have 'internalised an externality'.

Coase went further and showed that if firms were very small, if everyone had perfect information, and if there were no costs involved in negotiation, it would not matter which side was granted the legal right of use. The market price established for the property right would be the same in the two cases. But this is far removed from reality.

In the real world, people lack knowledge both about what happens and about likely consequences. In our mercury example, many people will not know about the activities of the firm. Some will become ill and die without the cause being established. It may not be known over what area fish will be contaminated or what levels of contamination will in the long term seriously damage people's health. The firm, too, may be large, with considerable resources at its disposal to influence the nature and the amount of information available to the public.

Further, the 'community' is not a single group. There may be conflict between the fishermen and the company's workers who will be worried that if the price for the right to use the river becomes too high the factory will close and they will lose their jobs. The local shopkeepers will have a point of view. Market negotiations will be long, complicated and costly. Some people will have more say than others. Future generations, who may well be affected by the outcome, will not be represented in the negotiations at all. Despite the existence of a clear property right, government intervention may still be needed to protect some groups of people.

Coase's argument, however, is an important one. We cannot simply say: 'Ah! here are some social costs. This is a case for the government'. Sometimes the market mechanism may provide the best solution to a problem involving externalities. Also, in some circumstances, although regulation of a market is required it may be best to rely on self-regulation, with the sellers controlling their own activities.

Nonetheless, in our complex world a good deal of government regulation of market activities is necessary in the interests both of some market participants and of people outside the market who are affected by what happens within it. No doubt you can think of many examples—consumer protection legislation, health and safety at work legislation, planning and zoning requirements are just a few. In recent years we have seen the growth of a strong demand for the removal of many of the regulations which limit market behaviour—the issue of 'deregulation' of markets. Some people indeed are in favour of the removal of almost all controls on markets. At a recent Conservative Party conference a participant was heard to say: 'The market is magic'. We shall return to the question of regulation frequently.

1.1.8 The importance of information

For markets to work well, market participants must be well-informed. To make sensible decisions, consumers should know the nature, quality and prices of available products both now and in the future, and be able to estimate accurately what is likely to happen to their incomes. Workers should know where jobs are available and what qualifications are required, in addition to the rates of pay, work conditions and future prospects in different jobs. Producers should know which products consumers wish to buy and the quality and cost of the labour and capital needed to produce them. Yet such things are commonly not known.

Market participants face three sorts of information problem. Firstly, information which is available free of charge takes time to collect and to analyse. But time itself is a scarce resource. Most people can readily think of things they would rather do with their time than stand in front of supermarket shelves reading labels on cartons, or reading advertisements pushed through their letterboxes. All information, then, has an opportunity cost (that is, to obtain more information one must give up something else—even if it is only an extra five minutes at home in front of the television with one's feet up).

Secondly, a lot of available information is not free. In order to collect it, one might need to buy newspapers or magazines, make phone calls, write letters, or travel considerable distances.

Thirdly, in many cases people do not know what information is available or where they might get it, or are not able to understand the information which is available. Since many products sold in modern markets are highly specialised and technical, it may require considerable training and experience to be able to assess them.

Sometimes experts—lawyers, accountants, consultants, brokers, agents—may be hired either to interpret material which is especially difficult to understand, or to provide information speedily and thus help to overcome the problem of the shortage of time.

This has all meant that one of the fastest growing markets in recent times has been that for information itself. Its rate of growth has been greatly increased by developments in communications satellites and computer technology. Change in the information industry has in turn led to changes in other markets, above all in financial markets.

Because information costs both time and money, participants in all markets have another decision to make. Buyers must weigh up the expected benefits from and costs of obtaining extra information. We all do this even if we do not think of it in quite this way. We may go to several shops to price a product we wish to buy, but then decide that it is not worth our while to go to yet more shops. Or we may collect twenty brochures on holidays in Spain but only read the first five.

The idea has been formalised in the proposition that people go on seeking information only as long as the expected benefits from doing so (the benefits resulting from being able to make a better decision) are greater than the costs involved.

1.1.9 Uncertainty and self-validating markets

It is true that the less information we have, the less certain we can be of the outcome of a decision. But even if we have a great deal of information, the results of market actions may be very uncertain. This is so because the wisdom or folly of most market decisions depends on future events. To help us make decisions we must make estimates of or guesses about the future.

Now it is a characteristic of all markets that market behaviour may be self-validating—if enough people in a market act as if something is true, their behaviour may make it come true. If enough people think a particular model of car is unreliable, its sales will plummet and it may have to be withdrawn from the market whether or not it is unreliable. Or again, if many people believe that the prices of shares on the stock exchange are about to fall and endeavour to sell their shares in advance of the fall, the increased supply of shares on to the market will force prices down.

It follows that anyone who wishes to make a consistent profit from buying and selling shares really needs to know how other people are going to behave: to know, in other words, how other people make their guesses about the future; or, to use the language of modern economics, how other people form their expectations about the future.

This has important implications for governments, since they are particularly interested in the behaviour of major markets in the economy. After all, unemployment arises from decisions made in the labour market; the exchange rate of sterling is determined in the foreign exchange market; the rate of inflation derives from product and financial markets. And all of these markets influence each other. The economic policy decisions of governments must necessarily be based on what they think is likely to happen in such markets.

This has led to a large growth in the forecasting industry which has been particularly important for governments. A government cannot decide effectively how to intervene in a market, how much or when to intervene, unless it is confident that it knows what is likely to happen in that market in the absence of intervention, and what effect intervention will probably have.

1.1.10 Uncertainty and insurance

In many markets, some form of insurance is available to help to reduce uncertainty. For example, people may take out health insurance to overcome the problem that they cannot know when they will become ill or what health care will cost. Shipowners insure their ships against all manner of hazard. Organisers of sports events insure against the possibility of bad weather affecting their attendances.

Markets develop for insurance itself. At Lloyds of London, insurance contracts are traded on the floor of an exchange just as any other product might be. Insurance premiums are then determined by the degree of risk involved, and by the amount of competition in the market.

People can insure against untoward future developments in other ways than through insurance contracts. We talked earlier of people selling foreign currency forward. Many who do this are engaged in speculation—trying to make a profit by outguessing the market. However, companies also use forward exchange markets to provide a form of insurance. Thus, an exporting company may know that it will receive a payment in US dollars in three months' time. It may then use the forward exchange market to protect itself against the possibility of a fall in the value of the US dollar over the next three months. The cost of this transaction is equivalent to an insurance premium. Insurance can be provided also through futures markets in commodities and financial assets.

Naturally, there are problems with insurance. In many markets, insurance is not readily available or is very expensive. Moreover, people who need most insurance often face the highest premiums. Anyone with a history of past illness usually can obtain health insurance (if at all) only at very high cost.

Insurance is extremely important in a market system, but it necessarily falls a long way short of completely overcoming the problem of lack of knowledge of the future.

1.2 DEMAND AND SUPPLY

1.2.1 Demand schedules and curves

Markets bring together people wishing to buy a product and those able and willing to supply it. Buyers show the strength of their demand by the amount they purchase at the existing price. It is possible to imagine people estimating the amount they would be willing to buy, in existing circumstances, at each potential price of the product. This would be a demand schedule. They could go further and convert the schedule into a demand curve, by plotting on a graph the quantity they would be prepared to buy at each price.

If we knew each person's demand curve for a product we could add together all the individual demand curves and construct a total demand curve for it. Each product sold has such a notional demand curve. Sellers cannot know precisely what this curve is like but they can obtain information about it through market research on the attitudes of would-be purchasers, or by observing what happens in practice to the amount of a good sold when its price is changed. Demand for almost all products is believed to be greater the lower are their prices. In other words, demand curves generally slope down to the right (they are negatively sloped) as with the line D in fig. 1.1.

12 *Understanding Markets*

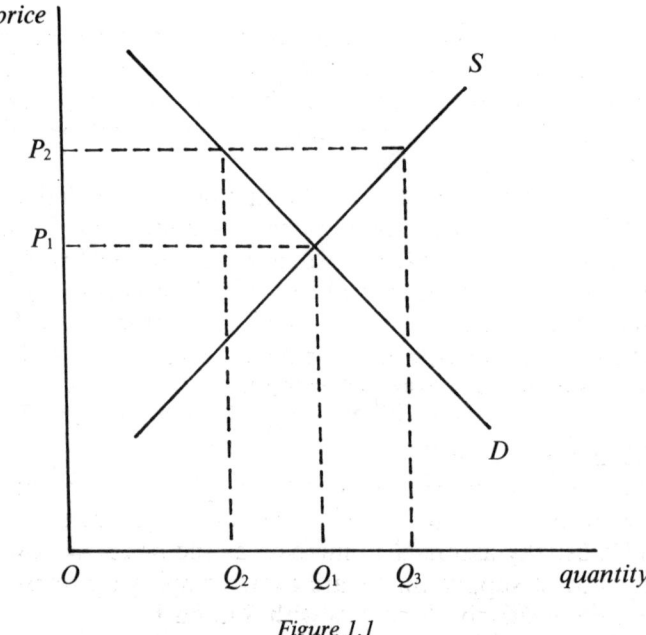

Figure 1.1

This is based on a particular view of the consumption choice. We imagine an individual consumer who has a given income and spends it on goods and services. We can broaden the picture by allowing the purchase of financial assets also (bonds, bank deposits, etc.). We can then regard these financial assets as current savings, while the purchases of goods and services constitute consumption expenditure. The aim of the consumer is to obtain as much satisfaction as possible (to maximise utility) from the available income.

The framework of analysis here is one of opportunity cost—the purchase of one product is at the expense of another. A decision to buy a financial asset rather than a good or service is a choice in favour of current savings at the expense of present consumption. However, since the purpose of current savings is to provide a future income, we can say that people using money to buy financial assets are sacrificing present consumption so that their future consumption will be greater.

To this is added a proposition about human tastes—that the more of a good one has, the less satisfaction one will obtain from an extra unit of it, and hence the less of other things one will be prepared to give up for that extra unit. Then we enquire into the effect of a change in the price of the product on demand for it, on the extremely important assumption that nothing else changes.

This form of analysis can be applied to the demand for anything. Thus, we can have a firm's demand curve for labour on the assumptions that the firm is seeking to maximise profits and that the stock of capital with which labour is to work is constant. Or we can have a demand for money or for foreign exchange. In all cases the framework is very rigid and, as we shall see in chapter two, rather limited.

1.2.2 Supply curves
In the same way we can construct a supply curve for a product, showing the amount sellers are willing to sell at each price. This is usually assumed to increase as the price on offer rises and so most supply curves are drawn sloping up to the right (they are positively sloped) as with S in fig 1.1.

1.2.3 Demand elasticities
For sellers, it is not enough to know that the demand curve for a product slopes down to the right. They need also to know how much extra of the product consumers will demand for each fall in its relative price.

If a small proportional change in the price of a product leads to a larger proportional change in the demand for it (say a 1 per cent fall in price leads to a 1½ or 2 per cent rise in the quantity demanded), we say that the demand is price elastic at this point. The more elastic demand is, the greater will be the change in the quantity demanded for a given change in price. But if demand changes by proportionately less than the change in price, demand for the product at its present price is said to be inelastic.

We can express this formally by saying that the price elasticity of demand for X equals:

$$\frac{\Delta Q_x / Q_x}{\Delta P_x / P_x}$$

where Q_x is the quantity of X demanded at price P_x and ΔQ_x is the change in demand for X which will follow from ΔP_x, a *small* change in the price of X. For a normal demand curve, this formula will produce a negative result, since an *increase* in the price of a product will lead to a *decrease* in the demand for it and vice versa.

But what determines how price elastic demand is likely to be? Consider the case of a rise in the price of a product. If people buy less of it but there is no change in the total amount of money they spend, they must be switching to some extent from the product whose price has risen to other things. The more they switch, the more the demand for the original product will have fallen and the more price elastic we can say the demand for it is. It follows that the price elasticity of demand for a product will depend on the extent to which people's wants can be satisfied by other things: that is, by the extent to which there are good substitutes for it. We shall expect the demand for products for which there are good substitutes to be price elastic; those with no close substitutes to be price inelastic. Let us take some examples.

We might expect the demand for Kelloggs cornflakes to be relatively price elastic. Why? Because there are other brands of cornflakes which seem to many people to be fairly similar and other types of breakfast cereal may also be a satisfactory alternative for many. Kelloggs cornflakes may not need to rise much in price before people start thinking about alternatives. Of course, Kelloggs try to persuade people through advertising, distinctive packaging and special offers on their packets that their cornflakes are very different from others. If they succeed in doing so, they will reduce the elasticity of demand for their product and be able to raise the price with less fear of losing sales.

Consider next the demand for breakfast cereals as a whole. There are still substitutes. Many people do not have cereals for breakfast, and people who do not have them may not be enthusiastic about a switch to pancakes and maple syrup, devilled kidneys or croissants. However, if cereals rise a good deal in price relative to other things, many people may switch away from them. But a small change in price may only lead to a small change in quantity demanded. Thus, we might expect the demand for breakfast cereals as a whole to be less price elastic than the demand for one particular brand of cornflakes. We can apply the same reasoning to other products. What would you say, for instance, about the likely price elasticity of demand for cigarettes, for caviar, for children's clothing, for shares in British Gas, for haircuts, for house mortgages? In some cases it is not easy to decide whether or not there are close substitutes for a commodity. Economists have argued amongst themselves for many years over whether or not there are assets which are close substitutes for money.

1.2.4 Supply elasticities

We can talk too about the elasticity of supply. Supply of a product at the existing price is said to be elastic if a small change in its price persuades sellers to change the amount they offer to the market by a relatively greater amount—where, for instance, at a 1 per cent higher price the seller is willing to increase supply by more than 1 per cent.

We can apply the same formula for calculating the elasticity of supply as for the elasticity of demand. Note here, however, that the answer is very likely to be positive since a small increase in the price of a product will usually lead to an *increase* in the amount of it offered to the market by sellers.

But what will determine how much extra will be offered for sale? Since most sellers are interested in making a profit, they will be concerned with the relationship between costs of production and prices. The elasticity of a supply curve will thus depend on the costs of providing an extra unit of the product.

For example, it is usual to accept that supply of many goods can only be increased quickly at great cost—by transporting additional supplies from elsewhere, or by paying workers high overtime rates of pay. Average costs of production will rise considerably as output is increased. In such circumstances sellers will only be willing to increase supplies at sharply higher prices. The supply curve will slope steeply up to the right (supply is highly price inelastic at existing prices). But given more time, sellers will be able to search for and find other cheaper sources of supply. Supply will become more price elastic.

In some industries, over a longer time period still, larger outputs will allow the purchase of better machinery, the construction of a new factory, or the reorganisation of production so as to increase productivity. In such industries increases in output may be possible with unchanged or lower average costs of production and the supply curve may become flat (with constant average costs) or even slope down to the right (with decreasing average costs).

1.3 PRICES AND MARKET CLEARING

We can see already that prices play a special role in the market process. The price level at which demand and supply curves cut each other (P, in fig. 1.1) is the only price at which the amounts demanded and supplied are exactly equal. It is known as the market clearing price. It is an equilibrium price both because at that price the market is in balance and because, unless something happens to shift the supply curve or the demand curve, there will be no tendency to move away from it.

1.3.1 Fix-price markets

Suppose, however, that the price being charged in a market is above the equilibrium or market clearing level. Say it is at P_2 in fig. 1.1. We can see that at this price the quantity of the commodity being demanded (Q_2) is less than the quantity which sellers are willing to supply (Q_3). Several things might happen here depending on the nature of the product and the characteristics of the market.

In many markets, nothing will happen immediately. The sellers will not sell all that they have for sale and will store what they do not sell. The market will remain out of equilibrium (or in disequilibrium). Naturally, this can only happen if storage is possible—there are obvious limits to the extent to which some goods can be stored. Sellers must also take into account the fact that storage costs money. They may not wish to store goods for long periods of time even if they could. What else can they do?

They may be able to reduce their future orders. Consider a

shop which has in stock ten short-sleeved shirts of a particular style and has plans to order an additional ten shirts of the same style per week for the rest of the summer. But currently the shop is only selling five of the shirts per week. The likely response is to reduce the weekly order. If a number of shops act in the same way this will affect the plans of the wholesaler and ultimately those of the manufacturer of the shirts. The styles of shirt produced may change, or workers may be moved to the production of other goods. If demand falls in all lines of production, the firm may lay off workers or even go out of business. There may be an increase in unemployment. All of this might happen without there having been any change in the price of the shirts.

Take as another possibility a company which prints Christmas cards. It is given a limited amount of display space in large retail shops and the shops buy designs of cards which they think will sell to the public. However, the card company

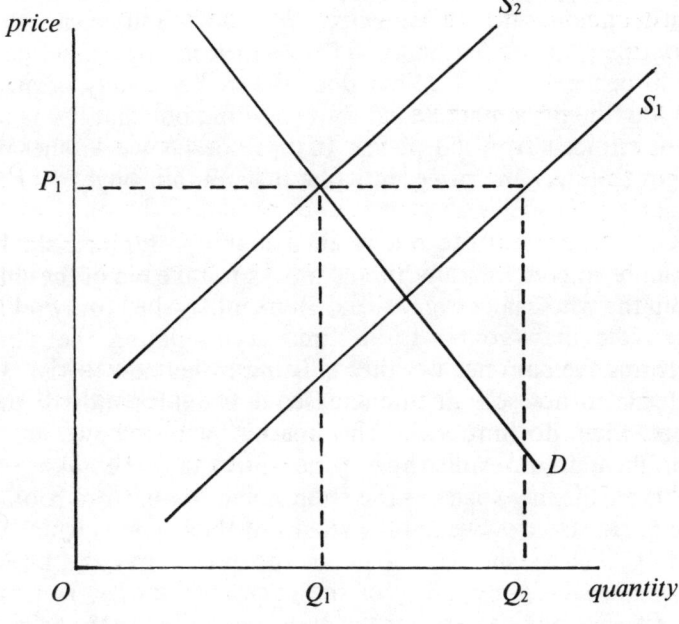

Figure 1.2

notices that a couple of designs are not selling well and are taking up too much of the limited display space. It responds by withdrawing those cards and replacing them with other designs which are selling well. What happens to the withdrawn cards? Usually they will be destroyed, with the company bearing the loss involved. Here too, the price does not change.

Both of these examples can be illustrated as in fig. 1.2.

The supply curve has moved up from S_1 to S_2. Both the price and the quantity sold have remained unchanged at P_1 and Q_1. Note that we have moved to a new equilibrium position (the quantity demanded again equals the quantity supplied at the existing price) but not through a change in price. Such a market is known as a quantity adjusting or fix-price market. There are many such.

1.3.2 Flex-price markets

But sometimes prices do change in response to market pressures. Take the case of a woman with a barrow in a street market at 5 p.m. on a Saturday afternoon. She won't be in the market again until the following Wednesday and has a tray of very ripe pears on her hands. There is little interest in her pears at 40 pence a pound. What does she do? She may begin by leaving the price unchanged, but shouting out that it has just been reduced from 50 pence. If that doesn't work, she may begin to lower the price until she does obtain buyers for the fruit.

Or we can return to our retailer of shirts. Suppose she has actually entered into a written contract to take ten of the shirts from the wholesaler every week. Remember, she is only selling five. She may go on for a time accumulating the shirts. Perhaps the summer weather is being rather too British and she thinks there will be an increased demand for short-sleeved shirts when it improves. If this doesn't happen, however, she will have to do something. The shirts may be taking up valuable display space in the shop. Even in the store room at the back, space is needed for stocks of those goods which are selling well. If she tries to cram too much into the limited storage space, the quality of the goods will suffer. Her only alternative may be to lower the price and advertise the shirts as a special offer. By trial and error, she may find the price which just equates supply and demand (that is, will sell ten shirts a week).

Now we have looked at two cases where we may have moved to a new equilibrium as a result of a changing price. In fig 1.1, neither the demand curve nor the supply curve has moved but we have gone from the original price of P_2 to the equilibrium, market-clearing price of P_1. A market where this occurs is said to be price-adjusting or flex-price.

1.3.3 Instantaneous market clearing

You will have noted, however, that in both flex-price cases, the price adjustment may have taken some time. Yet economic theory uses a quite different possibility to represent the ideal behaviour of markets, known as instantaneous market clearing. This means that if a market is out of equilibrium, the price in the market will change immediately so that we move without delay to a position like P_1Q_1 in fig. 1.1. This is equivalent to assuming that markets are never out of equilibrium. But it not easy to think of markets where anything like it occurs.

Perhaps the large-scale financial markets which operate in centres like the City of London come closest to it. Here the large number of very large deals, the operation of brokers, and the use of advanced communications technology which gives buyers and sells up-to-the-minute information about what is happening in the market, lead to constant small fluctuations in prices. But even highly sophisticated markets like these sometimes behave more like fix-price markets than flex-price ones.

1.3.4 Stability and Instability

Consider a market which is already in equilibrium. Suppose now that for some reason the price rises and the market moves out of equilibrium. Our flex-price assumption is that the price will eventually fall back to the original equilibrium level. If this does happen, the equilibrium is said to be stable.

However, even if we are temporarily at a stable equilibrium, demand and supply conditions may change rapidly (and demand and supply curves may shift about a good deal). Where this does not happen and thus the curves are thought likely to remain in the same places for relatively long periods, market conditions are also said to be stable.

It is important to know if market conditions are stable or not since, if things do not change over time, it is fairly easy to predict what is going to happen in the future. Thus, the words *stable* and *predictable* are often linked. But, there are certainly cases where a market equilibrium is unstable (if we move away from the old equilibrium price, there will be no tendency for us to move back to it) or where demand or supply conditions are volatile (that is, subject to frequent, rapid, and unpredictable change).

1.3.5 Prices as signals
Prices provide information from and to the two sides of a market. We have seen that the price at which a seller is willing to supply a good is likely to reflect the cost of producing an extra unit of it (that is its marginal cost). This, in turn, will reflect the prices which producers have to pay to acquire the resources (labour, capital, raw materials) needed to produce it. On the other hand, the price which the final buyer is willing to pay for a good indicates the satisfaction expected from it.

It is common to think of the basic economic problem in terms of how an economy can best use the resources it has available to meet the wants of its citizens. This is the problem of resource allocation. If prices signal to producers both what consumers most want and how scarce different resources are, then they play a major role in solving this problem. But to play this role fully, prices must be flexible.

It follows that people who believe that a market system does best solve the resource allocation problem are worried by intervention in markets which may cause prices to give people false information. In such cases, people are said to be confused; the signals being provided by prices are not clear. An analogy with radio signals is used, and anything which interferes with the role of prices as a signal is described as 'noise' in the market. An application of this has been the idea of inflation acting as 'noise' and interfering with the ability of people to observe correctly changes in relative prices.

If markets are fix-price, then the reality may be that there is so much 'noise' in markets that the price system has little chance of acting satisfactorily to allocate scarce resources. The choice then will be between trying to reduce the noise (by increasing competition or by regulating the market), and looking for an alternative way of allocating resources (such as government planning).

1.3.6 Prices as rationing devices

The same problem can be expressed in a different way. Given that we would like to consume more than we are capable of producing, we need some way of rationing the limited amounts available. Various rationing devices are used in our society. For example, some things are available on a first-come first-served basis—people queue for tickets to major matches at Wimbledon. One major way of rationing, however, is through the price charged for the product.

The argument for rationing by price derives from the notion that the price consumers are willing to pay for a product reflects the amount of satisfaction they hope to obtain from it. It seems to follow that we would create the greatest amount of satisfaction possible from our limited resources, by always allowing the product to go to those willing to pay the most for it.

But there is a catch here. Our framework for analysing demand assumed a constant income. Yet people have widely varying levels of income and this clearly affects the price different people are able to pay for a product. In what circumstances might it seem fair to have the distribution of income determine the pattern of consumption in an economy?

Think back to the notion that resources are limited. The scarce resources include human endeavour and talents. So, if it were true that the incomes people receive fairly reflect their contributions to production—through working hard, making use of scarce talents, using their money to produce goods other people want rather than spending it on themselves, and so on—the price mechanism would still be providing the link we want between our scarce resources and our unlimited wants.

In modern market economies, however, the distribution of income derives to a considerable extent from inherited wealth. Further, many people with scarce talents are not given the opportunity to use them. Thus the distribution of income is

22 Understanding Markets

unlikely to reflect at all accurately the nature of the economy's limited resources. The important link between resources and wants is broken. Consequently, on these grounds also, we may wish to choose some mechanism other than price to allocate the economy's scarce resources.

1.3.7 Shortages and queues

Let us look more closely at cases where the ruling price is below the market equilibrium price—say at P_2 in fig. 1.3.

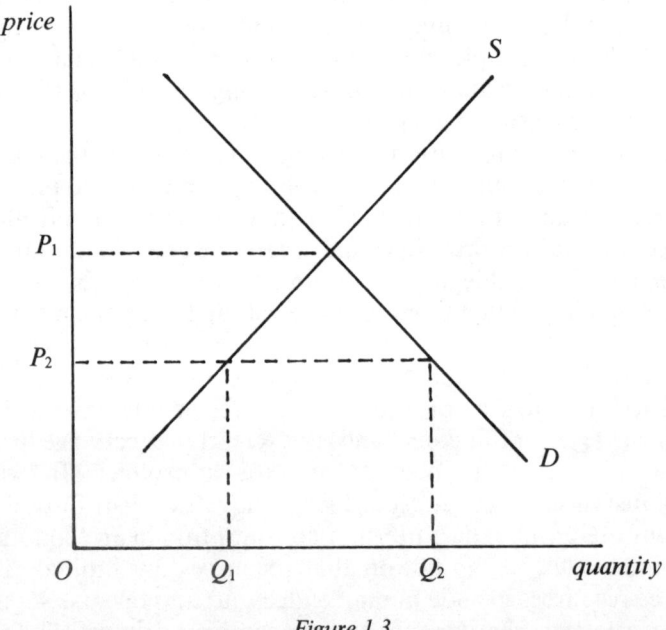

Figure 1.3

At this price, people are demanding more than sellers are willing to supply. If the price does not rise to the equilibrium level, P_1, what occurs?

Queues form, some people obtain the good at the existing price, while others who would have been willing and able to pay that price are disappointed, or have to wait. You can no doubt think of many examples. Sometimes there are mortgage queues. People are willing to pay the existing interest rate to obtain a loan to buy a house but insufficient funds are available at that rate of interest to meet the demands. Yet interest rates adjust only slowly and in quite large steps. The privatisation spree of the British government led to many queues. For the sell-off of British Telecom, the Trustee Savings Bank, British Gas and others, share prices were fixed lower than many people were willing to pay. An enormous number of applications resulted. Only a small proportion of them were successful. FA Cup finals provide another interesting example. Ticket touts obtain a number of tickets at the official price and then sell them at a much higher price to others who have not been able to get tickets.

This leads us to think of different people paying different prices for much the same product. Sometimes a seller will try to divide up a market so that it is possible to charge different prices to people depending upon their willingness to pay. This is the notion of price discrimination, the extreme form of which occurs when the price is determined through bargaining or haggling as in a middle eastern market. The skilled seller in such situations is always trying to assess the maximum price each individual customer is willing to pay.

Our FA Cup final example also introduces us to black or unofficial markets. The extreme cases here are where laws exist which prohibit the sale of the commodity but markets nonetheless operate outside the law as with the market for hard drugs.

1.4 PEOPLE AND MARKETS

Why, however, do people participate in markets at all? Let us accept for the moment that people live in clearly defined households and that each household has resources. These resources may be used in a variety of ways to give the members of the household satisfaction which, in turn, may take a number of forms. In broad terms we may say that people use their resources to enable them to consume (or to use up) goods and services now; or to save, allowing them to consume goods and services in the future, and thus to feel more secure.

Consumption *now* takes two forms. People may buy goods

and services in the market place, or they may consume goods and services which they produce for themselves at home or are produced by other household members or friends. Hence, we can distinguish between market and non-market production and consumption.

1.4.1 Household resources

The most basic resource of households is time. Without it we could neither produce nor consume. But in almost all uses of time, we also make use of goods which we purchase. Even on long, solitary walks we wear shoes and clothes.

As well as time, we have the ability to work and a mixture of skills and knowledge which we can sell in the labour market in return for income. Current incomes of households (and hence their ability to consume now) are affected by governments through taxation and transfer payments.

People also derive income from their wealth—their holdings of saleable real and financial assets. The funds to buy these assets may have come from gifts or inheritances, or from past savings of previous income. People may also consume now through borrowing against their expected (or hoped for) future income.

1.4.2 The decision-making unit

In practice, households may consist of several people and any household decision will be the result of interaction among its members. The economic behaviour of some people will depend upon the behaviour and/or the needs of other household members. For instance, children may have to leave school early because the breadwinner of the family becomes unemployed.

Further, we cannot be sure that a household decision really is in the best interests of all the people in the household. Parents may make decisions for their children against the children's wishes. Wives may be prevented from seeking work by the attitudes of their husbands. Households operate with widely differing financial arrangements and degrees of cooperation.

In any case, it is unrealistic to divide the population into separate households, each occupying its own little box. For example, expectations regarding future income may be influenced by anticipated inheritances or by how reliably an ex-spouse makes maintenance payments. Again, the decision of a neighbour to buy a home computer may persuade you to work overtime so that you, too, can buy one. Or your realising that your neighbour has taken up nude sunbathing may cause you to build a taller fence (or to buy a pair of binoculars).

What we have, then, is a large number of people whose decisions are to varying (but substantial) degrees influenced by the behaviour of others.

1.4.3 Restrictions on choice

We have talked a good deal about choices and decisions. However, people's market choices are restricted in many ways—by the resources they possess (time, skills, experience, health, financial and real wealth) and by the opportunities they have of acquiring them. Social norms may, for example, strongly limit educational and job expectations. Family backgrounds and friendships as well as 'old school ties' may be important influences on the range of opportunities available to people. Income and social background also affect both general health and life expectancy.

In addition to these and other social influences choices are constrained by lack of knowledge and by uncertainty about what will happen in the future. Consequently, people are often unhappy about the outcome of market choices—they are disappointed by the quality of the product they obtain; they discover that other people have bought the same thing more cheaply; what they thought were permanent jobs turn out to be temporary ones; the financial company with whom they have placed their lifetime savings disappears overnight.

In such circumstances, the standard assumptions of economics that people choose freely within markets and maximise their utility (that is, the satisfaction they obtain from their present consumption and their expected future consumption of products) have very little meaning. In real life, market decisions commonly relate to a vague and uncertain future and markets are often hazardous places. Prices convey a variety of economic, political and social information but only rarely adjust smoothly and quickly. Many markets are dominated by powerful buyers or sellers. Choices of individuals, firms and governments are heavily constrained. This is the world of this book.

2 Consumers in Product Markets

In chapter one we suggested that demand curves for most products slope down to the right, indicating that people are prepared to buy more of a good the lower its price. As we saw, this is based on the assumptions that income remains constant and that nothing else changes other than the price of the product itself. We also saw that the slope of a demand curve depends on the extent to which there are good substitutes for the product in question.

A very common form of economic analysis is being used here: people are assumed to be maximising something within a set of constraints or limitations. In the consumer choice case, they are said to be maximising utility or satisfaction given their income level, the set of existing relative prices of all products, and tastes. This is all very well as far as it goes, but it tells us little about consumer motivation or behaviour in real markets.

We have, after all, no indication of what gives people satisfaction. Some consumer choices are clearly intended to give the buyer personal pleasure. Others, however, seem to be based on altruism (a concern to help others) or on duty or obligation. Consider, for example, charitable donations, Christmas cards sent to people who have sent them to you, or wedding presents. Other consumer decisions appear to follow past habit. Yet no matter how strange a decision seems to be, the consumer in question is assumed to be maximising his or her satisfaction, in the existing circumstances.

Further, what people do and the satisfaction they obtain from their actions may well depend much more on the nature of the 'existing circumstances' than on whether or not they are maximising their utility.

For example, in 1985, the number of houses repossessed in the UK was seven times greater than in 1979. Yet presumably house purchasers were maximising utility every bit as much in 1985 as in 1979. Again, the attempt to maximise utility can lead to people sleeping rough through a London winter; killing themselves with drugs or cigarettes; buying products which quickly fall apart; or buying company shares the day before the stock market crashes. In other words, people may be maximising utility but the outcome may be a very low level of utility indeed.

If we are to understand consumer choices in real markets, then, we need to pay much attention to the constraints on people's choices. Let us begin by seeing what happens to demand curves for products when things other than the prices of the products themselves change.

2.1. CHANGES LEADING TO SHIFTS IN DEMAND CURVES

2.1.1 Prices of other products

We have so far been asking what happens to the demand for a product when the price of the product itself changes. But the idea of opportunity cost makes it clear that we are interested in the price of a product (say cheddar cheese) *relative* to those of other products, especially relative to the prices of good substitutes for it. Thus we need to consider what happens to the demand for a product when its price remains unaltered but the prices of other products change.

We shall expect an increase in the price of cheshire cheese while the price of cheddar remains unchanged to lead to an increase in the demand for cheddar. The demand curve shifts to the right. The closer a substitute cheshire is for cheddar in people's minds, the greater the impact of the price change and the further the demand curve for cheddar will shift.

The result is likely to be different if the price of a product which is used together with cheddar rises. Suppose cheddar is principally purchased to make cheese sandwiches and the price of bread rises. This may lead to a reduction in the demand for all sandwiches, including cheese sandwiches and the demand for cheddar may fall. There are only a few examples of these complementary goods, but some of them are important—consider the impact of an increase in the price of petrol on the demand for large, petrol-guzzling cars. The extent to which the demand for a good is affected by a change in the price of another good is known as the cross elasticity of demand.

2.1.2 Future relative prices
Here we have been talking about relative prices at a particular time. But as well as choosing which goods to buy, people may at the same time be choosing when to buy them. This will be very much influenced by what people think is going to happen to relative prices in the future. Thus, if a newspaper reports that a failure in this year's haricot beans crop will lead to a shortage next year of cans of baked beans on supermarket shelves, people may increase their present demand for them—not because the price of baked beans is currently high, but because they expect it to become so.

The issue is even more complex since consumers also take into account the possibility of new products coming onto the market; of existing products changing in nature or quality; and of products (for which spare parts may later be required) ceasing to be produced. Someone considering buying a personal computer may be influenced by views not only about their expected future price but also about likely improvements in next year's models. This introduces a large amount of uncertainty into consumer choice. Demand curves may move simply because people think things are going to change.

2.1.3 Income and consumption
Next we must deal with the assumption of constant income. Here we mean real income—the quantities of goods and services people can purchase. Real incomes change frequently, both because of changes in money incomes and through the effect of inflation. It is thus very important to consider how consumers are likely to react if relative prices remain unchanged, but real incomes rise or fall. Does the demand for each product change in the same proportion?

Clearly it doesn't. As people's real incomes rise, the type of products they buy changes. There are few products which people will actually want less of as they become richer but the demand will certainly increase much faster for some products than others. Remember our discussion of elasticities in chapter one? There we were discussing what happened to the demand for a particular good as its relative price changed and we used the term price elasticity of demand. Equally, we may ask what will happen to the demand for a good as the real income level in the economy changes (assuming nothing else changes) and we can summarise the answer in terms of the income elasticity of demand. That is, if a small increase in the average real income level in the economy leads to a more than proportional increase in the demand for a particular product, we can describe the demand for it as income elastic. Try to think of some products which seem to you to have a high income elasticity—restaurant meals, foreign holidays, wine, health care, video recorders...

We have only to look at what has happened to average real income levels in the UK since the second world war to realise how important the consequences of changing incomes are. Consider what has happened to the market for cheese. Any changes which have taken place in the relative prices of cheddar and cheshire cheeses have been insignificant compared to the impact of the appearance on supermarket shelves of foreign cheeses. The humblest supermarkets these days may well stock camembert or brie. What has been happening? As incomes have risen, consumer tastes have changed, strongly influenced by the much higher proportion of the population which has been able to afford foreign holidays.

How has the UK cheese industry responded? One major change has been the increase in the amount of superior traditional and farmhouse cheddars available in supermarkets at high prices. Again, the domestic cheese industry has felt the need to copy European styles of cheese. There is little doubt that a large reduction in the price of bland, heavily processed cheese will produce increases in its sales, perhaps large ones. That is, demand for such a cheese may be quite price elastic. Nonetheless, it remains that from the point of view of firms and industries, such possible effects may be swamped by the impact on demand of rising real incomes. In short, increases in income can lead rapidly to large increases in the range of goods from which people can choose. So much so, indeed, that the range of products available is often as important as the way in which people choose among that range.

Of course, cheese can't be taken as representative of all goods and services. There is presumably some limit to the total amount of cheese people are willing to buy. It is probably where the demand for a product is close to being 'saturated' that real income changes which allow people to buy more expensive varieties of the product become particularly important. In practice, changes in relative prices and in real incomes work together to influence consumption patterns as is shown in case study 2.1.

CASE STUDY 2.1: THE DEMAND FOR WORD PROCESSORS

In the early 1980s, home computers began to appear in the market for electronic goods. There were several reasons for this. Firstly, it was a new product which had a considerable novelty appeal. Secondly, as the teaching of computing increased in schools, many parents began to feel that their children needed access to some sort of computer at home. It was also important, however, that real incomes grew significantly from the depth of the UK recession in 1981, with earnings of people in work consistently increasing faster than the rate of inflation. This, together with the large increase in credit in the economy, led to a continuing boom in consumer goods markets. Finally, as is often the case with new and rapidly developing products, the price of home computers was coming down. Thus, the demand curve for home computers was shifting out to the right *and* there was a movement down to the right along the demand curve.

But producers misjudged the market. Initially home computers concentrated on computer games. This put them into competition with toys and games and with television and video—an extremely difficult and competitive market. An additional attempt to persuade people that they could use home computers for their household accounts was not successful. Once the novelty started to wear off, sales began to fall. The high level of competition led some firms into problems. Some withdrew from the home computing market, others cut back sharply. A market from which many people had expected big things appeared to be going nowhere very fast.

Then, in 1985, Amstrad, a small firm which had established a niche for itself in the audio market by selling low-priced stereo equipment, entered the market for home computers with a new product which had three notable characteristics.

Firstly, it was sold principally as a word processor. This made it a competitor for typewriters rather than for entertainment. Secondly, to support this, it was sold as a package including a printer and specialised word-processing software. People could see a clear use for the product because it was a substitute for an existing product, rather than one satisfying an entirely new want. Having a use for the product, people felt that they could then gradually learn to make use of the computing facilities offered, rather than feeling that they had to master strange, new skills before being able to do anything. Thirdly, the Amstrad PCW was priced to compete with electronic typewriters and was much cheaper than previous home computers which had offered word processing facilities.

Sales of the Amstrad PCW soared. On the basis of its enormous initial success in the computer market, the company was able in subsequent years to expand its range and to attack other parts of the market. The Amstrad experience clearly shows the importance of relative price in the demand for consumer goods. However, it also shows the importance of choosing the right time (one of increasing real incomes and a credit boom); of choosing the right market niche for a product; and of developing an overall design and marketing strategy.

It is worth noting here that just as consumers are influenced by expected future relative prices, they will also be affected by expected future real incomes. People worried about losing their jobs may change not only the balance between consumption and saving from their current income but also the type of products they buy. Since people's expected future incomes in part depend on their present level of wealth, a change in wealth (such as the fall in wealth associated with the 1987 stockmarket crash) may well affect demand patterns. Again, the demand for different products may vary depending on whether it is thought that the economy is heading for slump or prosperity.

2.1.4 The importance of income distribution

Since different types of goods have different income elasticities, the distribution of income is another important factor in the demand for particular goods.

Thus, two economies with the same average level of real income but with different income distributions—one with a less equal distribution of income than the other, with both more rich and more poor people—are likely to have different demand patterns. Again, in an economy which has a large amount of unemployment, but in which people with jobs go on steadily becoming better off, we can expect markets to become increasingly varied in the range of goods they offer, in the nature of their appeal to consumers and in the style of advertisements.

We should note that the distribution of real income in an economy may change because different households are affected in quite different ways by inflation. Suppose prices have on average risen over a year by 4 per cent but that price rises have been concentrated on those products which tend to be purchased more by people on lower incomes—basic foods, cheap imported clothing, council house rents. Then, the distribution of real income will have changed and this will have affected the pattern of demand.

2.1.5 Indebtedness and consumption

But in a modern economy consumption is not constrained by current income. One of the most important changes which has occurred over the last several decades is the extent to which people have gone into debt in order to finance the purchase of goods and services. Consumer debt has been rising rapidly in

Britain. Personal sector debt rose from just over 50 per cent of disposable income to nearly 90 per cent between 1979 and 1986. This in turn has meant that people's income gearing (that is, the ratio of interest payments to income) has reached record levels, at an average of around 10 per cent.

Current income is only one of the factors which determine how much people can borrow. Others include the amount of property people own and the expectations lenders have regarding the future incomes of borrowers (consider the willingness of banks to extend loans to students in higher education).

Equally, the willingness of people to enter into debt will be partly related to their expectations regarding their future incomes. But it will also be influenced by changing consumer tastes and habits and by changing attitudes towards being in debt. Further, the amount which people can borrow is affected by the size of the financial sector of the economy and by the competition within it. Thus the growth of banks, building societies, hire purchase companies, insurance companies and other financial institutions and the competition among them has made it much easier for people to borrow than it once was.

2.1.6 Interest rates and consumption

It is accepted that the level of interest rates has some impact on people's desire to save for the future and hence on present consumption. One might expect the impact to be greater when a high proportion of consumption is financed by borrowing, since going into debt involves risk in the form of the consequences of failing to meet future debt repayments (bankruptcy, repossession of goods, loss of reputation). However, this seems to be more than offset by changing attitudes towards indebtedness. The rapid increase in consumer debt mentioned above has been occurring during a period of high real interest rates. Thus it appears that both consumption and the demand for credit to finance it are relatively interest rate inelastic.

2.1.7 Tastes and advertising

Finally, we must consider tastes. The decisions of consumers are ultimately subjective. We all find it difficult to understand why other people buy the sorts of things they do (one of the few ways of making supermarket queues bearable is to puzzle over the purchases of other customers). When we have finished trying to explain consumption decisions on the basis of relative prices, real incomes, interest rates and so on we tend to fall back on individual tastes to explain the apparently inexplicable.

Economists usually do not attempt to explain tastes or changes in them, but pass the job on to social psychologists. But this is deeply unsatisfactory because a large part of modern economic activity is specifically concerned with trying to change people's tastes. Advertising has been one of the major growth areas of economies for a long time now. Tastes and fashions change in part because profits can be made by changing them. Indeed, J.K. Galbraith has proposed that advertising and other marketing activities have become so important in modern economies that producers as a group are now capable of determining what consumers wish to buy. This idea (named by Galbraith the dependence effect) is a reversal of the traditional notion of consumer sovereignty in which consumer choices are seen as determining what it is profitable for producers to produce and hence how the economy's scarce resources are used. Whether this is undesirable is another matter. It has been suggested, for example, that advertising and other marketing activities may perform a useful social function, by bringing the pattern of spending in an economy into line with what the economy is currently capable of producing.

There are many issues here. To some extent, advertising provides information (as we have seen an important factor in markets itself) but much of it is persuasion and successful persuasion at that—we are none of us as different from others as we like to think. It is important to discover how important advertising is in total as well as how successful particular advertising campaigns are. Are advertisers principally engaged in competing for an existing market of a given size, or do they influence the amount people buy in total, the way in which people think about the future, or the willingness of people to borrow? In case study 2.2. we consider the effect of advertising in the tobacco industry.

CASE STUDY 2.2: ADVERTISING AND CIGARETTES

The smoking of cigarettes by males in the UK reached its peak in 1960. The peak for women was reached in 1974. Since those years there has been a significant decline in both the percentage of men and women who smoke and in the average number of cigarettes smoked per day for the population as a whole. Similar declines have occurred in other developed countries. Meanwhile the smoking of cigarettes has continued to increase in developing countries. What forces have been at work in these changes in demand?

It is generally accepted that the demand for cigarettes is relatively price-inelastic. As nicotine is an addictive substance, heavy smokers find it very difficult to stop smoking. Nonetheless, the demand for cigarettes is to some extent price sensitive. Between 1961 and 1981, the price of cigarettes rose less than the average rate of inflation. That is, cigarettes became relatively cheaper and for this reason we would have expected the demand curve for them to move out to the right. If nothing else had changed, the demand for cigarettes should have increased.

Cigarette consumption should have increased as well because of the increase in real incomes which occurred during the period. This increase would also have been tending to shift the curve out to the right. But since the demand for cigarettes overall did not increase, something must have been happening to counteract these tendencies.

One major influence was the increased concern over the damage done by smoking to health, especially the now well-established link between smoking and lung cancer. That such concern has a *short-term* effect is shown by the fall in cigarette sales in the UK from 113 billion in 1961 to 109 billion in 1962, the year of the first authoritative report on the health dangers of smoking by the Royal College of Physicians. Cigarette sales increased again the following year to 115 billion. A similar pattern was observed in the US following the similar report of the US Surgeon General in 1964.

While the medical profession and others have been attempting to shift the demand curve for cigarettes to the left, chiefly through health education, the tobacco industry has been attempting to resist this shift through promotion of its products. The industry spends hugely on advertising — well over two billion US dollars world-wide. This is despite restrictions placed on it, including the ban on the advertising of cigarettes on television which has been in force in the UK since 1965.

The industry has always claimed that its advertising is aimed at persuading people neither to take up smoking nor to smoke more—that is, that it does not attempt to increase the total market for tobacco products, but is concerned only with the division of that market among existing brands. Is this distinction credible?

The answer appears to be no. Advertising appeals to images which have always been associated in many people's minds with the product in general, not just with particular brands—virility, sophistication, sexuality and success. For example, when Marlboro became a sponsor of Grand Prix racing in 1983, its associated publicity stated: 'We are the number-one brand in the world. What we wanted was to promote a particular image of adventure, of courage, of virility'.

Further, advertising has been particularly directed towards potential growth areas of the market—towards women (with appeals to desires to be attractive, slim, sophisticated and, later, desire for greater equality with men); towards people in developing countries (stressing the link between the success and glamour of Western living and cigarette smoking).

Although secure links between advertising and cigarette smoking in total are difficult to establish, evidence from Norway suggests that the total banning of advertising of tobacco products is likely to lead to a reduction in smoking in children and, since most adult smokers begin smoking as children, ultimately to a fall in the total number of smokers. Finally, the distinction which the tobacco industry tries to make between splitting up an existing market among brands and expanding that market is called into question by continued advertising in countries in which one company has a monopoly of the sale of cigarettes. For example, although British American Tobacco had a monopoly of the Kenyan cigarette market in the 1970s, it was the country's fourth largest commercial advertiser.

The cigarette market illustrates again that although the relationship between price and demand, assuming other things equal, is an important one, the most interesting and important aspects of consumer demand are factors which influence tastes.

Again, in examining tastes, we may wish to look beyond the activities of advertisers. The national and international transmission of tastes and fashions through newspapers, films and television is an important phenomenon today; consumption/savings decisions and consumption patterns may be influenced by these at least as much as by current income or interest rates. Of course, as we have suggested above in our cheese example, increases in real incomes have themselves played a major role in increasing people's exposure to other cultures and other tastes through expanding tourism.

Many other factors may influence the tastes of communities, including their changing age, social and racial compositions, their living conditions and their perception of future opportunities. The whole question is complex and difficult, but to understand fully a market economy, we must understand why tastes are what they are and how they are changed.

2.2 A SUMMARY OF INFLUENCES ON DEMAND

We began with the notion of a demand curve for a product, expressing the view that for almost all goods and services, a fall in price would lead to an increase in the quantity demanded (and vice versa) on the strict assumption that nothing else which might affect the demand for the product changed at the same time. We went on to point out that the amount demanded of some products would vary more at existing prices in response to a small change in its price—that is, that the demand for some products is more price elastic than for others.

In this chapter we have added that the demand for a product

Table 2.1: Effects of changes on demand

Change	Effect on the demand for a product
1. An increase in the price of the product	quantity demanded falls
2. An increase in the price of a substitute	demand rises
3. An increase in the price of a complementary good	demand falls
4. An increase in income	demand rises
5. An increase in the rate of inflation	demand falls
6. A change in the distribution of income	effect uncertain
7. An increase in net indebtedness	demand rises
8. An increase in wealth	demand rises
9. A change in tastes	effect uncertain

will vary as several other factors vary. The above table indicates the direction of change we shall expect in demand for a product from a change in each of these, always assuming that nothing else changes at the same time.

There is an important analytical difference here between change 1 and all the others. If the price of the product itself changes, the effect on demand is shown by moving along an existing demand curve. Thus an increase in the product's price from P_1 to P_2 in fig. 2.1 will reduce the quantity of the product demanded from Q_1 to Q_2.

Any of the other changes will cause the whole demand curve to shift. Hence, an increase in the price of a substitute moves the demand curve in fig. 2.1 out to the right, causing the amount demanded, at the unchanged price of the product, to increase to Q_3. On the other hand, an increase in the price of a complementary good will move the demand curve in to the left, and the amount of our product demanded at its unchanged price, will fall (to Q_4 in fig. 2.1).

In reality, several factors will be changing at the same time, making it difficult to isolate the size of the impact of any one change on its own. Consider the following case. There is inflation, but nominal incomes are increasing faster than the price level; both private sector wealth and net indebtedness are rising; a firm which produces washing powder increases the price of its product by more than the rate of inflation and by more than the rate of price increase of its competitors; at the

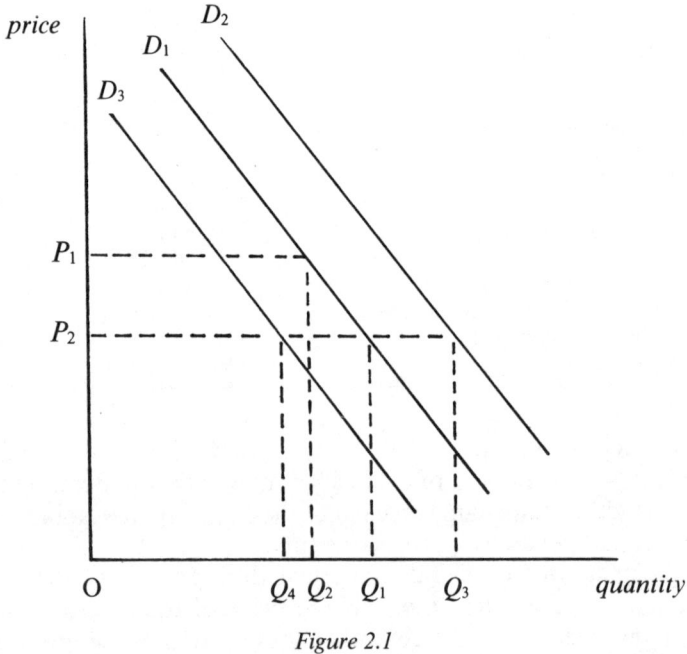

Figure 2.1

same time it mounts an advertising campaign proclaiming the introduction of a new and improved formula and puts on the pack a coupon which will give 10p. off the price of the next packet purchased. You should try to consider the conflicting forces here in terms of the analysis above.

2.3 SOME ALTERNATIVE NOTIONS

We have worked our way through the usual view of consumer demand, raising a number of difficulties on the way. There are some important issues, however, which cannot be considered adequately within that approach. In particular, we need to think about consumer motives and the judgement of product quality.

2.3.1 Consumer motives
We have accepted the proposition that consumers do the best

they can for themselves in the existing circumstances. But this leaves several questions unanswered. Firstly, what is meant by 'best'?

We can begin with the idea that what consumers are seeking to judge is how well a product carries out the functions for which it was designed. For example, in buying a cassette player, consumers might consider sound quality, size and weight, and ease of use of controls as well as price. The American economist, Harvey Leibenstein, referred to this as the functional motivation behind consumer demand. In itself, it seems reasonable, but there is much more to consumer motivation. People who buy fur coats do not do so simply to keep warm!

Several additional notions have been advanced by economists. The major group of these (classified by Leibenstein under the heading external effects on consumption) relates to the fact that people's consumption choices are in varying ways affected by the behaviour of other consumers. The group includes:

a. *Bandwagon effects*: people buy a product because other consumers are buying it. There are various possible reasons for bandwagon effects. As demand for a product increases, it may become fashionable. Again, in the absence of adequate information about product quality, it may be accepted that the other people buying it must have some privileged information (a very common assumption in betting shops).

b. *Social taboos*: negative bandwagon effects—people reject a product because no one else is buying it.

c. *Snob effects*: some people buy a product because they think ownership of it will distinguish them from other people. Thus, if the price of the product falls and, as a result, more people buy it, some of the previous purchasers will cease doing so. This is the motivation exploited by the 'limited editions' offers of plates and medallions which are so common in the colour supplements of Sunday papers.

d. *Veblen effects*: this is based on the idea of conspicuous

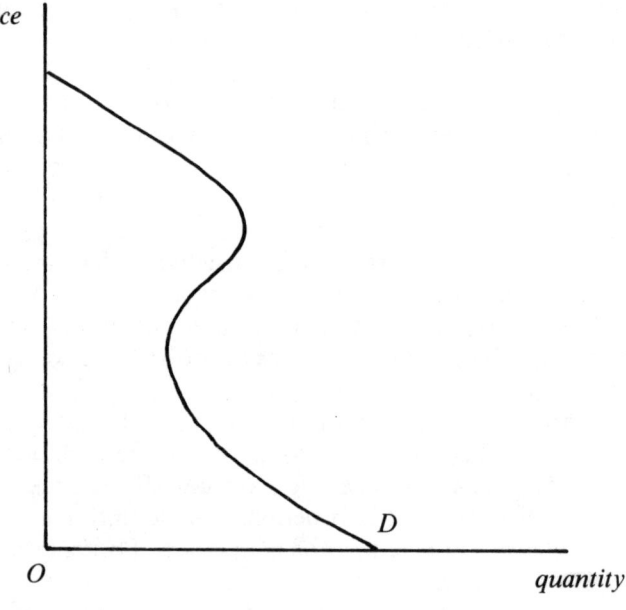

Figure 2.2

consumption, developed by Thorstein Veblen, an American social scientist. This suggests that a major motive for consumption is to be seen consuming. Hence, people may buy products because other people believe them to be highly priced. Consumption is used as an indicator of wealth and hence of success.

Leibenstein showed that these effects could be analysed within the framework of demand curves. Incorporating bandwagon and snob effects and social taboos still leaves us with downward sloping demand curves. All that is altered is the steepness of the slopes. Veblen effects, on the other hand, may produce demand curves which slope upwards or downwards, or which combine both negative and positive slopes as in fig. 2.2

However, the analysis of consumer behaviour becomes much more complex once such motives are admitted. Further, there can be seen to be a much greater role for packaging and advertising. It may be important that a product looks expensive (whether or not it is). Firms may hope to sell by persuading consumers that other people are buying the product (whether or not they are). It may be important to distinguish a product clearly from those of competitors in order to perserve an image of exclusiveness. More types of information (to many of which again a consumer may not have ready access) become important in consumer decisions. Marketing becomes much more important relative to production.

Leibenstein also proposed two other types of consumer motivation. One of these (speculative demand) we have come across in section 2.2.2—the purchase of extra amounts of a product now because its price is expected to rise in the future. The other (irrational demand) covers unplanned purchases which do not derive from an attempt to maximise utility.

As well as people's levels of utility being influenced by other people's behaviour and attitudes (as in bandwagon or Veblen effects), it may be affected by factors which influence other people's utilities (formally we would say that welfare functions are interdependent). People may make altruistic purchases (they will buy things to please or to help others); consumption decisions may be the result of compromises among several people; or they may be made deliberately to excite or to avoid the envy of others. It is possible to include all such influences on decisions under the heading of tastes. However, the more complex the notion of tastes becomes, the more difficult it is to say anything sensible about it.

Further, the more factors there are which have an impact on consumer decisions, the less satisfactory it is to centre the examination of consumer behaviour on the effect of changing relative prices, on the assumption that nothing else alters. If consumer choice involves many elements which are subject to change, it becomes extremely difficult for firms to know precisely what effect a change in price of their product will have on demand for it. This is just one reason among many why firms may set a price using a standard formula (cost plus a profit mark-up) and then try to influence demand in other ways, rather than being particularly concerned with the price elasticity of their product. To put it another way, we might say that firms may be more interested in what shifts the demand curve for their products rather than in the shapes of the demand curves.

2.3.2 The judgement of quality

Let us now revert to the notion that people are principally interested in the qualities of products themselves (that is, their motives are functional). After all, a lot of everyday shopping for detergents, toothpaste, or deep-frozen chips might seem to have very little to do with snob effects or social taboos. The question we are left with is how, in a world of many competing products, of much technical information, and where time is scarce, do we judge quality?

With products we buy regularly, trial and error is always a possibility, although matters can become very complicated as firms frequently introduce new brand names and new formulas. With products which are bought less often (for example, consumer durables such as washing machines), personal experience is hardly likely to be sufficient.

Many other sources of information exist—the testimony of friends, articles in consumer magazines, advertisements. However, for many people the price itself becomes an important indicator of quality. There are two extreme positions. We may buy expensive goods in part because we believe that the high prices are a form of guarantee of quality. When we are travelling abroad, we may reject the cheapest hotels or restaurants on the grounds that they are not likely to have clean bed linen or kitchens.

On the other hand, faced with a number of brands of a product, we might deliberately buy the cheapest on the grounds that since we have no information about their respective qualities, there is no logical reason why we should assume the cheapest to be worse than any of the others. In such a case, our bargain-hunting instincts win out. This applies too to cases where we buy because we believe the price of a product has been reduced considerably from its previous level. Sellers of products are aware of the strength of this feeling among purchasers—just think how common it is to see goods advertised for sale at, say, 30 per cent or 50 per cent off.

However we choose, there are problems for our earlier analysis. It depends, remember, on the proposition that people start with views about the qualities of products and then, given their incomes and the relative prices of the products, they seek to maximise utility. But if the relative prices themselves are a major influence on the judgement of quality, some markets may produce decidedly odd results as relative prices change. The best-known example of such a possible result occurs in the analysis of 'lemons' by the American economist, George Akerlof.

'Lemons' are second-hand cars of doubtful quality. The second-hand car market is a very good example of a common situation in markets—one where the seller knows a good deal more about the quality of the product than the buyer (there is asymmetric information). Second-hand cars may have suffered long-term damage in serious accidents but this may be disguised by clever repair work. Again, assume that randomly distributed among new cars are a certain number of 'rogues' ('Friday afternoon cars'). Assume also that buyers of these are much more likely to wish to re-sell them quickly than are buyers of reliable new cars. It follows that second-hand cars being sold might include a considerably higher proportion of 'rogues' than new cars. Akerlof uses the justifible suspicion of buyers of second-hand cars to explain why the price of a new car falls so much as soon as it leaves the showroom.

Further, he uses the idea of 'lemons' to explain why the market may not clear. Suppose you advertise a second-hand car for sale for, say, £2000. It does not sell at that price. You drop the price to £1800. At the lower price, however, prospective purchasers may feel that it is more likely that the car is a 'lemon'. In such circumstances, demand may not increase as price falls. We may not be able to move to an equilibrium price at which demand equals supply. The market may become jammed.

2.4 REGULATION OF CONSUMER MARKETS

There are three separate arguments for the regulation of consumer markets. These concern: (a) the extent to which consumers can be assumed always to act in their own best interests; (b) the extent to which consumption decisions of some people may affect the welfare of others; and (c) the extent to which consumers are at a disadvantage in consumer markets. Let us deal with each of these in turn.

2.4.1 Merit and demerit goods

It is a basic assumption of economics that people always act in their own best interests. However, governments everywhere quite frequently decide that consumers are not making wise consumer decisions.

There are several possible reasons for this. For example, it may be felt that people are badly informed about the true benefits and costs to them of consumption; that they are subjected to strong social or personal pressures to consume; or that the product is physically addictive. Thus, consumption may be made illegal (drugs); access may be restricted (age limits on and licensing hours for the purchase of alcoholic drinks); advertising may be limited (cigarettes); products may be taxed to raise prices and reduce consumption (cigarettes; alcoholic drinks); educational campaigns may be undertaken (cigarettes, alcoholic drinks, drugs); and so on.

All of our examples above are of demerit goods. But there are also many merit goods which people are compelled or encouraged to use. Obvious examples are helmets for motor cyclists; seat belts; condoms; and basic education.

In all of these cases, the judgement of individual people is being replaced or modified by the judgement of the government. One complicating factor, however, is that governments may have a number of motives (which sometimes conflict) in making such decisions. Further, governments may reflect the views of only part of the community or may themselves have inadequate information. We cannot say that governments necessarily make better judgements than do individual citizens. However, very few people believe that everything should be traded completely freely.

2.4.2 Social costs and benefits

In section 1.3.7 we looked at the problem of social costs and benefits and at the idea that it might be overcome by a clearer definition of property rights. However, this notion is hardly applicable in many cases of consumption externalities.

Imagine, for instance, a smoker in a crowded pub having to negotiate with the other drinkers a price for making use of the communal air, before lighting up. You can no doubt think of other equally absurd cases. An alternative is for governments to use their taxation and subsidy powers to make some products more or less expensive.

This can be shown on a normal demand and supply diagram. In fig. 2.3 supply conditions are shown by the supply curve S_1; demand, in an unregulated market, is shown by D_1. Q_1 of the product is sold at a price of P_1.

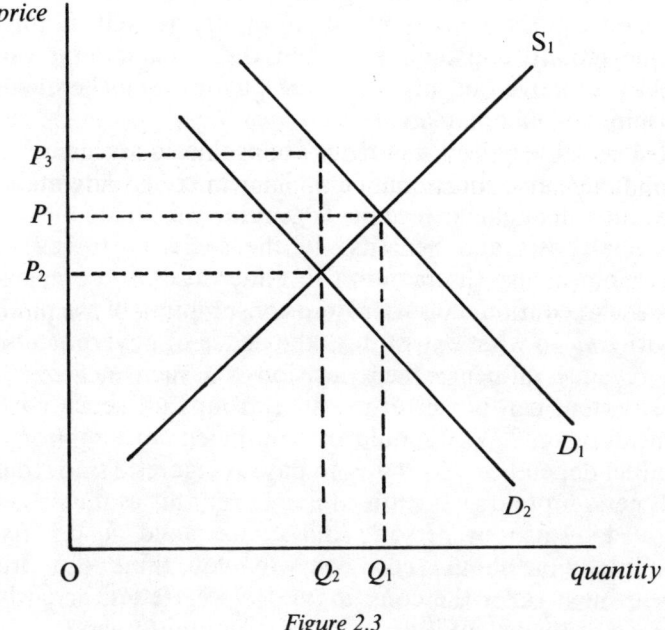

Figure 2.3

Now, a government decides that consumption of the product creates a public nuisance for which its consumers should pay. It imposes a tax on the product, causing its price to rise. Demand at each pre-tax price will fall and the demand curve will, in effect, shift to the left to D_2. Only Q_2 will be consumed. The supplier of the product will receive only P_2, but the consumer will pay P_3. The difference between P_2 and P_3 is the tax which goes to the government.

It is clear in this example that part of the burden of the tax falls on the sellers of the product (they receive a lower price and sell less as a result of the tax). How much does so depends on the slope of the supply curve (the elasticity of supply). You should experiment with differently sloped supply curves, compare the results and see what general conclusion you reach.

All of this is couched in terms of social costs. We could, however, reverse everything in the case of social benefits. Thus, a government could subsidise a product (say, higher education) in the belief that greater consumption of it would be good for the community as a whole, as well as for the people actually consuming it. Then, the demand curve would effectively move out, people would pay less and the quantity consumed would increase.

This is all very well, but there are problems associated with using taxation and subsidies in such a way to regulate markets. To what extent can governments genuinely estimate the extent of social costs and benefits? In the social costs case, can governments use the taxation revenue raised to compensate those who continue to suffer from consumption of the product by others? To what extent does the desire of governments for tax revenue influence their decisions on such measures? To what extent can powerful pressure groups influence government decisions? Why should the continued consumption of a product depend on the ability to pay? A cigarette smoked by a rich person pollutes the atmosphere every bit as much as one smoked by a poor person. And so we could go on. As an example, you should consider why you think the British government taxes the consumption of cigarettes, and why it does so to the extent it does. Why not more? Or less?

What else could we do? We could simply restrict by law the amount consumed to Q_2 by controlling supply. But this may be difficult to do and leads to other problems. Do we let the price rise to P_3? If so, who benefits? If, instead, we keep the price at P_2, how do we ration the limited supply among people wishing to consume?

The overriding difficulty is that just as unregulated markets present problems, so too do all the available forms of regulation. This is not necessarily an argument against regulation of markets. But it is a reminder of the complexity of the issue. It is easy to understand the heat of the controversy between those who prefer largely unregulated markets (market optimists) and those who favour heavy regulation (market pessimists).

2.5 THE FAIRNESS OF CONSUMER MARKETS

In theory, we have said, consumers exchange part of their incomes in return for goods in order to obtain utility. The price paid for a product should reflect the utility expected from it. In this sense, every exchange between buyer and seller is a fair one. Consumers who do not think they will obtain sufficient utility from the product to justify the price need not buy. We have seen that consumers may obtain much less utility from purchases than they expect. Equally, however, they may obtain more satisfaction than they expect. Market optimists, then, take the view which is bound up in the Latin phrase *caveat emptor*—let the buyer beware. Exchanges are voluntary and no one should intervene between buyer and seller.

It is possible to argue, on the other hand, that consumer markets are such that buyers are at a disadvantage. We have seen that buyers may have inadequate information to enable them to make sensible decisions. In particular, we have suggested that sellers may have more information than buyers about the quality of products. We might argue then that exchanges are not fair and that regulation is needed to overcome the imbalance.

2.5.1 Self-regulation
Sellers who wish to remain in a market for a long time have an interest in being thought reliable and trustworthy by consumers: they have reputations to worry about. We might, then, expect them not to take advantage of the extra information they have available to them. This assumes that there is sufficient competition in the market and that there are good communications among consumers.

Firms with little or no competition or which are only likely to provide their services once to each consumer (such as double glazing firms) may not be unduly concerned about their reputations. There is yet another problem. Some sellers may be 'fly-by-night operators': happy to enter a market, make full use of their advantages, and soon quit.

Consequently, we have the common phenomenon of established traders attempting to regulate a market by setting up a trade association. Membership is meant to act as a guarantee of the quality of the product or service. Some trade associations, for example the Association of British Travel Agents, go further and offer consumers compensation if they suffer from the failings of members. Both consumers and producers benefit.

But problems remain. To what extent can consumers rely on such associations to control members? The only sanction the association has is to expel misbehaving members. But expulsions reduce the size of and weaken the association and frequent expulsions would destroy the value of membership to those who remain in. Again, if a trade association successfully imposes a code of practice on its members, the outcome may simply be more uniform practice, not necessarily fairer practice from the point of view of consumers. Yet again, membership of the association may be used as a way of restricting competition within the market. Aggressive competitors may be excluded on the pretext that they are not conforming to desired practices; new firms may take time to be accepted; membership fees and insurance arrangements may be very expensive for small firms. Ultimately, the interests of sellers are different from those of buyers and no group of sellers is likely to give up voluntarily all of the advantages over buyers which the nature of the market gives to them.

2.5.2 Government regulation

The alternative to self-regulation is, again, government regulation. It may take several forms. In most countries there is a general law which requires products sold to be 'fit for sale'. This embodies a number of ideas—that restaurant and hotel kitchens should be hygienic; that firms marketing medical drugs should have sufficiently investigated the possible side-effects of the drugs; that products which may deteriorate with time should have 'sell-by dates' attached to them; that there should be limits on the number of people carried on public transport; that coach drivers and pilots should have passed special tests of their competence and so on.

All of these in some way relate to the question of information—that consumers should know precisely what they are buying. To try to achieve this, we have definitions of products and content requirements. The European Commission, for example, is worried by the use of the word 'ice cream' to describe much of what is sold under that title in the UK, because it contains no cream, only vegetable fats. In many countries there are rules about the percentage of meat in sausages and meat pies. Rules about the required qualifications of dentists, doctors and vets are of this kind.

Then, there is a multitude of labelling requirements. Here we are saying that it may not matter what the contents of products are, but consumers should be in a position to know. Thus, we have labelling on food products; requirements that the strengths of alcoholic drinks should be stated, that all conditions should be printed on airline tickets, that advertised price reductions should be genuine and many more.

All types of consumer markets, then, are regulated. A controversial question in recent years has been whether these markets should be more or less controlled. Let us consider briefly some of the objections to regulation.

2.6 THE PROBLEMS WITH GOVERNMENT REGULATION

Regulation makes products more expensive. Labelling and product control increases the costs of production and uses resources. The setting of required qualifications for providers of services (doctors, dentists, pilots, etc.) limits the supply of the service in question. In both cases, the effect in fig. 2.4 is to shift the supply curve of the product up to the left. Prices rise. Consumers indirectly pay for the information they are given.

It seems clear that in most markets, most people want some regulation. The problem is to determine precisely how much

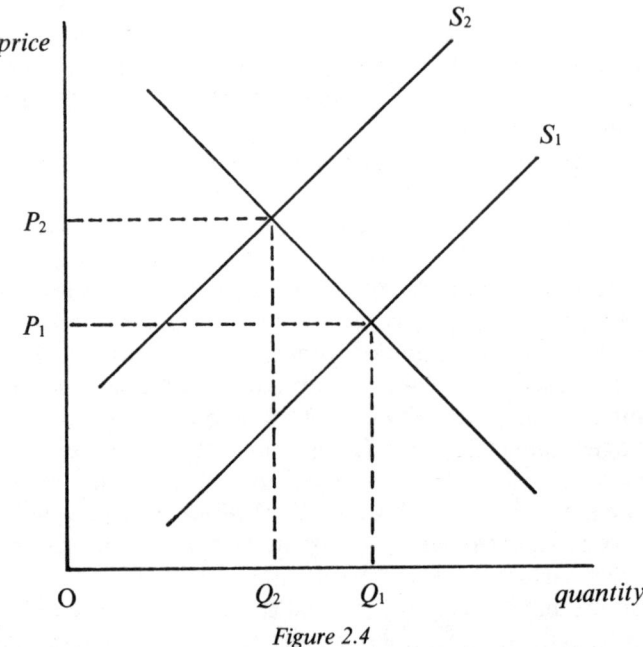

Figure 2.4

should be provided. Here we run into another difficulty. Economists are fond of assuming that there exists something called the 'national interest': that a particular action (or a lack of action) might be judged to be in the interests of the country as a whole. This is an old idea. Adam Smith used it in 1776 in his book *The Wealth of Nations* when he talked of the 'invisible hand' of the market—an early reference to the idea that the market is magic. Smith proposed that if markets are (with a few important exceptions) left to operate freely without government intervention the results will be the best possible one for the economy as a whole even though people in markets act only out of self-interest.

This is all very well as far as it goes. The problem is that once we accept any degree of regulation (and even Smith did this) how do we judge how much regulation is in the 'national interest'? The nature of markets is that there will always be winners and losers. Further, in an unregulated market, people with limited information will be systematic losers. From their point of view, regulation is very desirable.

Thus, any decision either to regulate or to deregulate markets not only will affect the total costs of supplying goods but also will alter the distribution of utility among people and groups of people.

Market pessimists argue that governments, chosen as they are by a political process in which each person has one vote, better know the needs and interests of the community than a market system driven by the forces of supply and demand. The market system, they argue, can also be seen as a voting process, but one where the number of votes people have increases with their incomes, particularly as incomes can be used to acquire information.

But it is easy to find cases where regulation seems to be in the interests of a few rather than in the general interest of market participants; where markets are over-regulated with a consequent mass of bureaucracy; or where regulation which is said to be in the interests of consumers in fact serves entirely different purposes. For example, most governments use consumer protection legislation to protect domestic industries from foreign competition. One recent example was a decision by the Japanese government to change the requirements for skis in Japan partly on the grounds that Japanese snow was different from snow in other countries!

There is no easy answer. The magic of the market is a magic which fails rather too often and which leaves some of the participants sawn in half. Equally, excessive or wrong-headed market regulation may reduce the entertainment and even put magicians out of business.

3 Firms in Product Markets

Product markets are frequently portrayed as dull and bloodless, involving few choices, relative certainty and management by the application of a few rules.

In reality, this is anything but the case. Product markets are characterised by complex and changing relationships among firms, by the rapid growth of some firms, and by many bankruptcies. Many firms produce a wide range of products in a variety of markets and across national boundaries. They have numerous and sometimes conflicting objectives. They need to deal with constant market changes and, at the same time, to be planning their actions well into the future. Simple rules can't be applied in such circumstances. Even if they could be, firms would often lack the information necessary to use them. Instead, they develop market strategies which are broad, subject to varying interpretations, and often fluid.

However, the notion of perfect competition, with large numbers of small firms provides a standard with which we can compare the behaviour of firms in product markets.

3.1 COMPETITION IN PRODUCT MARKETS

3.1.1 The small competitive firm

Imagine a market with a large number of small producers, all selling an identical product to large numbers of consumers. Everyone in the market has perfect knowledge of present and future prices and there are no transactions or transport costs. In these circumstances, the price of the product is determined by the interaction of demand and supply in the market and each firm sells at the going market price. Firms, in other words, are price takers.

For the market as a whole, the demand curve slopes down to the right as in our diagrams in Chapters one and two. But the demand curve facing each individual firm is a horizontal straight line at the market price. Any firm which attempts to raise its price above the market price will lose all its custom, since consumers will instantly be aware that the same product can be purchased at a lower price elsewhere in the market.

New firms can freely enter and leave the market and thus firms earn what are known as normal profits—profits which are just sufficient to persuade owners of firms to remain in the industry since they could not do better elsewhere. If profits in the industry rise, new firms will seek to take advantage of the improved conditions within the market and profits will be forced back down to the normal level.

Suppose the product suddenly becomes more popular with

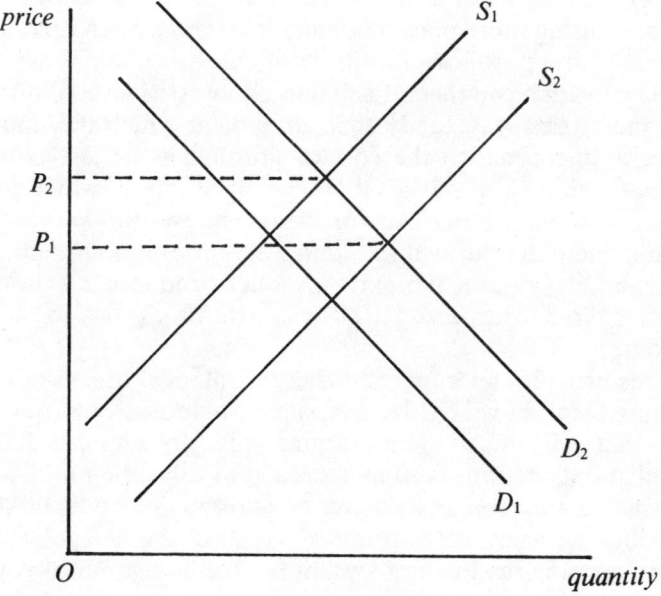

Figure 3.1

consumers. Demand increases. In fig. 3.1 the market demand curve moves out from D_1 to D_2 and price rises from P_1 to P_2. Profits for each firm in the market rise above the normal level (they are earning super-normal profits).

As a result, new firms enter and add to the total supply in the market. The supply curve shifts down from S_1 to S_2. Price falls back to P_1 and normal profits are re-established.

Firms in such a market are completely constrained. They produce only one commodity and have no choice over where or to whom to sell it. They seek to maximise profits but in the long run can make only normal profits. To earn these, they must charge the going price. They are not able to vary the quality or nature of the product. Because everyone knows that all firms in the market are producing an identical product, there is no point in advertising.

Because firms are only earning normal profits, there are no funds available for spending on research and development. To survive, firms must produce at minimum costs and so each firm will produce the product in exactly the same way as all others—there is no scope, for example, for some firms to produce using more machinery and less labour than others.

Firms simply follow a number of rules to make those few choices available to them. Each one 'chooses' its level of output but must produce exactly that amount at which the market price is just equal to the cost of producing the last unit of output (that is, it produces that level of output at which price equals marginal cost). Again, firms 'choose' the amount of labour they hire but will hire that amount of labour at which the market value of the extra product produced by the last worker hired is just equal to the wage they must pay to obtain labour.

This provides an important theoretical ideal because of the pricing formula which firms in such a market would have to use: that price must equal marginal cost. In section 1.3.5 we pointed out that this is what is needed to solve the problem of how to use the economy's scarce resources to satisfy as far as is possible the wants of consumers. Much of the defence of the market system as the best system for the allocation of scarce resources depends on the assumption that firms are perfectly competitive and do follow this rule.

However, perfectly competitive markets do not exist. This is probably just as well since in such a world there would be no art to management. Product markets would be very boring.

3.1.1 Other market types

We can move closer to reality by looking at other market types based on the number of firms in the market and the degree of competition among them. Thus, we have imperfect (or monopolistic) competition in which we still have many firms but they produce slightly different products from each other; oligopoly where a market is dominated by a small number of large firms; and monopoly where there is only one seller of a product.

Firms may also have a variety of relationships with their suppliers or with the labour market. Thus, a firm manufacturing motor cars may be purchasing its gear boxes in

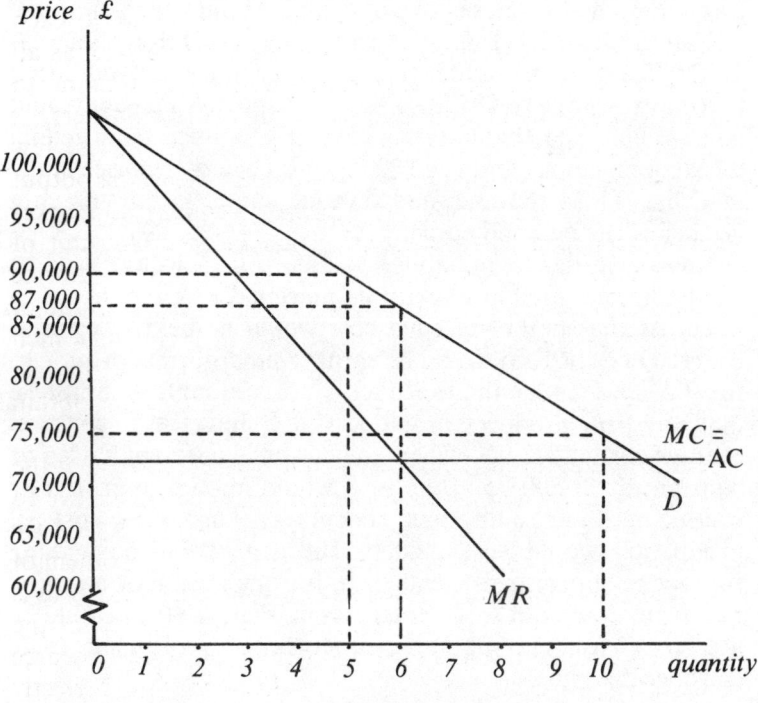

Figure 3.2

another market. Most likely, the car manufacturer will be one of only a few buyers in the gear box market, or, in the extreme case, it may be the only buyer (this is known as monopsony). For each of these market types, rules which will enable firms to maximise profits can be derived. These rules relate to the costs of production, the prices charged and the quantities produced of single products within single markets.

Thus, once we depart from perfect competition, the demand curve facing the firm will slope down to the right since a firm will be able to increase its sales of the product by lowering the price it charges. This in turn means that the extra or marginal revenue which it generates from the sale of an extra unit will be less than the price.

Fig. 3.2, for example, represents the demand curve facing a manufacturer of automated blood cell counters for medical laboratories.

We are making here the very unrealistic assumption that the firm knows that it can sell five of these machines per year in the UK at a price of £90,000, producing a total revenue of £450,000, but that in order to sell six machines, it would need to lower the price to £87,000. Total revenue in that case would be £522,000, and the marginal revenue obtained from selling the sixth machine would be £72,000, well below the price of the machine. Thus, the marginal revenue curve on our diagram lies below the demand curve.

Now, in order to maximise profits, a firm would need to equate its marginal costs with its marginal revenue, not with price. At that point marginal cost would be below the price charged and the firm would be earning supernormal profits. In fig. 3.2, let us make the thoroughly unreasonable assumption that our firm produces its blood cell counters at a constant average cost of £72,000. Then, the marginal cost would also be constant at £72,000 and the firm would maximise profits by producing and selling six machines. The total cost of production would be £432,000. The firm would be making supernormal profits of £90,000. If, for one reason or another, new firms could not easily enter this market, the firm would be able to go on making these supernormal profits for some considerable time.

3.1.2 Some real world choices

More important, however, this example introduces the possibility of a choice of strategies for the firm. It may choose *not* to maximise profits. For instance, it may be a foreign firm wishing to break more strongly into the British market. Thus, it may choose to price the machines at £75,000, planning to sell ten per year. At this price, total revenue would be £750,000, total costs would be £720,000 and the supernormal profits would be only £30,000. However, the firm may feel that its greater number of sales might lead to the machine becoming better known and might lead to an outward shift in the demand curve facing it in future years. This would be an example of penetration pricing—pricing with the particular intention of penetrating the market.

Yet again, the company may also produce biochemical analysers which are already doing very well in the British market and may be prepared to use its profits from these to subsidise its blood cell counters for some time. Thus, it may lower its price for them to below £72,000, actually making a loss on the machines in order to make a large splash in the market.

These possibilities lead us a little closer to reality—but only a little. Exactly what would happen when the firm lowered its price to say £70,000 would depend on how other firms in the market responded. They might try to prevent the new firm from making large inroads by temporarily lowering their prices also. In other words, our original firm would need to make some assumptions regarding the likely behaviour of its rivals before it could estimate the likely shape of the demand curve it faced. It would also need to make guesses about other things, including what was likely to happen to the funding of National Health Service hospitals.

Further, it could attempt to compete in other ways than lowering its price. It might leave the price unchanged and seek to get its name known by financing medical conferences and dinners, by encouraging trials to be carried out on its machines in the hope that favourable articles would be published in medical journals, by advertising in those journals or by increasing its salesforce. In other words, it might deliberately attempt to move the demand curve for its product out, rather than moving down an existing but uncertain demand curve.

Other possibilities might include: (a) keeping its short-run prices and profits high and spending those profits on additional research in an attempt to obtain a technological lead over its rivals; or (b) taking over a British company already in the market. Instead of importing machines for sale in Britain, it might then manufacture its own machines here, perhaps avoiding tariffs by so doing.

And so we could go on. There is, no doubt, some value in understanding rules such as 'firms maximise profits when marginal revenue equals marginal cost', but they provide little guidance to the way in which product markets work. It is far more important to recognise the wide range of actions open to many firms and the complexity of the interrelationships among them. We provide an example of alternative strategies chosen by industries in case study 3.1.

CASE STUDY 3.1: DIFFERENT STRATEGIES IN KITCHEN FURNITURE

The kitchen furniture industries in Britain and West Germany provide an excellent example of different strategies and attitudes among firms. A report published by the National Institute of Economic and Social Research (NIESR)[1] points out the importance of the industry in both countries—kitchen cabinets make up 23 per cent of all furniture production in West Germany and 19 per cent in Britain. But that is about all the two industries have in common.

The West German industry aims for the top end of the market, using high quality materials and offering a wide range of colours, finishes, and accessories. It mainly produces complete kitchens which are installed whole by the suppliers. It is characterised by a well-trained labour force, high productivity, highly automated computer controlled machinery, and sophisticated production planning which is geared closely to orders from customers. Little is manufactured for stock. A third of all output is exported. At least 90 per cent of shop floor workers have had three year training courses. The NIESR investigation of nine plants in Britain and eight in West Germany reported that productivity in West German plants is 66 per cent higher than in British plants. By contrast, the UK industry produces for the bottom end of the market, producing principally self-assembly units, most of which are sold by the large do-it-yourself stores. Thus, it makes mass-produced cupboards of standard sizes with a limited range of cabinet fronts. Companies produce in large batches for stock, using out-dated machinery, with very little use of computers. Only 4 per cent of output is exported. Fewer than 10 per cent of shop floor workers have relevant qualifications. A complete kitchen costs around £1000 compared with over £10000 for some German kitchens.

The British industry is currenty highly profitable—more so than its German counterpart. The differences in strategy of the two industries have partly historical explanations. However, much stems from the different attitudes of the companies in the market. It is the British industry which is closest to the text-book model of profit maximisation. In recent years, it has seen many takeovers and reorganisations of firms. There are a number of young, rapidly expanding firms. One of the authors of the NIESR report, Hilary Steedman, has said: 'The West German companies have a completely different outlook. Their aim is to survive with a name and a tradition, as a sort of institution. British companies are concerned with making profits. To them it does not matter who runs it and what the name is—as long as it makes money'.[2]

The British industry has, however, two long-term problems. Firstly, as real incomes rise more people in Britain are likely to move away from the lower end of the market. This will mean an increase in imports of kitchens (already imports take 23 per cent of the British market and 63 per cent of imports are from West Germany). Secondly, they are increasingly likely to be challenged in the lower end of the market by kitchens from developing countries which have lower-cost labour. A concentration on short-term profits may ultimately turn out not to be the best strategy.

Whether it does or not, the industry gives some indication of the range of choices facing manufacturing companies.

NOTES

1. H. Steedman and K. Wagner: 'A second look at productivity, machinery and skills in Britain and Germany' NIESR Nov. 1987. London.
2. As quoted in R. Atkins: 'Now the heat is on in the kitchen' *Financial Times* November 20, 1987.

3.2 PRODUCT MARKETS IN PRACTICE

There are many small businesses but, despite their numbers and the great attention paid to them in recent years in politicians' speeches, they play only a minor role in many product markets. In all industrialised economies, a high proportion of sales and of employment is in the hands of large companies. Most product markets are dominated by a small number of large firms. This domination continues to grow through merger and takeover activity among firms. Where small firms continue to exist alongside large ones, the nature of the market is determined by the actions of the large companies.

Of course, the position differs considerably among markets. The domination of a market by large firms is often measured by the five-firm concentration ratio which shows the proportion of output in an industry accounted for by the five largest firms. This varies widely from industry to industry, being, for example, very high in the man-made fibre industry but quite low in general printing and publishing. Despite such variations, it remains that over half of the industries in the UK have 5-firm concentration ratios of more than 50 per cent.

Small firms may still expand rapidly and have considerable impact in particular markets—witness the performance of Amstrad within the computer market which we discussed in case study 2.1. However, such growth is likely to require one or more of: a distinctive product; heavy advertising; aggressive pricing policies; a takeover of or merger with other firms. Amstrad followed all of these lines of action. Further it was only able to enter and succeed in the microcomputer market on the back of profits made in another market. In any case, despite its impressive performance, the computer market worldwide is still dominated by IBM. There are very few markets indeed where firms which correspond even remotely to the price-taker image of section 3.1 play any significant role. The most interesting question indeed about small firms is why so many of them fail.

Many large firms are active in several markets. Rules developed concerning the production and sale of a single product in a single market simply do not apply to them. Further, all large firms are also financial enterprises. They raise funds in order to finance investment or takeovers. They do this by issuing new shares, or by borrowing from banks or directly from financial markets as issuers of bills or commercial paper. They engage in international trade and therefore necessarily engage in foreign exchange transactions. As owners of large buildings or large-scale purchasers of raw materials they may speculate in property or commodities markets.

The significance of this is that in many cases the profits of large companies may in particular years have relatively little to do with their efficiency in their principal lines of production. In recent years, Lufthansa, Alitalia and Volkswagen have all made large losses in foreign exchange markets. In the 1970s Rowntree, which buys large amounts of cocoa on world markets in order to produce their chocolates, purchased much more than they needed in the hope that the price would rise and they would make a speculative gain. The price fell. Midland Bank profits fell in the middle 1980s, not because of any inadequacy in its UK banking operations, but because it purchased Crocker, a loss-making United States bank.

Naturally there are many success stories also. The point is that to look only at a firm's production and sales activities is often to ignore an important part of the picture. A firm may be forced to raise its prices, not so as to maximise profits, but to raise cash in order to meet losses made in financial transactions.

Finally, we need to stress here the internationalisation of product markets. We can see from United Nations surveys,

Transnational Corporations in World Development, that many firms have become truly international. For example, the third survey (published in 1983) showed that in 1980 46 per cent of IBM's assets were held outside the United States and 43 per cent of its employees were employed abroad; the equivalent figures for International Harvester were 48 per cent and 35 per cent; 61 per cent of the assets of the French firm St Gobain were held outside France and 53 per cent of its employees were employed outside France. Many other examples could be given.

This development of transnational corporations has resulted in some very complex production and marketing arrangements. A single product may be produced by one firm but might consist of component parts produced in a number of countries. Ford UK is simultaneously the UK's largest importer and largest exporter of motor vehicles.

Again, what happens to a subsidiary of a transnational company may have little or nothing to do with its performance within the market in which it is operating. The closure of the Caterpillar tractor factory in Scotland did not result from inefficiency and losses within the factory but was the result of problems faced by the Caterpillar company in the United States.

3.3. FIRMS AND THEIR OBJECTIVES

It is commonly assumed that firms seek to maximise profits. This is logical as long as we think of firms as small, since it is likely that a small firm will be largely managed by its owners and it seems reasonable that the owners of a firm will be principally interested in the rate of return they can obtain on their capital.

Once firms become large, however, ownership is likely to be separated from control. Large companies quoted on the stock exchange are owned by their shareholders. Typically, a firm will have many thousands of shareholders, most of whom will own a very small proportion of the company indeed. In these circumstances, shareholders can have very little influence on how the firm is run and on what the objectives of the firm are. There are basically two reasons for this.

The first is purely organisational. Small shareholders are unlikely to know each other. They live in various parts of the country (or abroad) and would find it almost impossible to organise sufficiently to put pressure on the company's board of directors for the firm to follow a particular course of action. In any case, small shareholders have relatively little information regarding the running of the company and are in no position to know whether a company is maximising profits or not.

Consequently, they must delegate authority to the board of directors. It is generally assumed that small shareholders will be happy as long as the firm seems to be doing reasonably well—well enough to pay out a satisfactory dividend and to ensure that the company's shares maintain their relative value on the stock market. All firms have annual general meetings, but usually only a small proportion of shareholders attend. Thus, when votes about company policy are taken, many shareholders either do not vote at all or give their proxy vote to the board of directors.

It is true that larger shareholders are very likely to be represented on the board of directors but here our second argument enters. Modern firms are frequently very complex—perhaps producing specialised and technologically advanced products, selling in many markets, negotiating complicated deals with suppliers and large numbers of workers, operating in a big way in financial markets. In these circumstances, to understand fully the management choices facing the firm, a great deal of technical knowledge is needed relating to production, marketing, distribution, finance, tax laws, labour laws and so on.

Members of boards of directors who are not full-time employees of the company simply cannot have this knowledge. Boards may formally make decisions regarding the operation of the firm, but they are usually dependent on the advice of the full-time management of the company (named the technostructure by the American economist, J.K. Galbraith). In some cases the board of directors may have very little idea at all as to what management is doing.

Now it is possible that management advice may be based on quite a different set of objectives from those of the shareholders. It is true that senior management rewards are likely to be in part related to the profit performance of the company—they will usually be small shareholders themselves and may be granted by the company options to purchase shares at set prices. In this case, they may stand to make considerable capital gains if the stock market perceives the company to be doing well and the firm's share price rises well above the price at which management may buy. For all that, other objectives may be important to management.

For example, management prestige may be related to the size of the company. Some managements will be aggressive and seek to takeover other firms and to cause the company to grow, even if that involves a sacrifice of some profits. Again, management may have a longer term view than shareholders and may be particularly concerned with protecting the firm from takeover by others. Or, it may principally want an easy life. Instead of pushing for ever-higher profits, it may be concerned simply to achieve a satisfactory level of profits and to maintain its position in the markets in which it operates, rather than attack other firms and risk counter-attack. In other words, large firms take on lives and characters separate from their owners, the shareholders.

We have talked generally of 'management' here. This plays down rather too much the role of individuals. Firms are sometimes dominated by one person. This person may be the founder of the company and have a large shareholding in it (as with Rupert Murdoch and News International). But in other cases the dominant personality is a full-time employee of the company with a relatively small shareholding, as with R.D. Elliott, the chief exexcutive of the aggressive Australian company, Elders IXL. Mr. Elliott owns rather less than 0.5 per cent of Elders' shares, but plays a major role in determining the strategies of the company. Sometimes, a firm's strategy changes as the balance of opinion changes among full-time employees; or when one chief executive retires and is replaced by another.

All of this indicates that although the behaviour of a firm may in some cases be closely related to purely economic questions of marginal revenue and marginal cost and a desire to make as much profit as possible, in many cases company policy will have quite different bases and concerns.

3.4 RIVALRY AND COMPETITION

Economists are particularly concerned with the extent of competition within markets. When people talk of competition, they mostly have in mind price competition—that is, the attempt by a firm to increase its share of the market by charging a lower price for an identical or similar product. Yet competition within markets can take many other forms. Firms may attempt to compete through product quality; image and brand name; after-sales service; or presentation and salesmanship.

But even this broader view of competition represents only a small part of inter-firm rivalry. For instance, firms may seek to merge with or take over other firms with the specific intention of reducing the need to compete in markets or to enable them to compete more effectively with other companies. On the other hand, a merger or takeover may have relatively little to do with competition—a firm may merge with another in an attempt to protect itself from takeover by some other firm. Mergers and takeovers may take many forms. Let us consider some examples.

3.5 CHOICES AND STRATEGIES—FIRMS IN PRACTICE

3.5.1 Horizontal integration of firms

Horizontal integration occurs when firms which are producing the same product are combined—for example, the takeover of Acorn Computers (the makers of the BBC mircocomputers) by Olivetti; the takeover of the *Today* newspaper by Rupert Murdoch's News International; the merger of the Alliance and Leicester building societies.

Such an integration may have several outcomes. It immediately gives the combined firm a higher share of market sales and reduces the number of firms competing in the market (in other words, it increases the concentration of the market and increases the market power of the combined firm). The greater size of the firm may enable production, management and/or marketing to be carried out more efficiently, thus reducing the firm's average costs (that is, it may lead to internal economies of scale). The bigger firm may have greater bargaining power in dealing with suppliers of raw materials and intermediate goods, and may be able to obtain these at lower prices. It may be able to borrow more easily from financial institutions, possibly at lower interest rates.

Such benefits from the merger or takeover lead them to lower costs and possibly to higher profits and higher dividends to shareholders. However, the firm may take advantage of its improved position by lowering prices, or by increasing spending on advertising or on research and development in an attempt to increase its market share further. But many other possibilities exist. A firm taking over a competitor may completely close down the operation of its victim—its motive may simply be to reduce competition. This is what occurred when the London *Evening Standard* took over its rival the *Evening News*. As we show in case study 3.2, the *Evening Standard* was later able to defend its position in the market.

CASE STUDY 3.2: COMPETITION IN ACTION—LONDON EVENING NEWSPAPERS

For many years London had two evening newspapers—the *Evening Standard* and the *Evening News*. Then, the two companies merged and the *Evening News* was closed down. For several years, the *Evening Standard* had the market to itself.

In February 1987, Robert Maxwell, the publisher of the *Daily Mirror*, entered the field with the *London Daily News*—a paper which was intended to have several editions and to be a '24-hour newspaper' but which was in essence in competition with the *Evening Standard*.

The response of the management of the *Standard* was to resurrect the old *Evening News*. This was hurriedly done and a slim paper was put on the streets. This caused confusion over newspaper titles and attempted to appeal to any lingering loyalty which remained to the old *Evening News* title. As well, the resurrected *Evening News* appeared at a price lower than the 20 pence of the *Standard* and the *Daily*

News. This could all be seen as a particularly clever, if a little belated, barrier to entry.

Having failed to obtain a position in the market, Maxwell was forced to cut his price also, and a short price-cutting war followed, adding to the losses which the *London Daily News* was making. After only six months, it was closed down and Maxwell at least temporarily withdrew from the market. Although the resurrection of the old *Evening News* was clearly a spoiling tactic, the management claimed otherwise and suggested that they would continue to operate the two papers. However, once a respectable time had elapsed and the challenge from the opposition had been beaten off, the *Evening News* was again closed down, once again leaving the *Evening Standard* in sole possession of the market.

Here we saw an attempt to use pricing policies to establish a market niche; a short price war; and a successful attempt to obstruct a competitor. Maxwell's response was to threaten the establishment of a new free newspaper in London to challenge the *Evening Standard's* monopoly by another route.

Or it may be acting to enter a new segment of the market in the cheapest or easiest possible way. Thus, a large brewer may take over a small regional brewer principally because this enables it to sell its products in an increased number of pubs in the region. This would be an example of a takeover where the predatory firm is only interested in some of the assets of its victim—not in the whole business.

When News International took over *Today*, it gave as its aim the desire to enter the middle-brow daily newspaper market in contrast with its existing papers *The Sun* and *The Times* which are aimed respectively at the lower and upper ends of the market. This meant that it could use its spare printing capacity and its own distribution network, while building on the existing readership of *Today*.

3.5.2 Vertical integration

This involves the merging of a firm with one of its suppliers (backward integration) or with a firm which markets or distributes its product (forward integration). An interesting recent example of backward vertical integration occurred when Rupert Murdoch acquired the Hollywood film company, Twentieth Century Fox, principally to obtain its vast film library for his American and Australian television stations. The brewing industry in Britain provides a good example of forward vertical integration with a high proportion of pubs and off-licences being owned by brewing companies.

Vertical integration may be undertaken to make it more difficult for new firms to enter a market and compete with existing firms. The early 1980s in Britain saw the establishment of large numbers of new, small breweries. In many cases, they found it difficult to market their products precisely because so many beer outlets were owned by the firms already in the market. In other words, vertical integration may act as a barrier to entry for new firms.

On the other hand, vertical integration may be defensive. It may be aimed at protecting supplies of materials and market outlets from other aggressive firms. Like other forms of integration, vertical integration may allow cross-subsidisation. Suppose a brewer owns a very high proportion of pubs in one area, but faces very stiff competition in another. It may be able to raise its prices in the area which it dominates, and use the additional profits there to cut prices and attack its rivals in the second region.

3.5.3 Lateral integration
Here we are concerned with the merging of firms whose products have little or nothing in common with each other. A much publicised example was the takeover of the retail store group, the House of Fraser (whose stores include Harrods) by the Al-Fayed brothers, whose other commercial interests were in shipping, oil and the ownership of hotels.

Lateral integration may also influence competition in a variety of ways—for example through the benefits of size, especially in financial markets. Lateral integration may, however, have relatively little to do with questions of technical efficiency of firms. Sometimes they are undertaken in order to obtain tax advantages; or to allow the stripping of the assets of the firm taken over, perhaps in order to provide necessary cash flow for the company.

3.5.4 Influence on government and protection
Faced with foreign competition, a firm may, instead of attempting to lower costs and prices, try to influence the government to impose tariffs or quotas on foreign firms or to subsidise the domestic product. Again, the requested government action may be more subtle. It may employ one of those many devices collectively known as non-tariff barriers, which act by increasing the administrative or production costs of rival foreign producers. Perhaps the most famous example of the past decade was the decision of the French government in the early 1980s to require all foreign videos to be transported to the inland town of Poitiers for customs clearance. The customs office in Poitiers was very small and could not cope with the extra workload. This led to considerable delays for importers and large increases in transport, storage and administrative costs.

3.5.5 Foreign trade versus investment
Protection is one of many factors which influence a firm's choice of strategy in relation to foreign markets. Basically, a firm wishing to enter a foreign market has one of four choices. It may produce at home and export its products. Instead, it may sell licences to other firms permitting them to manufacture and market the product in other countries; thirdly, it may invest abroad, establishing a subsidiary company which produces and sells the product in the country in which it is established. Finally, it may enter into co-production arrangements with firms in other countries, as with the arrangements in the UK between Austin-Rover and Honda.

Firms may, of course, follow different strategies at different times. The Australian brewing company, Elders IXL, initially entered the British market by selling to the UK firm, Grand Metropolitan, the right to manufacture and sell Fosters Lager within the UK. Later, Elders acquired the UK brewer, Courage, but then found that it was too difficult to buy back from Grand Metropolitan the right to produce Fosters. Consequently, Grand Metropolitan continues to produce Fosters, but it is now marketed here by both companies.

Such choices may be influenced by many things—

protection, taxation laws, the availability of capital; the nature of the product; the nature and level of the competition and so on. Again what we wish to stress here is the complexity of such decisions. Static cost and demand curves may be only one small part of the total information considered by the firm. Further, the management of large firms is necessarily dynamic—the actions which a firm sees as necessary to maintain or advance its position in a market this year may be different from those followed last year or those which will be followed in two or three years time.

3.6 SMALL FIRMS AND FAILURE

Firms fail, it is usually said, because they are inefficient. Their costs are too high and they fail to make normal profits. Hence they leave the market. Competition acts to weed out the inefficient. Only the efficient firms survive. As with our earlier rules, there is no doubt often an element of truth in this. But it is again too simple. We can allow for the possibility that large firms may be able to operate at lower average costs than small ones. Then, new, small firms in a market may be unable to compete because they are too small to reap these economies of scale. This still does not take us far enough.

Above all, it concentrates too much on production and insufficiently on the marketing and distribution of products and on the financial aspects of firms. We have already considered an example (in the brewing industry) where vertical integration makes it difficult for new firms to obtain outlets for their products. We have mentioned the possibility of large firms artificially lowering prices in a market through cross-subsidisation in order to see off new rivals.

There are other possibilities. We have suggested that product differentiation is important in new markets. A new product has to become known. In today's world, this almost invariably requires large scale advertising. In April 1987, a new Sunday newspaper, the *News on Sunday*, was launched. There were many problems with the paper and arguments over what sort of newspaper it should be. Such problems clearly contributed to its failure. However, there were other elements.

The paper was initially under-capitalised. It lacked the funds needed to advertise at the level required. Surveys shortly after its launch showed that only 12 per cent of people were aware of its existence.

Yet another major problem of new firms is cash flow. Firms may have considerable future prospects. But they need funds to tide them over initial losses. Banks and other financial institutions are often cautious in lending to new firms. The result may be that the company lacks the funds needed to give it time to succeed. This was yet another problem of the *News on Sunday*. Some of its arranged bank loans were tied to its reaching a particular circulation level. Because this was not reached the bank loans were not forthcoming. After a change of ownership, the paper finally closed down in November 1987.

Firms may start small and successfully. Their success requires them to expand. This expansion requires further loans which may then be tied up in the form of illiquid assets such as machinery. Again they may fail because they cannot generate the necessary cash flow to meet payments on borrowings, rather than because the firm is not efficient or not profitable. Successful firms may fail because they attempt to expand too quickly.

3.7 GOVERNMENT INTERVENTION

Government intervention may affect production in many ways. For example, governments may: (a) tax citizens and use the proceeds to provide commodities produced by the private sector; (b) subsidise private firms or give tax allowances to them; (c) impose tariffs, quotas or other protective devices on imported goods; (d) invest in the infrastructure of the economy (for instance, in transport networks, communications, housing or education); (e) employ labour themselves to produce commodities which may be sold or distributed without charge to the public; (f) legislate to control the behaviour of private firms towards their customers, their competitors, their workforce or the government.

The last two of these have been particularly controversial in recent years. Many nationalised industries and government-held shares in private corporations have been sold, and services previously provided directly by the public sector have been contracted out to the private sector. Many government controls have been abolished or reduced. Here, however, we shall particularly concern ourselves with government policy relating to competition within markets.

3.7.1 Monopolies and restrictive practices

We have seen that competition within product markets is generally regarded as desirable. It follows that where markets come to be dominated by a small number of large firms with market power, it is often thought that social welfare is reduced. Thus it is argued that there is a role for government intervention to reduce the number of mergers and takeovers. Such action alone, however, may only lead to firms agreeing formally or informally to act *as if* mergers or takeovers had taken place; that is, firms may remain in separate ownership but may voluntarily restrict competition.

Since the outcome from the point of view of the economy as a whole is the same, any legislation aimed at inhibiting the tendency towards monopolisation will need to be supported by legislation preventing the restrictive practices of firms (that is, acts which restrict competition and are thought to be against the public interest). Naturally, governments will also be interested in likely future developments in markets and will thus be concerned about any restrictions on the ability of new firms to enter markets (barriers to entry).

Now it is far from clear that monopolisation of markets is *necessarily* a bad thing. The reduction of competition produces larger firms and these larger firms may be able to reap economies of scale not available to small firms. Again, the existence of supernormal profits may lead to extra spending on research and development, with consequent more rapid technological advance. An increase in market power, that is, may be associated with a reduction in costs.

On the other hand, it may be associated with a restriction of output leading to higher costs and prices and/or a failure to produce at minimum cost because of lack of competitive pressure (X-inefficiency). The outcome may be different in different cases. A government must decide, then, whether every single case has to be judged on its individual merits or whether certain types of market structure are sufficiently likely to be against the public interest that they should be ruled out automatically.

In fact, there is little evidence that profitability and efficiency of firms are significantly improved as a result of growth through mergers. The most profitable firms are not necessarily large. In addition, the majority of firms which take over other firms seem to be growth-maximisers rather than profit-maximisers. Only a small number of mergers seem to be made to reap the benefits of technical economies of scale. Indeed, many mergers do not result in larger plant sizes. The growing firm may simply acquire more plants. There may be economies of scale in management or in the rationalisation of plant activities within the now larger firm, but it is not at all certain that mergers lead to greater efficiency.

The link between size and technical innovation also seems to be insecure. In many industries it is the smaller, sometimes newer, firms which lead the way. Larger firms in some cases lack the necessary flexibility or have too much of their capital tied up in existing technologies. Large firms which do invest heavily in research may establish a lead in the invention of new products and processes. It does not necessarily follow, however, that they will choose to put these inventions into practice (that is, invention may not be followed by innovation).

In sum, the practical case in favour of movements away from competition is not strong. But this does not mean that movements towards greater competition are always desirable. Such movements may involve redistributions of income, and where these occur it may be impossible to decide whether the country as a whole is better off as a result of the change.

These arguments seem to reinforce the view that individual cases should be investigated, rather than having blanket legislation which assumes that increased competition is necessarily good and that the reduction of competition beyond some particular point is necessarily bad. However, the investigation of individual cases takes considerable time and uses resources. As well, it raises difficulties over the basis of choice of the cases to be investigated, and introduces the possibility of political influence on this choice or on the subsequent investigations.

Nonetheless, British legislation has accepted this selective approach to the judgement of the impact on competition of mergers and restrictive practices. In 1948, the Monopolies Commission was established. Since then there have been several changes in name, powers and operation. Since 1973, it has been known as the Monopolies and Mergers Commission. The decision to refer mergers to the Commission is now taken by the Director General of Fair Trading. The Secretary of State for Industry can, however, overrule the Director General's decision to refer or can decide to make references against the advice of the Director General.

Once the Commissioners have examined a merger, their acceptance or rejection of it can be overruled by the Secretary of State. It is hardly surprising that in these circumstances there has over the years been a great deal of confusion and controversy over the operation of the act.

In 1980 the Competition Act gave the Director General of Fair Trading new powers to examine anti-competitive practices of individual firms. However, there was no explicit indication of the sort of practices the government had in mind. The Act also allowed the investigation of nationalised industries and trade unions. It provided strong support for the text book competitive ideal and gave the government considerable potential power over the activities of individual firms. But uncertainty and controversy have remained.

In practice, the government has been particularly concerned with the activities of nationalised industries and with the question of competition in the labour market. No coherent or strong policy has emerged towards the growth of corporate power in the private sector of the economy. Even where government corporations or government-held shares in private corporations have been sold off to the private sector, there has been little attempt to ensure an increase in the level of competition.

4 The Labour Market

It is possible to think of labour as a factor of production along with capital and land, and to analyse it in the same way as anything else which is bought and sold. Then, the demand for and supply of labour interact to produce an equilibrium wage rate (the price of labour). This framework can be used to investigate wage relationships among different groups of workers in an economy.

For this purpose, workers can be classified in a number of ways. They may be divided by type of occupation into manual and non-manual, with manual workers, in turn, being split into skilled, semi-skilled, and unskilled. Or the wage relationship between specific occupations, for instance teachers and policemen, may be considered. Alternatively, we may be interested in industrial or regional wage differentials, asking, for example, about the relationship between the wages of machinists in the textile industry and in the footwear industry, or workers doing the same work in London and Dundee. Again, we may wish to enquire into wage differences between men and women or white and black workers.

Economists also use demand and supply analysis to try to explain unemployment. Gluts occur in all markets and unemployment can be seen as a glut of labour services—supply is greater than demand at existing wage rates. However, supporters of the standard approach hold that labour markets are competitive, that wage rates are flexibile and that they change in order to equate demand and supply. Thus, wage rates should fall to bring about full employment.

There are problems here. Labour has many characteristics

which make it different from other factors of production and, in many ways, real labour markets are much closer to fix-price markets than to flex-price ones. Thus, although we shall begin by looking at the demand for and supply of labour, we need then to consider the factors which make labour markets different from others.

4.1 THE DEMAND FOR LABOUR

Let us assume that firms are profit maximising and that a firm faces an ordinary downward sloping demand curve for its product. We assume further that it can use any combination of labour and machines (capital) in production. That is, it may produce labour intensively, using a lot of labour relative to capital or capital intensively. Its choice will be influenced by the level of technology available to it and by the cost of labour (the wage rate) relative to the cost of capital. We can assume either that funds have to be borrowed to buy capital equipment or that the firm re-invests its own profits, rather than using them in some other way. In either case, we can take the cost of capital to be the rate of interest available in the economy on long term financial assets. If we assume that there is no technological change and that the cost of capital is constant, it follows that the higher the wage rate, the less labour the firm will wish to hire relative to capital; that is, the more capital intensively the firm will choose to produce the good.

It is usually assumed also that a firm can change its capital stock only slowly, but that the quantity of labour employed is easily varied. Thus, at any particular time, the amount of capital used by the firm will be fixed and the higher the wage rate, the less labour the firm will use with that capital stock. In other words, the higher the wage rate, the less labour the firm will employ. The firm's labour demand curves slopes down to the right as most other demand curves do. In principle, we may add up the labour demand curves for different firms to produce labour demand curves for each industry and even a labour demand curve for the whole economy, although no one pretends that this is possible in practice.

We can apply the same notion to the demand for different

types of labour—the higher the wage rates of unskilled workers relative to those of skilled workers, the smaller will be the proportion of unskilled workers hired.

But many other factors enter into the demand for labour. Let us look at several of them.

4.1.1 Hiring, training and firing costs

Labour is not fully variable. We can extend the idea of labour as a factor of production by thinking of the acquisition of work-related skills and experience as an investment (or an increase in the worker's human capital). Some of this investment in labour is paid for by firms because the learning of new skills increases a worker's value to the firm.

As well as training costs, firms face hiring costs in employing new workers. They advertise, interview applicants, and seek references from previous employers. This costs time and money. And no matter how careful they are in making new appointments, they cannot know in advance the exact quality of labour they are hiring. There are also costs in getting rid of workers. It may take time to follow laid down procedures for declaring workers redundant. Compensation may have to be paid to those made redundant. Trade unions are likely to resist.

All this means that firms will be very unlikely to respond at all quickly to a wage increase by reducing their workforces. We have seen that it may be costly to do so. Further, if other conditions were to change soon after so that it again made sense to increase their workforces, they would face additional hiring and training costs. Wage rates may have to rise very sharply before employers reduce their demand for labour (the demand curve for labour, especially for skilled labour, may be very steeply sloped).

Often firms have greater scope for flexibility than this perhaps implies. In some industries, overtime working is a regular practice and firms may be able to reduce their demand for labour quickly not by declaring workers redundant but by cutting back on overtime hours worked. Again, some firms are able to put their workers on short-time working without losing their experienced and skilled workforces. Nonetheless the size of a firm's workforce is far from being easily variable.

4.1.2 Primary and secondary labour markets

The notion of a firm investing in its labour force raises the possibility that there are in practice two (or more) quite separate labour markets—the primary labour market and the secondary labour market.

Primary labour markets are markets for jobs which require knowledge, skills and/or experience. Firms seek to retain the types of workers who fill such jobs. One way of doing this is to develop promotion ladders. A firm's primary workers are organised into a hierarchical structure, broad at the bottom and tapering towards the top, like a pyramid. Workers are employed from the external labour market at only a few levels (or ports of entry) in this pyramid. Jobs at other levels are filled by promotion from below. It is then hoped that skilled workers will not leave the firm, even if they can obtain higher wages elsewhere, because they may lose their place on a promotion ladder. In any case, if all large firms are organised in a similar way, there will only be a few points at which workers can enter other firms. This type of structure is known as an internal labour market—internal, that is, to each firm.

Secondary labour markets, on the other hand, are markets for jobs which do not require skills or experience. Firms invest little in workers who perform these jobs and so wish to be easily able to get rid of them when the firm's position worsens or if wages rise. They will thus seek to hire them part-time or on short-term contracts which provide less legal protection for the worker than longer-term contracts. Secondary workers are also less likely than primary ones to be protected by strong unions or professional associations. Thus the view that the size of a firm's labour force can be easily varied is more likely to apply to secondary workers than to primary ones.

4.1.3 The relationship between labour and capital

There will often be technical reasons why a firm cannot vary its labour force, while keeping capital stock constant. Labour and capital work together in production. Operations may need to continue until a decision is made to shut down or to cut back greatly a whole section of a company. Redundancies are commonly announced in large numbers—a plant closes down or a workforce is reduced by several hundred. Such changes do not suggest precise responses in labour demand to wage rate changes.

4.1.4 Shifting labour demand curves

Let us accept, however, that an increase in wage rate, while nothing else changes, will cause a movement along a downward sloping labour demand curve. How important is this in any attempt to understand how real labour markets work? After all, labour demand curves, like demand curves in other markets, may move around a good deal.

An increase in demand for the firm's product will shift the curve out to the right. We have seen in Chapter two many reasons why this might happen—a change in tastes, increases in the prices of other products, an increase in the economy's real income, an increase in total consumption at the expense of saving, a change in the distribution of income, a change in wealth. We can add to those. Many UK companies produce tradable goods or services. The demand for them will change with changes in exchange rates or with changes in the tariffs of different countries. Can you see why a trade union is usually strongly in favour of tariffs to protect its industry?

Another problem is that we began with the assumption that firms maximise profits. We have seen in Chapter 3 that firms may not do so, and hence may respond to a change in wage rates in a variety of ways. If the product market is not price-competitive, a firm may be able to offset an increase in wages by increasing the price of its products without much affecting the demand for them. Or it may respond by making a greater sales effort or re-organising production so as to raise productivity. Either of these actions will move its labour demand curve to the right. Yet again, given the costs of union resistance, a firm may prefer for a short period of time at least to accept a decline in profits rather than attempt to reduce the size of its workforce.

Large companies (including transnational corporations) complicate things further. They may transfer production from one plant to another for reasons which have very little to do with the efficiency of operation or the wage level of the plant which is losing production. For example, jobs may be moved from one region to another or one country to another because of changes in the subsidies provided by different governments. Countries and regions within countries actively compete for jobs in this way. The taxation and tariff policies of governments may also strongly influence where jobs go.

Finally, the assumption of no technological change avoids what has been the single most important labour market issue for over two hundred years.

4.1.5 Technological change and the demand for labour

Technological change may influence the demand for labour in two conflicting ways. Firstly, less labour is needed to produce the existing level of output. Labour is replaced by capital and labour demand curves shift left. If nothing else changes, employment falls. It was this sort of view of the likely effects of technological change which led the Luddites to destroy machines in the eighteenth century and has worried all trade unions since.

However, technological change allows the existing workforce to produce more. Thus, there is a *potential* for increased output, increased real income and an increased demand for all goods. If this potential is realised, then all product demand curves and labour demand curves shift right. As long as the second effect is at least as strong as the first (as it has been for much of the past two centuries) and output grows at least as fast as the rate of increase in labour productivity, then total employment in the economy will not fall.

But what if all of the *potential* additional output cannot be sold? Then actual output in the economy might grow more slowly than the ability of the economy to produce and the number of jobs in the economy would fall. At present, labour productivity is growing at a rate of about 3 per cent per year. Output must, therefore, also grow at 3 per cent a year if the number of people employed is not to fall.

Of course, even if this occurs, the same people might not be employed. As we saw in Chapter two, when real incomes rise, demand patterns change. Some industries expand, others decline. Further, some industries are much more affected by technological change than others. Old skills are no longer required. Older workers, in particular, will find it very difficult to re-train or to move from one region to another to find work

The labour market 83

in the expanding industries. Average incomes in the economy will rise but some people will be worse off. This explains why particular groups of workers will resist technological change in their industries, even if it is thought to be a good thing for the economy as a whole. We consider the question of winners and losers in case study 4.1.

CASE STUDY 4.1: TECHNOLOGICAL CHANGE AND THE PRINTING INDUSTRY

Changing technology began to revolutionise the printing industry in the 1970s. Papers used to be produced by being set in hot metal by linotype operators. The metal type was then formed into pages by compositors and proofs were run off. These were checked for mistakes by proof readers before corrections were made by the linotype operators and the paper was printed. Printing workers thus played an extremely important part in newspaper production and were able in many cases to build up a good deal of industrial strength and to obtain good wages for their key members.

Computerisation allowed journalists and typists to input material directly into computer terminals. Computer controlled printing presses did away with the need for hot metal—the jobs of linotype operators, compositors and proof readers disappeared. Standard labour market theory would argue that this was of benefit to the economy as a whole. The output of the newspaper industry could be produced with fewer workers. The displaced workers would move into other jobs in the economy or would choose to leave the labour market. There would be no increase in unemployment.

This was not, however, the way printing workers saw the issue. From 1981 on, when computerisation really started to take hold in most countries, the world was undergoing a major recession with many people being unemployed. Redundant workers over forty years old were finding it increasingly difficult to find work. Printing workers knew that, at the very best, they would find work which made little or no use of their skills or experience. They would thus only be able to earn much lower wages.

Consequently, they sought to resist automation. The highly unionised workers in the national newspapers in Fleet Street succeeded in doing so for some time. However, gradually provincial newspapers changed. With the help of strong new anti-trade union legislation and heavy fines imposed on the National Graphical Association, one of the main printing unions, Eddie Shah, the proprietor of the *Stockport Messenger*, won a major victory over the unions. With the national prominence which this gave him, he was able to raise funds and move to London, establishing the new daily paper, *Today* using new technology and non-union labour. Shortly afterwards, Rupert Murdoch, proprietor of the *Sun* and the *Times* moved to a new plant at Wapping and defeated the printing unions after a prolonged dispute. The new technology moved in everywhere.

Who gained and who lost from this change? Clearly, the printing workers lost. Many workers retired earlier than they would otherwise have done. Some moved to other jobs which did not pay as well. Some remained unemployed for long periods. Some workers, of course, gained—the non-union men employed by *Today* and the workers from the Electrical Trades Union employed by Rupert Murdoch at Wapping, but they were much fewer in number than the displaced printers. Journalists gained to the extent that they felt that the new technology improved their working conditions. Industries providing the new printing presses and computers gained, although a good deal of this equipment was imported. The newspaper owners gained in the form of lower costs and higher profits. To the extent that that led to greater investment in the UK there was a subsequent gain. However, several UK newspapers are largely owned by foreign companies.

What of newspaper readers? Newspaper prices did not fall. It was strongly suggested that the new technology would lower costs to such an extent that new owners would enter the markets, new papers would appear and choice would increase. But as we have seen elsewhere in the book, several of the attempts which have been made have failed, with the papers either quickly closing down, or, as with *Today*, being taken over by existing newspaper owners. The

new printing presses allow colour printing and thus more colour appears in newspapers. There are now fewer interruptions to production as a result of industrial disputes but that may have occurred in any case with the much changed industrial relations legislation of recent years.
In other words, the gains appear to be small, uncertain, and widely spread. In a world in which labour is not particularly mobile, the principal effect of technological change will frequently be income redistribution—with some gaining at the expense of others. It is often far from clear to what extent the economy as a whole benefits.

There is yet another issue. Is the rate of technological change related to the level of wages in an economy? High wage levels may lead firms to adopt new technology more quickly than they might otherwise do. Then an increase in wages might cause both a movement along a labour demand curve *and* a more rapid shift in the curve than would otherwise occur. In this case, the size of the shift is very likely to be more important than the movement along the existing curve.

4.1.6 The demand for labour in the public sector

We have so far seen the demand for labour as being *derived* from the demand for products which are sold in product markets. But much of the output of the public sector is not sold. How can the productivity of public sector workers then be measured?

We can divide public sector output into two types. Some could be sold. Thus, schools and hospitals can be run for profit. The interesting questions here concern the aspects of their output which are highly valued by markets and the extent to which market values differ from those of the public sector. For example, how would a fully private health system compare with the present system? This is a large and difficult question which we cannot deal with here but it is a vital one. You should think back to our discussion in Chapter one of public goods, externalities and income distribution.

Some public sector output could not, however, be sold: the output, for example, of the armed forces or of prisons. For people employed in these areas there can be no objective measure of productivity and no sensible labour demand curve.

It is, of course, true that for any given level of public expenditure, the higher are public sector wages, the lower will be the level of public sector employment. But much more important than this is the question of what determines the level of public expenditure. Recent experience shows that the demand for public sector labour in fact depends on a mixture of political views and macroeconomic judgements regarding the desirable level of public expenditure.

4.2 THE SUPPLY OF LABOUR

The theory of labour supply assumes that people work only so as to be able to buy goods and services. The choice which they face in deciding how much labour to supply at different wage rates is a choice between goods (or real income) and leisure. The price of leisure is thus given by the existing wage rate. That is, the wage rate represents the opportunity cost of leisure. Only two uses of time are considered—market work and leisure. An extension of the theory introduces a third use of time—non-market work to cover activities such as housework, travelling to work, and studying for exams. Here we shall keep to the simple view and allow only for work and leisure.

People are assumed to try to maximise their own individual utility, although the theory can be adapted to consider interactions between the labour supply decisions of different members of the one household.

The labour supply question is asked in terms of the number of hours a week a worker will offer to the labour market at different wage rates. Once workers are in jobs they may have little control over the length of their working week. But if we take a period of time longer than a week (perhaps as long as a lifetime) we can see that workers may vary the amount of work they do in several ways—through, for example, the length of holidays and of unpaid leave or engaging in moonlighting (having more than one paid job). Further, the length of the working week (or working year, etc.) may strongly influence a worker's decision as to which job he or she takes.

Now consider the position of workers whose wage rate has just been increased. The wage rise means that leisure has become more expensive, since taking an hour of leisure now means giving up more goods than it did previously. We shall therefore expect that the wage rise will cause workers to give up some of their newly more expensive leisure (that is, working more hours in a paid job). This is the substitution effect—the substitution of work for leisure because of the change in their relative prices.

However, as a result of the wage rise, any given expenditure of effort will yield more goods and services. This change in potential real income is the income effect of the wage rise. If we assume that extra goods and services and extra leisure are both attractive to workers then they are likely to take this income effect partly in the form of each of them. The wage rise should then produce an income effect leading to fewer hours being worked.

Thus we have two effects—the substitution and income effects—tending to influence the number of hours worked but in opposite directions. What will the total effect of the wage rise be? On theoretical grounds alone we have no way of knowing. The answer will be different for different people depending on how they value goods and leisure. Some may work more (the substitution effect is stronger than the income effect); others less (the income effect is stronger than the substitution effect).

It is commonly assumed that workers on low wage rates will respond to a wage increase by offering to work longer hours but that the outcome is less certain for workers on higher rates of pay. It is often assumed too, that at some high rate of pay the income effect dominates the substitution effect and workers offer fewer hours of work as wage rates rise even further. This can be shown by a labour supply curve. In fig 4.1 we have the wage rate on the vertical axis and the hours of work offered on the horizontal axis.

Above the high wage rate W_1, the labour supply curve bends backwards as the income effect outweighs the substitution effect.

This analysis of individual labour supply could be made much more complex. We could assume that the worker

88 Understanding Markets

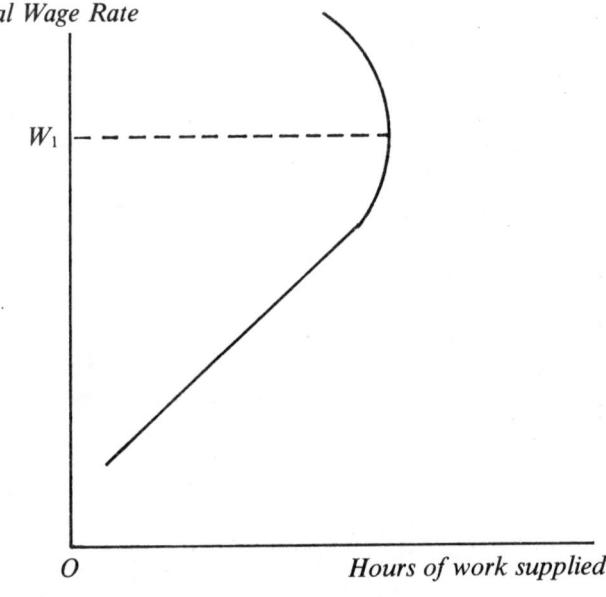

Figure 4.1

receives income from sources other than work; introduce overtime rates of pay and allow for increasing tax rates as income rises; and include unemployment benefits and the cost of transport to work. But these changes do not alter the conclusion that we cannot know from theory how workers will respond to changes in wage rates.

We can produce a labour supply curve to firms or industries or to the economy as a whole by adding together individual supply curves. It is generally assumed that when this is done the backward bending section of the curve disappears. This is because any tendency for some workers to work less as wage rates rise will be more than offset by those workers who wish to work more and by new entrants to the market who are only attracted into it at higher rates of pay.

Thus, in fig. 4.2, we put together a conventional upward sloping labour supply curve with the normal downward sloping labour demand curve to produce a labour market diagram which looks like that for any other market.

The labour market 89

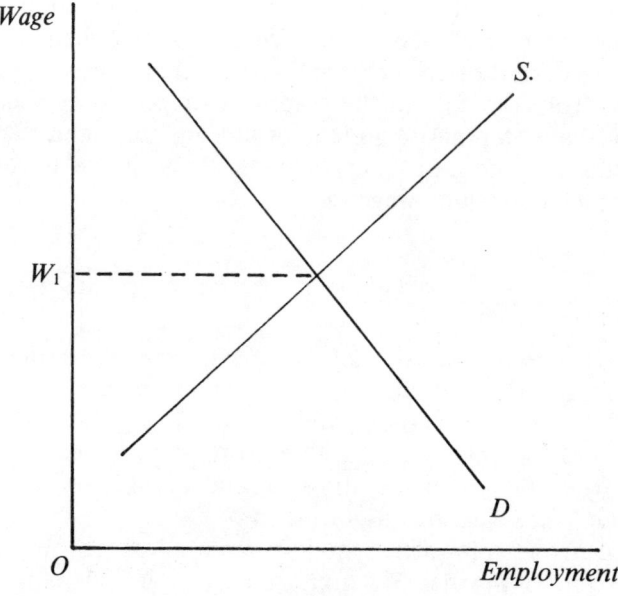

Figure 4.2

Then if wages change to equate the demand for and supply of labour we will have no unemployment. As wage rates fall, some people decide that to maximise utility they should leave the labour market rather than to continue to work in paid employment. They no longer have jobs but if one thinks of them as unemployed one has to think of them as voluntarily unemployed. They would no doubt prefer a world in which wages were higher, but in existing circumstances they can be seen to be exercising a choice.

There is something odd about fig. 4.2. Can you work out what it is? Think about the labelling of the vertical axis. What influences the demand for labour? In our discussion of labour demand, we were dealing with the money wages paid to workers (before income tax is paid). But to be realistic, we should include other costs to employers of hiring labour—the cost of providing fringe benefits such as company cars; employers' national insurance payments and contributions to employeee superannuation schemes. When we were dealing with the supply of labour, however, we were talking about the real wage rate (net of income tax). We should also include the value to workers of fringe benefits (and that may be quite different from the cost to the employer of providing them). Thus, we have to practise quite a lot of sleight of hand to put labour demand and supply curves on one diagram and to come up with an equilibrium 'wage rate'.

4.3 UNEMPLOYMENT AND THE ROLE OF SEARCH

No one suggests that the labour market works perfectly. Everyone accepts that there is always some unemployment, even if it is only frictional (unemployment existing because the matching of the unemployed with existing job vacancies takes time). How then can we draw a realistic picture of an essentially price-clearing labour market?

The principal approach in modern economics is through the development of the idea of search—a particular application of the importance of information and lack of it in labour markets. Consider an example.

A worker becomes unemployed and wants another job. Based on her previous experience of the labour market she has an idea of the wage she is prepared to work for—her reservation wage. She looks for jobs and receives a number of job offers but at wage rates lower than her reservation wage. Consequently she rejects them (voluntarily remaining unemployed) so that she can search the labour market for better offers. However, there are costs in searching the market—she has to live; there are costs in applying for jobs and attending job interviews. Gradually she lowers her reservation wage. With time, she is finding out more and more about the present state of the market and is bringing her expectations into line with reality.

Meanwhile employers are not able to fill their job vacancies and are experiencing costs in the form of lost production. They gradually raise the wage rates attached to their job offers. Eventually our unemployed worker receives an offer with a wage rate equal to her now lower reservation wage and accepts the job.

Unemployment exists in this view because workers do not immediately accept job offers. This is not pigheadedness on their part but an attempt to maximise utility in a market with imperfect information. Workers know that if they accept the first job offer they receive (at a low wage) they may miss out on a better job at a higher wage which they have not yet discovered.

This approach has been developed in many ways. For example, the level of unemployment at any time depends on how long, on average, workers keep searching before accepting a job offer. Thus, it is argued, we can investigate increased levels of unemployment in an economy by analysing the factors which influence the average length of search time for jobs. From here it is only a short step to saying that the more income workers have from sources other than work, the longer they will be willing to search, the longer will be the average duration of unemployment, and the higher will be the level of unemployment. This will be especially true if people lose some of their present income when they find employment. This has led to the theory that high unemployment benefits lead to high unemployment.

What we have here then is an expansion of the notion that labour markets are price adjusting. Wages do ultimately change to clear them, but they certainly do not clear instantaneously because of imperfect information and because of government intervention in the form of social security benefits.

4.4 THE NET ADVANTAGES APPROACH TO WAGE DIFFERENTIALS

Why do workers choose to work in one job rather than another? The supply of labour to different jobs is held to depend principally on the wage rate and on the nature of the job. This leads to the theory of net advantages—the notion that the various advantages or disadvantages of different jobs (including the wage paid) will tend to be equalised.

Thus, a job which is physically dangerous or dirty should, other things being equal, be paid more highly than one which is pleasant. The same should apply to jobs which are insecure, which give little chance of promotion, or which carry considerable responsibility. Finally, jobs for which people must train should be paid more highly. This is based on the notion that education and training involve two types of costs— the cost of the training itself (fees; cost of books and other materials) and income foregone—the income the person might have earned if he or she had been working rather than studying.

We can modify this net advantages approach by allowing for non-competing groups. In its simplest form this acknowledges differences in natural ability and suggests that these differences limit the range of jobs which people can obtain and hence limit competition for many jobs.

We finish up with upward sloping labour supply curves for all occupations with the slope and position of each curve depending on the nature of the occupation, and on the number of people with the required natural ability. We shall expect the labour supply curve to the medical profession to be steeply sloped (price inelastic) because the job requires a certain level of natural ability and many years of study involving expense and foregone income. The labour supply curve to unskilled jobs may, for the opposite reasons, be expected to be very price elastic.

Putting together demand and supply curves for each occupation produces a set of equilibrium wages and hence a set of wage differentials. In a dynamic economy, because patterns of productivity and of demand for products change rapidly, we should expect the relative demands for different types of labour to be changing rapidly and hence wage differentials to be constantly changing. Equally, because wages represent an important element in the attractiveness of a job, we should expect relatively small changes in wage relationships to alter the pattern of labour supply to different occupations, and wage changes thus to play an important role in labour mobility.

4.5 PRICE ADJUSTING LABOUR MARKETS AND THE REAL WORLD

It is hard to relate the view of a price-adjusting labour market to reality. In any economy there are always people who are unemployed and who do not see their lack of a job as stemming from a free exercise of choice on their part. The majority of the unemployed, far from being able to reject some job offers because the offered wage rate is too low, receive none at all. During the 1980s, the level and persistence of unemployment has seemed far too great to be written off as merely frictional.

Again, many wage relationships seem to change only very slowly, if at all, over time. Different workers doing the same job often receive quite different rates of pay yet this does not always produce movement of labour.

Many dangerous and unpleasant jobs remain lowly paid. If there is a shortage of workers for such jobs it is commonly met not by wage increases but by bringing into the labour force poor or underprivileged workers—the worst jobs in society are often done by migrant workers or women.

These jobs may become part of the unofficial or informal economy, enabling employers to continue to pay low wages because employees do not pay tax and because government regulations concerning minimum wages, health and safety are ignored. Much of this work is part-time and temporary. It is extremely difficult to measure the amount of it occurring. There may, however, be as many as 2.5 million workers in the unofficial economy in the UK.

In contrast, highly paid workers frequently receive high fringe benefits and other advantages. Advantages and disadvantages of jobs do not offset each other in the real world.

4.6 DISTINCTIVE FEATURES OF LABOUR MARKETS

We noted at the beginning of this chapter that labour differs in a number of ways from other factors of production. Let us look now at these differences.

4.6.1 Some problems with the notion of labour supply

In most markets it is clear how much of a commodity is available for sale. It is not difficult, for instance, to discover how much wheat was grown last season or how many word processors were produced. It is not nearly so certain how many people in an economy wish to take paid jobs.

Let us begin with the usual definition of the labour force: people in paid employment + the self-employed + the unemployed. Then we define the unemployed as those people without jobs who are actively seeking work. But there our problems start. Some people may be applying for jobs but making little or no attempt to be appointed to them. Other people may wish to work but may have stopped actively seeking jobs.

Consider an old-fashioned statistician's family of husband, wife and 2.4 children, with the husband in regular employment. The wife is not currently working but has worked in the past for local factories. The family is not well off and she would like to work. But the factories in her area have no vacancies. There may be jobs available in other towns but her family circumstances rule them out. There are jobs for secretaries in her own town, but she lacks the necessary skills. Consequently, she does not actively seek work and by our definition above is not unemployed or part of the labour force. Yet she is certainly willing to supply her labour and to do so at the existing wage rate. She is what is known as a discouraged worker.

Think next of a family in which the wife chooses not to work although there are jobs available. Later, the husband becomes unemployed but remains part of the labour force. The wife responds by seeking and obtaining a job but with the intention of quitting it when the husband again obtains work. In this case (the added worker effect) the labour force has temporarily grown in size.

Both of these cases illustrate an important point—the size of the labour force at any time depends on the conditions in the labour market at that time. We can express this formally by writing:

$$\text{Unemployment} = \text{Labour Force} - \text{Employment}$$

Normally we would expect changes in unemployment to be the result of either: (a) a change in the size of the labour force; or (b) a change in the level of employment. But we have seen that a change in the level of employment may itself cause a change in the size of the labour force. In Britain matters are confused even more by counting as unemployed only those people registering for unemployment benefit. Undoubtedly, some people who register for unemployment benefit prefer not to work if they can possibly avoid it. But others who wish to work and who are actively seeking work do not register for benefit because they are not eligible for it, are not aware of their entitlement to it, or choose not to claim it. Further, we have seen that people may be willing to work but may not easily be able to show that willingness in the labour market.

We can say that the size of the labour force at any time depends on the size of the population and on the labour force activity rate (that is, the percentage of the population active in the labour market). The problem is to discover who is active in the market and who is not.

There are other difficulties. For example, there are large numbers of potential workers in full-time education or training. They are not counted as part of the work force. But people may stay on in education (or take places on government training schemes) not because they really wish to study but because they are unable to find jobs.

A rather different worry is that when labour market conditions are bad, many workers may be working fewer hours than they would like to. Official figures of the numbers of people in the labour force or unemployed do not address this question at all. Yet it is very important to know what percentage of the officially employed are working short-time or part-time and what proportion of these would prefer to be in full-time employment.

4.6.2 Labour market stocks and flows
To understand how well the labour market works, we need to be interested not just in stocks (the number of unemployed or the size of the labour force at any one time) but also in flows (the number of people becoming unemployed or finding jobs over a given period of time).

People are constantly moving into the labour force from different sources and out of it to different destinations. Thus there are flows into the labour force (either into employment or directly into unemployment) of school leavers or immigrants; of people returning to the labour force after an absence to raise a family, to undertake more education or because of illness; or from the informal economy. People leave the labour force through retirement, emigration, death, illness, voluntary separation, or to join the unofficial economy. Within the labour force people are constantly moving between employment and unemployment.

These flows are important because we need to know the average length of spells of unemployment, and how frequently the unemployed become unemployed, if we are to appreciate the nature of the problem of unemployment. It is quite different becoming unemployed but obtaining a new secure job in, say, six weeks, from becoming unemployed several times in one year or becoming unemployed and remaining so for over twelve months. One interesting phenomenon of the end of the 1970s was that the big increase in unemployment in the UK was associated not so much with more people becoming unemployed but with people remaining unemployed for much longer periods of time.

4.6.3 The inseparability of the worker from labour provided
In almost all jobs, a worker has to be physically present at a place of work to be able to work. This has two important consequences.

Firstly, people are brought up in particular regions and often become strongly attached to those regions socially and psychologically. But to change jobs may mean moving from one region to another and breaking such ties. Moving jobs from Sunderland to Milton Keynes is far different in nature from producing a good in one place and selling it somewhere else. Again, moving home from one region to another means finding somewhere new to live—buying or renting a new house. Consequently, there are important links between the ability of people to move to find a job and the state of the housing market in different areas. Yet again, family responsibilities frequently prevent people from moving from one area to another in search of work.

Some years ago, the unemployed were advised by a government minister to 'get on their bikes' to look for work. Alas, this sensitive piece of advice ignores many difficulties.

Secondly, working conditions are very important but workers thinking of changing jobs may find it much more difficult to obtain information about them (including such difficult-to-measure things as friendliness and promotion prospects) in other firms than about wage rates. Thus there is inertia in labour markets—workers are much less mobile in response to wage changes than the net advantages theory suggests. Labour markets, even more than others, are strongly influenced by that very academic theory: 'the devil you know is better than the devil you don't'.

4.6.4 The perishability of labour

Many commodities which can't be immediately sold can be stored for future sale. Labour cannot. People can only work for a certain number of years (at a maximum from 16 to 65); for only a certain number of weeks in each year and hours in each week. An unemployment spell of six months is six months out of a lifetime's work. It cannot be put to one side for later sale. Unemployment is then from the points of view of both the individual worker and the community a waste of productive potential.

As well as labour itself being perishable, skills decay. This presents a particular problem to the long-term unemployed. The longer workers are out of work, the more difficult it becomes to obtain work of the type and level which they had in the past. This applies too to people who leave the labour force for a time (perhaps to raise a family) and then seek to rejoin it later.

4.6.5 Work, identity and the work ethic

For many people a job is much more than a way of earning income. It provides regular contact with other people and may lead to broader social relationships outside of work. In a modern urban setting a good proportion of friendships develop at or through people's work.

Further, the idea of work is so central to industrial societies that unemployment is commonly regarded both by the unemployed themselves and by the community as a sign of failure. Work also may provide a major channel for individual expression; and the type of work you do frequently plays a significant part in the way you are regarded by others. 'What type of work do you do?' is one of the first questions asked by almost all new acquaintances.

Thus, what happens to people in the labour market is of great importance in many people's lives. Labour is hardly just a commodity like any other.

4.6.6 Further reasons for non-competing groups

We have mentioned the idea of workers being divided into non-competing groups by differences in natural ability. This is not really any different from dividing tomatoes in a street market into 'rock-hard' and over-ripe. But in labour markets, non-competing groups also arise from different access to information, education and training and this in turn may depend on differences in wealth, income and social class of parents.

The labour market is strongly social in character. Labour markets have become more open, and intergenerational social mobility has increased, but social background still plays a major part in determining the sorts of jobs people do and their chances of being successful in the labour market. In our society, success does literally still breed success.

People may also be prevented from competing for certain jobs because of their gender or race. For instance, social expectations still have a strong influence on the amount and type of education females receive.

4.6.7 Bargaining power and trade unions

There is another more basic reason why labour markets cannot resemble perfectly competitive models. Although, as we mentioned in 4.6.5, jobs may mean a lot more to people than a way of earning income, it remains that most workers have to work in order to have an acceptable standard of living. The majority of workers have few, if any, resources beyond their 'human capital'—their ability to earn income through the labour market. Employers own a much higher proportion of the nation's wealth.

The labour market 99

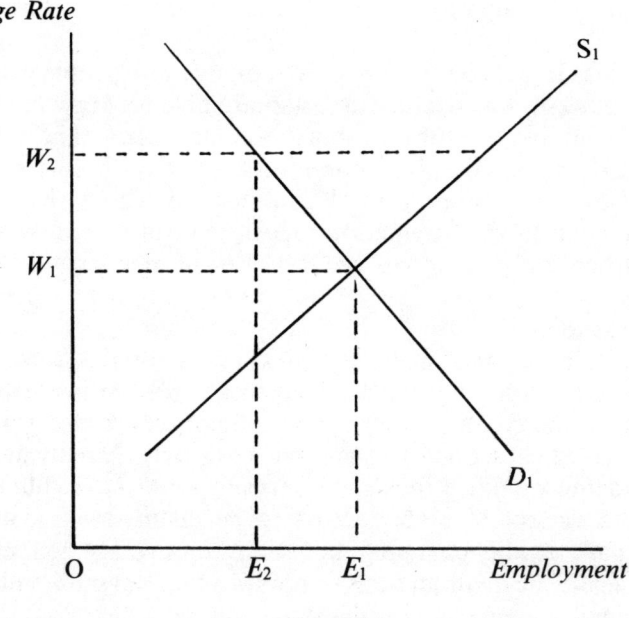

Figure 4.3

Necessarily, a market in which labour is not organised is one in which bargaining power between employees and employers is unequal. Given that the organisation of production brings workers together and provides scope for combining and taking collective action, the growth of trade unions can be seen as a logical outcome of the nature of labour markets—an attempt to redress the balance in favour of workers.

But trade unions (and professional associations of accountants, lawyers, doctors, etc.) are not just concerned with the relationship between wages and profits. They are vitally concerned with the wages of their members, *relative* to the wages of other workers. Their presence in the market changes the nature of labour supply.

In order to improve their relative wage position, workers attempt to limit the supply of labour to their occupations. In fig. 4.3, S_1 is the labour supply curve to an occupation. The market-clearing wage rate is W_1. Workers, however, wish to raise their wage to W_2 and limit the number of people able to work in the occupation to E_2. We have a quantity-adjusting labour market.

But it is clear that at a wage of W_2, many more people would like to work in this occupation than are able to. How are the limited number of jobs rationed among them? There are several ways, but the most common these days is to require people to obtain some formal qualification before they can obtain a job in the occupation. Then, control of numbers is established by controlling the number of people who are allowed to sit the necessary exams or the number of people who pass them.

For example, the medical profession negotiates with the government over the number of places available in medical schools in the country. Every year, many more students wish to enter medical school than are able to. Entry is largely based on academic qualifications and interview performance but this allows a variety of other factors to be taken into account. Things are steadily changing, but males, on average, still need lower academic qualifications to obtain a medical school place than females.

Accounting and other professional bodies frequently have very high failure rates in their exams—much higher than seems justified by the difficulty of the subject matter. All professions attempt to control the acceptability of foreign qualifications. Trade unions attempt to control labour supply in various ways. For example, to follow many trades, it is still necessary to obtain an apprenticeship ticket and these are limited. To practise as a professional actor, a person must obtain a union card from Actors' Equity and this is often difficult. This is an example of the operation of a closed shop, where workers must be a member of the relevant union in order to work in a job. In the past, especially in the United States, there have been many examples of closed shops being used not only to limit the total number of workers, but also to discriminate between male and female workers, or between white and black workers.

But trade unions are interested in much more than wages. Working conditions and the extent to which workers have a say in those conditions are a vital concern. Thus, many industrial disputes are not about wages but about the speed with which a production line moves, the length of the washing up time available to workers at the end of a shift, the safety of machinery or of working practices, the attitude of managers to workers and so on. Many of these things affect the cost of hiring labour and hence the demand for labour.

With the development of employers' organisations and the growth in size of both firms and trade unions, national agreements became very common in labour markets. Their importance has tended to decline in recent years but there is still a great deal more uniformity in the results of labour market negotiations than in most markets. Labour economists sometimes talk of *bilateral monopoly*—with a monopolist seller of labour (the union) facing a monopolist buyer of labour (the firm). This applies strictly to very few labour market bargains but it is closer to reality in much of the labour market than the notion of perfect competition.

Of course, some groups of workers are much more able to influence labour supply and working conditions than others. Thus, there are great differences in the amount of market power which different groups have. The labour market is very unequal among workers, as well as still often being unequal between employers and employees.

4.6.8 Government and labour markets

We have seen that government is involved in some way in all markets in mixed economies. This is particularly true, however, of labour markets. This has partly been because work is so important a part of people's lives in an industrial society that strong community feelings have been aroused by some results of labour markets. Children working in nineteenth century factories and mines is an obvious example. There are many others. Governments have acted (not always with great speed) against low wages and poor work conditions in 'sweatshops'; long working hours; the use of dangerous machinery and work practices; conditions leading to industrial diseases such as abestosis; sex and race discrimination, etc..

Government involvement has also reflected the participation of representatives of workers in politics—partially to overrule what they have seen as undesirable results of the operation of labour markets. Government interest in labour markets has grown greater since government itself has become by far the single largest employer of labour in the economy and since central government has taken on the responsibility of managing the national economy.

Just as with other markets, there has been a movement in recent years to reduce the level of government intervention. No matter how far this movement goes in the years to come, however, a great deal of government regulation, from rules governing the employment of children to statutory retirement ages, will remain.

4.6.9 Labour contracts and real wages

Labour contracts usually specify fairly loosely the amount and type of work to be exchanged for a particular level of money wages and other employment conditions. We have mentioned the uncertainty faced by employers regarding the exact nature of the future exchange. But workers too face much uncertainty.

Firstly, they do not know the real wage for which they will exchange their labour because it will depend not only on the money wage but also on the future rate of inflation. Equally, they cannot know in advance what will happen over the life of a contract to their wage relative to the wage rates of other workers. Real take home pay will also depend on what happens to direct tax rates.

Workers concerned with their real wage need to try to guess the future rate of inflation. If it has recently been very high, they may seek to include in the contract a clause requiring the money wage rate to rise in line with inflation (an escalator clause) or to shorten the length of the contract period. Workers will also not know in advance their money earnings, since these will depend on such things as the amount of short-time or overtime working, or of bonus or other incentive payments, as well as on promotion prospects, all of which are variable.

Labour contracts seldom spell out precisely the conditions under which work will be done—shift patterns, the intensity of work, times for tea breaks and so on. We have seen that trade unions attempt to limit the power of management to change such things but cannot be sure of success.

Our picture so far has been one not only of great uncertainty but also of necessary antagonism between employees and employers. Yet this is far from always the case. Employees seeking promotion may attempt to impress employers by their efficiency and effort; employers may pay great attention to worker morale. Many employees stay a long time with a single employer. We have seen that this may be important for employers in regard to highly skilled or experienced workers. Job security means a great deal to most workers. The employee/employer relationship is quite different from that between buyers and sellers in other markets.

4.7 A QUANTITY ADJUSTING LABOUR MARKET

It is now time to put many of these ideas together and to present a realistic overall view of the operation of the labour market.

4.7.1 Wage differentials

One of the several theories which doubt the existence of a clear link between pay and productivity is based on the idea of internal labour markets. It proposes that the wage a large employer is willing to offer particular workers depends on the hierarchical needs of the organisation. For example, set relationships will develop among the wage rates paid to people at different points on a promotion ladder. Or a worker in charge of other workers will need to be paid a certain amount above that paid to the workers below him. Pay, in other words, may be related to the need to maintain worker morale or may reflect prestige rather than productivity.

This is related to a much broader theory which argues that different jobs are accorded different status by society and status is then reflected in the wages offered for those occupations. Status itself is determined by social and historical factors. High social status occupations are awarded high rates of pay, with relatively little attention being paid to productivity.

If this is so, wages do not act to allocate labour among different jobs. Labour markets are quantity adjusting and available labour must be allocated in some other way than through the price (wage) mechanism. We can picture a job being advertised at a fixed wage. If interest in the job is high, large numbers of people apply and the employer, rather than lowering the wage, picks and chooses among them. The employer may be thought of as forming a notional labour queue based upon certain characteristics of the applicants. The most likely characteristics are sex, race, age, previous employment record, and educational background. Some of these may be related (at least in the mind of the employer) to likely productivity. However, judgements may relate to perceptions the employer has of the type of employee likely to be accepted by the rest of the workforce or by clients or may be straightforward expressions of prejudice. In this way we may have labour market discrimination against women and minority groups.

These ideas can be linked with the notion of primary and secondary labour markets or more broadly labour markets may be thought of as segmented into a number of groups which do not compete with each other. Some groups of workers (for example black women, the unskilled, older workers, school-leavers without educational qualifications) may be condemned to lowly paid insecure jobs, irrespective of their personal qualities.

4.7.2 Unemployment

Wages also do not adjust at all smoothly to equate the total demand for and supply of labour in an economy. Unemployment occurs because there are insufficient jobs in the economy to meet the available labour supply at existing wages. For the most part then it is *involuntary*. We have seen several reasons why wages might not fall. For instance, unemployed workers may be unwilling to lower their reservation wages because of the possibility that higher offers might soon be forthcoming (see 4.3.). Again, firms prefer to retain their existing workforce even if other people would be willing to work for less because of the existence of hiring, training, and firing costs (see 4.1.1).

It is the workers in secondary labour markets who are most likely to become and to remain unemployed. This in turn reinforces the existing patterns since employers are generally unwilling to hire workers with a history of unemployment.

In these circumstances, if unemployed workers offer to work for less than the going market wage they are still unlikely to obtain jobs. Indeed, if unemployed workers offer to work for less than the going rate, this may be taken by employers as an indication of their low quality. In other words, the notion of lemons (see our discussion in chapter two) applies to labour markets as well as product markets.

It may be true that if real wages generally could fall in an economy more jobs would be created. However, this is far from certain since wages are workers' incomes and a fall in wages represents a fall in spending power and may also lead to a reduction in firms' confidence and hence in the level of investment in the economy. In any case, many of any new jobs created would be taken by people re-entering the labour market rather than by the existing unemployed workers.

Workers do not, in any meaningful sense, maximise utility. The nature of labour markets is that they are in no position to do so. People no doubt do have some vague notion of a preferred relationship between work and leisure but this is not simply a relationship between goods and leisure, since there are other reasons for working than to obtain goods. Further, they have little influence over the real wage they obtain for their work, since this depends on many variables over which they have no control.

To the extent that there could be said to exist a labour supply curve which represents a utility maximising choice on the part of workers, there is no reason to believe that workers ever are, in practice, on that curve or that they can do anything to get themselves there. Labour markets, then, are chaotic and are much more likely to re-inforce existing inequalities in society than to provide a rational reward for ability and endeavour or to lead to the best use of society's scarce human talents.

5 The Markets for Money and Bills

In the next three chapters we shall look at the ways in which a number of financial markets function. In the UK today there are many different types of financial market, and as new financial instruments are being continually developed the number of markets in which they are traded will continue to increase. We have chosen just four of those markets; for money, for bills, for bonds and for equities. In this chapter we shall look at the first two together because the markets for money and for bills are so closely related in their operations that we cannot discuss one without at least implying something about the other. For example, money and bills are such close substitutes that a decision to hold more of one is often a decision to hold less of the other. Furthermore, government efforts to control the growth of the money stock involve continuous bill market operations.

We said in Chapter 1, that financial markets are often claimed to provide the best examples of perfect markets. This claim is only partially justified. What we shall see in the next three chapters is that financial markets are often dominated by a few major traders amongst whom the authorities themselves sometimes feature largely; that prices respond to factors other than just the desires of buyers and sellers; and that relevant information is often in very poor supply.

5.1 CHARACTERISTICS

5.1.1 Money
Money is anything which settles ('extinguishes') a debt. That is

to say, it is something which is acceptable as a means of payment. Notice, this is more restrictive than something which functions as a medium of exchange. Many things, credit cards and hire purchase agreements for example, enable us to acquire goods and services legitimately. But they do this by converting our obligation to pay the seller into an obligation to pay the credit company. They transfer the debt, they do not extinguish it. Eventually, as we all know, the day of reckoning will come when we have to settle our debt with the credit company and for that only one thing will do—money.

So much for theory. What in practice meets this requirement? Plainly notes and coin do so. Indeed, their universal acceptability is guaranteed by their status as 'legal tender'. However, while legal status may be a guarantee of acceptability, such status is clearly not *necessary* in order for something to function as money. By far the greater part of transactions (measured by value) in modern economies is carried out through the use of cheques, direct debits, standing orders and similar devices. What these do is to cause a change in the ownership of bank deposits. Such deposits are not 'legal tender' but they are perfectly acceptable as a means of payment and must be included in our definition of money.

Four points of considerable importance follow from this definition. Firstly, if 'acceptability' is the test of 'moneyness', then convention and custom are in effect responsible for defining money. Once, only coins were money because only precious metals were acceptable. Now we accept bank deposits, recorded and transferred by electronic means. What might be acceptable in future?

Secondly, if money includes bank deposits then it includes something which can be created and destroyed by the actions of banks. Like other private sector commercial organisations, banks have an interest in expansion. Subject to considerations of prudence, therefore, they will want to increase their volume of loans and deposits. Inevitably this tends to expand the money supply and immediately gives us an insight into why the authorities have such difficulties in controlling monetary expansion.

In recent years banks have begun to pay interest on an increasing range of bank deposits, including those 'current account' or 'sight' deposits against which cheques can be written. Thus, a third consequence follows from including bank deposits in our definition of money. This is that some part of the money stock now yields interest. The significance of this will become apparent later in 5.9.

Lastly, defining money as 'notes and coin plus bank deposits' begs a number of further questions. There are various types of bank deposit; should they all qualify? For that matter, what is a bank? At the moment a number of building societies are on the verge of formally becoming banks. But for many years people, depositors in particular, have seen little difference in practice and economists have argued over whether or not their deposits should be included in official measures of money.

The Bank of England collects and publishes data on six detailed definitions of money. These are set out in table 5.1. Of these, M1, M2 and M3 are close to our 'notes and coin plus bank deposits' formula; M4 and M5 are wider.

Table: 5.1: *Relationships among monetary aggregates and their components*

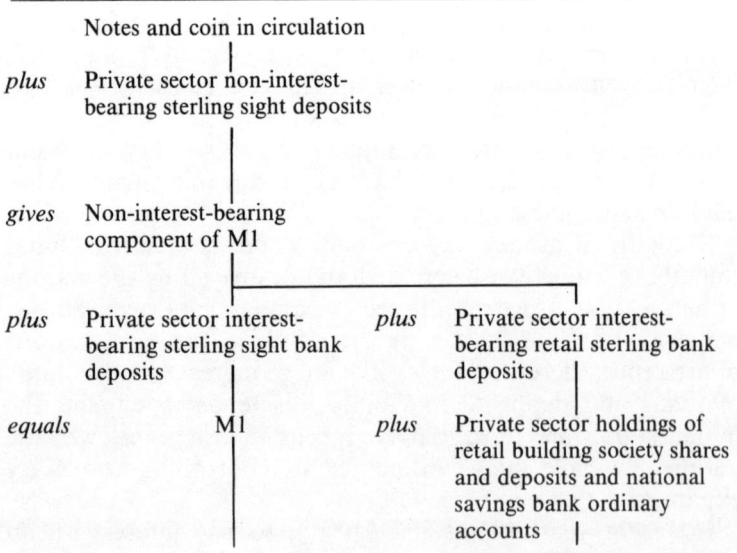

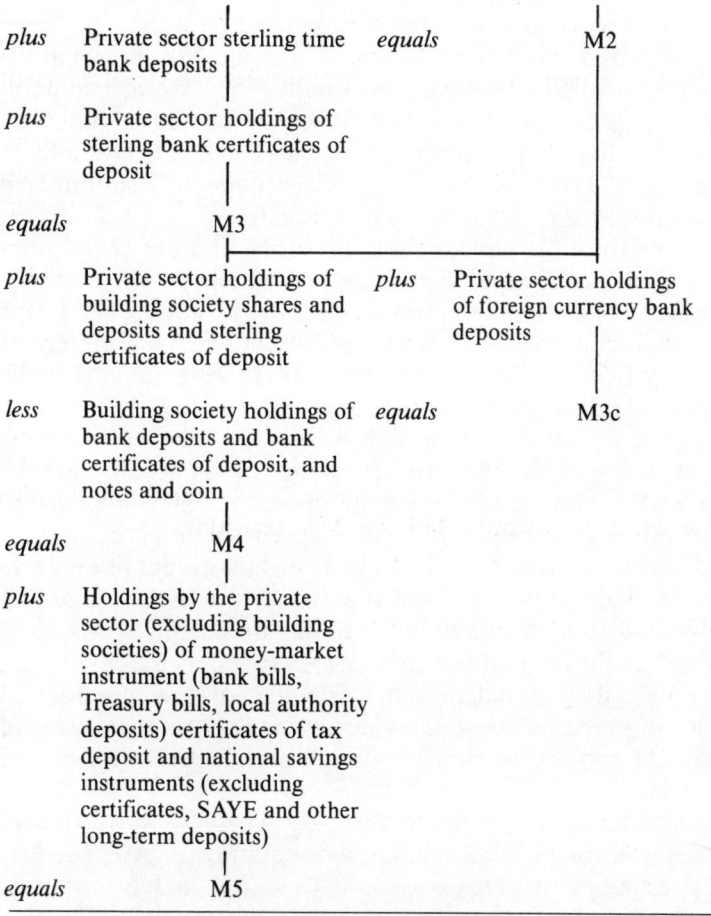

Source: Bank of England Quarterly Bulletin, May 1987.

5.1.2 Bills

A 'bill' is a certificate containing a promise to pay a specified sum of money at a specified time in the future. Bills may be issued to someone either in exchange for goods and services received or in exchange for money, and are therefore a means of obtaining credit or borrowing money. In theory a bill can be issued by anyone but in practice most are issued by large corporations (commercial bills), by the government (treasury bills) and by local authorities (local authority bills).

Compared with other financial instruments, bills have a number of distinctive features. Firstly, they are of comparatively large denomination. Few treasury bills, for example, are issued with a denomination of less than £50,000. This tells us immediately that the market for bills is going to be dominated by institutions rather than by individuals.

Secondly, bills have a short maturity and are therefore a source of short rather than long term credit to their issuers. Treasury bills have an original maturity of 91 days (three months); commercial bills are issued with various maturities ranging from one month to one year. If we assume that the issuers of bills are unlikely to default, as is plainly the case with the government and only slightly less so in the case of large firms, then, from the holders' point of view, bills are an extremely liquid asset. They will always be redeemable in the near future and their capital value at redemption is certain.

Thirdly, the return to the holders of bills comes in the form of a discount. Bills are issued at a discount to their redemption value and so someone holding a bill to redemption will get a reward in the form of the difference between its purchase price and its value at redemption. The size of this discount in relation to the redemption value can be expressed as a rate of discount and is then similar, though not identical, to a rate of interest.

Consider as an example the case where the government issues a 91-day, £100,000 bill at a discount of £5,000. The first step to finding the rate of discount, as we just said, is to express the discount as a proportion of the redemption value. Thus:

$$5,000/100,000 = 0.05$$

However, this discount was paid on a loan of only three months while it is usual, as with rates of interest, to express discount rates in annual terms. Here we must multiply 0.05 by 4, or what amounts to the same thing, divide the denominator by 4:

$$5,000/(100,000/4) = 0.20 \text{ or } 20\%$$

By comparison, a rate of interest would normally be calculated on the initial outlay. In this example we should be interested in £5,000 as a proportion of £95,000:

$$5,000/(95,000/4) = 0.21 \text{ or } 21\%$$

Notice that for this reason a rate of interest will always appear higher than its corresponding rate of discount.

In general terms, therefore:

$$d = (R-P)/R.n$$

while

$$r = (R-P)/P.n$$

where d is the rate of discount, r is the rate of interest, R the redemption value, P the initial price and n the period to maturity in years.

Fourthly, bills can be resold before their maturity date. Clearly, this adds even further to their liquidity. Assuming that interest rates and therefore yields on all other assets are given, we must expect the value of a bill to increase with time. As time passes and the maturity of the bill approaches, the difference between its purchase price and its redemption value is a return for a shorter and shorter period of waiting. This can be seen formally from the expression above. With the passage of time, n gets smaller. So consequently does the denominator and thus if (R−P) stays constant the rate of discount will rise. For the rate of discount to stay constant P must approach R as n diminishes.

Fifthly, the market price of bills will vary inversely with interest rates. Suppose interest rates rise. New borrowing and lending will have to take place at the new rates and so newly issued bills will need to carry a bigger discount than existing ones. By comparison, existing bills will be less attractive; holders will sell in order to buy new bills. In theory, this generalised selling will push the price of existing bills down to the point at which their discount to redemption matches that on new bills. This inverse relationship between interest rates and asset prices we shall observe in many contexts.

Lastly, the existence of a market for existing bills together with price fluctuations caused by changes in interest rates creates a second reason for holding bills, quite independent of the gain that would be made by holding them to maturity. This is the prospect of capital gain, made by buying when interest rates are high (and bill prices low) and correctly anticipating a fall in interest rates (rise in bill prices).

5.2 THE SUPPLY OF MONEY

In this section we shall outline the theory of money supply determination as it appears in many economics texts. This standard presentation is far removed from what happens in practice in the UK and in many other countries and this will become apparent as we set it out.

In most macroeconomic texts, the supply of money is treated as though it were exogenous. That is to say, it is

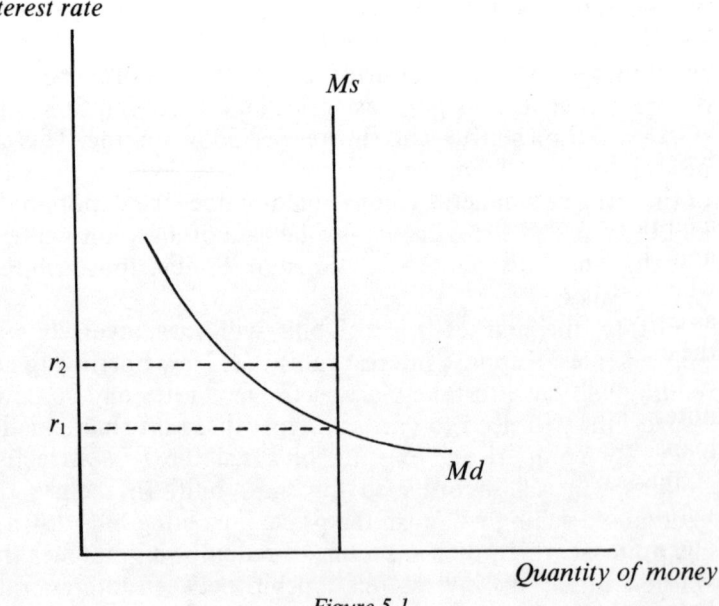

Figure 5.1

determined independently of other variables in the economy, like the demand for money, the demand for lending, the level of interest rates and so on, and is determined by the actions of 'the authorities'—the Bank of England and the Treasury. When it is presented diagramatically, as it is in figure 5.1, it is usually combined with a demand curve to show equilibrium between the supply of money and the demand for it.

The next point to appreciate is that the supply of money, unlike the supply of other goods, is not a flow which takes place over a period of time. It is a stock. If no 'new' money were being created there would still be a supply of money, the existing stock. This stock will change over time of course as a result of flows.

Notice that the supply curve, Ms, is drawn vertically, showing that the level of interest rates has no effect upon the supply of money. The quantity of money supplied will change only if the supply curve *shifts*, and this will happen only if something outside the diagram changes, i.e. only if the authorities so desire.

Notice too, that, given the demand curve Md, the equilibrium rate of interest is the *result* of the predetermined money supply. The causal sequence, in other words, runs from the money supply to interest rates and not from interest rates to the money supply. What principles underlie this presentation of an exogenously determined money supply? Essentially, there are three.

The first involves the 'reserve ratio'. We begin by imagining a bank's balance sheet in which, as in all balance sheets, assets and liabilities are equal. Banks' liabilities consist overwhelmingly of customers' deposits, which may be withdrawn as cash or transferred between banks or even transferred from the commercial banks to the government's account at the Bank of England. By contrast, banks' assets are diverse, consisting of notes and coin, deposits at the Bank of England, securities, loans, etc. Table 5.2 presents a simplified version.

Table 5.2 reveals an important, relationship. Notice that *within* the balance sheet there is a ratio of 10 per cent of notes and coin plus deposits at the Bank of England ('the Bank') to deposit liabilities. The purpose of the notes and coin and balances at the Bank is to function as 'reserves' from which to

Table 5.2

Liabilities	£m.	Assets	£m.
Deposits	100	Notes and coin	5
		Balances at Bank of England	5
		Securities	20
		Loans	70
	100		100

Ratio of deposits: reserves = 10:1

meet customers' withdrawals and transfers. Given the size and sophistication of the UK banking system now, and the fact that each of the major banks has a very large number of account holders, it follows that the withdrawals and outward transfers of one group of customers will be largely matched by the deposits and inward transfers of others. Nonetheless, each bank has to be ready to meet any *net* withdrawals/transfers. Reserves are held for this purpose and since they earn no interest and banks are concerned with profit, it is a reasonable assumption that banks will hold the minimum ratio consistent with commercial prudence.

The second principle we need to grasp is that banks can create deposits, and therefore money, by making loans. Imagine a customer applies successfully for an overdraft. He now has the ability to write cheques in excess of his existing deposit. He uses this facility to buy goods and because the bank honours the cheques, the seller of the goods receives an addition to his bank deposit. Notice that the loan does not appear as an addition to the borrower's deposit, it appears as an addition to someone else's deposit when it is spent. Notice also that it does not matter if the recipient banks with some other bank, provided we are considering an individual example of what is happening in the system as a whole. Bank A's loans may finish up increasing the deposits of customers of banks B and C but bank B will be making loans, some of which will be deposited with A and C and some of C's loans will go to A and B. A general increase in loans will result in a general expansion of deposits and therefore of money.

The third principle is that government departments bank with the Bank of England and not with the banking system. Consequently *net* payments to the government by the private sector have *two* effects. Firstly, the private sector's deposits with banks fall by the amount of the net payment. Secondly, the reduction in their liabilities is matched on the asset side of banks' balance sheets by a reduction in their balances at the Bank of England. The Bank of England in effect debits the banks' accounts and transfers the funds to an appropriate government account. Of course the reverse would also apply: if the government made net payments to the private sector, bank deposits would rise as customers paid in their cheques from the government and the Bank would credit banks' balances and debit the government.

This analysis begins by assuming a stable, financial relationship between reserves and deposits, and the ability of the government to influence the size of these reserves through its transactions with the private sector. It follows as a matter of fairly simple arithmetic that if the stock of reserves changes by a given amount, then the quantity of deposits must change by some multiple in order to preserve the relationship. With the aid of some more simplified balance sheets we can follow through a typical sequence of events.

Imagine that the government repays £2m of past borrowing by buying bonds from the public, other things remaining unchanged. Banks' liabilities increase by £2m as the public pays the funds into its bank accounts. Of course, bank assets must also increase by £2m and this happens as the Bank of

Table 5.3

Liabilities	£m.	Assets	£m.
Deposits	102	Notes and coin	5
		Balances at Bank of England	7
		Securities	20
		Loans	70
	102		102

Ratio of deposits: reserves = 8.5:1

England transfers funds from the government's account to banks' deposits at the Bank. In table 5.3 assets and liabilities have risen to £102m.

But look now at the ratio of reserves (£12m) to deposits (£102m). This ratio, which was originally 10:1 has fallen to 8.5:1. If banks were previously confident that 10:1 gave them adequate security, they must now take the view that cover is overprovided and that they should expand their balance sheets to take advantage of the extra reserves.

Table 5.4 shows one way in which this expansion might take place. Banks have increased their lending to customers and the result of these loans is inevitably an increase in deposits. With reserves at £12m and a ratio of 10:1, banks can afford deposit liabilities of £120m, i.e. an increase of £18m on the position in table 5.3. Table 5.4. shows an increase in lending and deposits of £18m and the balance sheet in equilibrium at £120m. With a ratio of 10:1, a unit increase in reserves leads to a tenfold increase in deposits. In fig. 5.1 the supply curve, Ms, would shift to the right. Obviously, we could reverse this process. The government could sell bonds to the public, draining deposits and reserves from the banks. An equal drain of deposits and reserves, would, however, reduce the reserve ratio and banks would have to undertake a further, multiple, contraction of deposits.

Table 5.4

Liabilities	£m.	Assets	£m.
Deposits	120	Notes and coin	5
		Balances at Bank of England	7
		Securities	20
		Loans	88
	120		120

Ratio of deposits: reserves = 10:1

The tenfold increase in the example above is obviously dependent upon the size of the reserve ratio. It is in fact the reciprocal of the ratio of bank reserves to bank deposits.

$$\Delta D = \Delta R \times \frac{1}{R/D}$$

where D is deposits, and R is reserves.

This is a very simple version of the *bank credit multiplier* or *monetary base* approach to the determination of the money supply. It is highly simplified because it treats deposits as the sole form of possible increases in money supply and changes in banks' deposits at the Bank of England as the ultimate source. Since we have included notes and coin in our definition of money, and since notes and coin are also part of banks' reserves, we ought also to include changes in the quantity of notes and coin in our multiplier analysis. Doing this would lead us eventually to an expression:

$$\Delta Ms = \Delta MO \times \frac{1+b}{a+b}$$

where Ms is the money supply; MO is the monetary base (total notes and coin plus banks' deposits at the Bank of England); a is the banks' reserve ratio (their holdings of notes and coin and deposits at the Bank of England to total deposits); and b is the public's cash ratio (their holdings of notes and coin to their deposits).

This is more realistic than the simple expression that we had before. Even so, this too can be further expanded in a number of ways. The banks' reserve ratio, b, for example could be broken down into two ratios reflecting differential reserve requirements for time and sight deposits. None of these increasing sophistications, however, changes the essential features of the multiplier approach.

These are, firstly that it assumes two or more crucial ratios to be stable. Banks are assumed to have stable reserve ratios and the public's cash preferences are stable. Secondly, it assumes that the authorities can and do control with reasonable precision the supply of monetary base. Thirdly, it assumes that it will always be profitable for banks to expand deposits to the limit set by the monetary base.

As assumptions about what actually happens these are simply false.

5.3 THE DEMAND FOR MONEY

It is tempting to think of the question of why there is a demand for money and the related question of what determines its magnitude, as two of the sillier questions in economics. It seems obvious that people want money because they wish to buy things. To think like this, however, is completely to misunderstand the meaning of the demand for money and if we go on thinking like this we shall make no sense at all of the arguments.

Of course in everyday language we say to ourselves that we would like more money because then we would be able to spend more, but this is not strictly a demand for *money* on our part. It is a demand for more *goods and services* or a desire for more *real income*. When economists talk about the demand for money they are talking about people's desire for 'unspent' money.

Imagine a person with a given income paid monthly, in money from. On pay day, this individual will have a stock of money which will diminish over the month as expenditure takes place. Prior to the next pay day the stock may be very small indeed. We could, if we wished, calculate the average holding of money over the month.

We now have three magnitudes in the picture; the *flow* of money income per month, the *flow* of money expenditure during the month, and the average *stock* of money held during the month.

Imagine that we aggregate everyone's average money holdings and do it over a year. This then is what economists mean by the demand for money or 'liquidity preference'. Text books refer to the demand for money 'to hold', though the demand for money 'to hand' might be a better expression. The 'demand for money' is the amount of money people wish to have 'to hand' and therefore unspent, averaged over a period of time. What factors influence the community's 'liquidity preference'?

The most obvious, is the level of aggregate real income. It is obvious because of the means of payment function of money. A higher aggregate income means a higher level of economic activity, a greater volume of transactions taking place and so a greater need for money. What we are saying here is that there is a *transactions* demand for money and this is positively related to income.

The transactions demand is also related positively to the level of prices. For a given volume of transactions, the more money will be required the higher is the average price of those transactions.

However, people do not generally organise their expenditure so as to start the period only with their latest instalment of money income and end on the night before pay day with zero money balances. In aggregate, people hold money balances which are greater than necessary to finance their expenditure. In addition to a transactions demand for money there is a *precautionary* demand.

Precautionary balances are held as protection against unforeseen events. Such events might have to do with the uncertainty as to *timing* of major payments and receipts, particularly for firms which can have very uneven patterns of cashflow.

People's demand for precautionary balances is normally assumed to be related to their holdings of transactions balances and therefore ultimately to the levels of real income and prices. For explanatory purposes, therefore, this means that the demand for transactions and precautionary balances can be combined. We can henceforth refer to them as *active* balances (or 'L1') and express the quantity demanded as a function of real income and the price level. If we assume a given level of prices, then the demand for active balances can be written:

$$L1 = f(Y)$$

The demand for active balances originates in money's role as a means of payment. But those assets which function as money also function as a store of wealth. People can hold money as an alternative to other financial assets and even as an alternative to real assets such as consumer durables or capital equipment. Money's use as a store of wealth gives rise to what is variously called the speculative or asset demand for money. We shall refer to it as the demand for *idle* balances (or L2).

Recognising that people hold money as a form of saving and that some balances are therefore 'idle', is not in itself controversial. However, in the 1930s, the idea was taken up by the famous British economist J.M. Keynes and extended in a quite controversial direction. Keynes was to argue that the quantity of idle balances people wish to hold would be elastic with respect to interest rates.

In deciding how much of one's wealth to hold in money form, Keynes thought the choice lay between money and financial (as opposed to real) assets. He did this on the grounds of liquidity. Money is the perfectly liquid asset in that it can be readily exchanged for any other good or service and its money value is (by definition) certain. This is not true of any other asset but there are some financial assets for which it comes close. Bills and bonds are examples. These can be turned into money fairly quickly, though of course one cannot be certain of their value until the sale takes place.

Because of their comparative liquidity, therefore, Keynes argued that financial assets were close substitutes for money. By contrast, real assets were a very poor substitute. Real assets could be sold for money but this could not normally be done quickly. Nor was the value assured.

The next stage is the argument is that market interest rates fluctuate and that therefore people will be uncertain as to the future movement of interest rates. We have also to recall from section 5.1.1 that when interest rates change the price of fixed-interest assets like bills and bonds changes in the opposite direction. Thus, a person may be holding an asset and enjoying the interest advantage that it possesses over money, but if interest rates rise the price of the asset will fall and the holder will incur a capital loss.

The decision to hold financial assets or money therefore becomes one of balancing the interest advantage against the risk of capital loss. Obviously, if one knew when their price was going to fall (interest rates rise) one would sell such assets prior to the price fall and hold money instead. Conversely, if one expected prices to rise (interest rates fall) one would buy such assets and hold less money. But all one can do is to make uncertain estimates.

The question is: how do we make such estimates? The basis on which Keynes thought such estimates might be made was the current level of interest rates in relation to what one thought was normal in the circumstances then facing the economy. If the current rate seemed high, one might expect a fall. This would suggest a rise in asset prices and encourage a movement out of money and into assets. The higher the current rate, thought Keynes, the more people would expect a fall and therefore the lower would be the demand for idle balances. Conversely, the lower interest rates were, the more people would be expecting a rise and the greater the demand for money would be as people moved out of assets.

All of this suggests that we could treat the demand for idle balances at least as a *negative* function of the current rate of interest.

$$L2 = f(r)$$

where r is the rate of interest.

If we then assume that the demand for active balances is given (by assuming a given level of income, prices and so on) we could even treat the whole of the demand for money as a negative function of the rate of interest. This is what is shown by the downward sloping demand curve in fig. 5.1.

5.4 MONEY MARKET EQUILIBRIUM

In fig 5.1, the supply of money, exogenously determined, is shown by the curve Ms. The demand for money is shown by the curve Md. Obviously, the quantity demanded matches the quantity supplied where the curves intersect. At this point the market is in equilibrium and that equilibrium is associated with a rate of interest, r1.

Before going any further, we should check that we understand what this means. We have a *stock* of money whose magnitude is fixed by the authorities. On the demand side, some part of this stock is held by people as active balances. Its magnitude is determined by the level of expenditure they intend to undertake, i.e. it is fixed for so long as we assume a given level of prices and real income. What about the rest? Since we are in equilibrium, it must not only be held, it must be willingly held and as idle balances. But what mechanism exists to ensure that part of the money stock not held in relation to expenditure is exactly what people wish to hold as a way of storing wealth? The answer lies in the rate of interest.

We said the community as a whole would decide on its demand for idle balances in the light of what it expected to happen to interest rates (and therefore asset prices). If the residual part of the money stock is willingly held as idle balances it must be because there prevails a rate of interest (level of asset prices) such that the balance of opinion anticipating a price fall is just sufficient to take up the balances. This is the significance of the interest rate $r1$.

Suppose that the interest rate were at some other level, say $r2$, above $r1$. The diagram tells us that the demand for money would be less than the existing stock. What would happen then? Firstly, notice that if there is excess supply of money this means that the balance of opinion fearing an interest rate rise (asset price fall) is insufficient to hold the available idle balances. There is too great an expectation on balance that interest rates will fall (asset prices rise). Next consider that if this is the case, people will want to hold assets rather than money in order to make a capital gain. Thus they will buy assets. The stock of money will not change of course. That is fixed. But, the buying of assets will push up their price, lowering the current level of yields and interest rates. $r2$ will begin to move towards $r1$. As this happens the balance of opinion about future movements will change. As asset prices rise and yields fall opinion will tend increasingly towards the view that the next move will be in the opposite direction. As this happens, the demand for idle balances is increasing. As we said, the supply of money remains fixed but the fall in yields and rise in prices causes the demand for money to expand.

5.5 SOME DIFFICULTIES

How easy is it reconcile this account of the market for money with what we observe in practice? Some basic features are plainly satisfactory. The demand for money expands as the level of prices and real income rises. There is evidence also that the demand for money varies inversely with interest rates, though the elasticity is low. Asset prices and interest rates certainly move inversely. But we know we encounter difficulties when we try to interpret current events through this framework, and it is time to consider what these difficulties are and perhaps to suggest something more helpful.

Firstly, the emphasis upon ratios in the money supply process is misleading. Banks *do* observe certain ratios but not for monetary control purposes, nor do the authorities rely upon the ratios for that purpose. Banks which are members of the Monetary Sector are required to hold 0.5 per cent of their eligible liabilities (roughly, their deposits) as balances at the Bank of England, but this is solely to provide the Bank with income and resources. These balances are strictly non-operational and therefore banks have to hold additional balances for liquidity purposes. What is more, they are free to make their own judgement about the appropriate, or prudential, ratio of operational balances to liabilities. A ratio which the banks decide for themselves would scarcely be stable enough for control purposes. What is more, the ratio in practice varies between 1 and 2 per cent. With a multiplier value of over fifty, the authorities would have to be very accurate indeed in their control of the monetary base if the money stock is not to vary wildly. Yet further, *for a given monetary base*, fluctuations in the multiplier (from c.50 to c.100) would also produce massive changes in the money supply.

The fact that supply does not and under present arrangements cannot behave as the textbook multiplier describes, prepares us for the second difficulty. This is that the supply of money is very poorly controlled indeed. As table 5.5 reveals, in spite of setting themselves quite wide target ranges, the authorities have not often been successful.

Thirdly, the conventional money market account leads us to

Table 5.5: Money supply: targets and outturns

Target announced	Target period	Target variable	Target range (% p.a.)	Outturn (% p.a.)
June 1979	June 1979–April 1980	£M3	7–11	10.3
March 1980 (1)	Feb. 1980–April 1981	£M3	7–11	18.5
March 1981	Feb. 1981–April 1982	£M3	6–10	14.5
March 1982	Feb. 1982–April 1983	£M3	8–12	11.1
		M1	8–12	14.3
		PSL2	8–12	11.3
March 1983	Feb. 1983–April 1984	£M3	7–11	7.9
		M1	7–11	8.5
		PSL2	7–11	12.8
March 1984	Feb. 1984–April 1985	£M3	6–10	11.9
		M0	4–8	5.7
March 1985	Feb. 1985–April 1986	£M3	5–9	14.8
		M0	3–7	3.4
March 1986	Feb. 1986–April 1987	£M3	11–15	18.3 (2)
		M0	2–6	4.9 (2)

Notes: (1) periods overlap because targets are revised before the expiry of each period
(2) twelve months to Dec. 1986.
Source: Bank of England Quarterly Bulletin, various issues.

associate expansions in money supply with falling interest rates and vice versa. In practice, the relationship is reversed. Rapid expansion of the money supply leads the market to anticipate, often correctly, a *rise* in interest rates. Either the demand curve in fig. 5.1 has the wrong slope or interest rates are determined in some way quite unlike that suggested by the diagram.

Fourthly, as represented by fig. 5.1 what is demanded and supplied is a *stock*, the existing stock of money. However, what the market responds to is information about *flows*, and frequently flows of bank lending rather than of new bank deposits. In August 1987, for example, UK financial markets were thrown into confusion by figures showing a flow of new bank lending in July of £4.9bn. Nobody mentioned the size of the money *stock*.

5.6 THE IMPORTANCE OF FLOWS

Like any other stock, the money supply changes because of flows. If

$$M3 = C + D$$

where C is notes and coin in circulation with the non-bank private sector and D is deposits, then it follows that

$$\Delta M3 = \Delta C + \Delta D$$

Why do C and D change? Notes and coin are issued by the Bank of England. They are liabilities of the Bank and are, in effect, one of several contributions to the financing of the government's borrowing requirement. In practice, the Bank issues notes and coin on demand from bank customers. In terms of bank balance sheets, deposits (liabilities) fall as people draw out cash and this is matched by a fall in balances at the Bank as banks draw cash from the Bank of England. Clearly, if the flow of cash being paid into banks exceeded the quantity being withdrawn we could have a negative value for ΔC.

The stock of bank deposits, we know from table 5.2, changes as a result of banks' lending. At any time, some people will be paying off past loans while others will be taking out new ones. Again, the importance of flows is apparent. If the flow of new loans exceeds the termination of existing ones, the net new lending will result in an expansion of deposits. More formally, banks' balance sheets have deposits, D, as liabilities. These are matched by assets all of which constitute lending in some form. Balances at the Bank are held by the Bank of England against government bonds. Such balances are, therefore, a form of lending to the government. Banks' holdings of securities constitute lending to the government (bonds and treasury bills) and to the private sector (equities and commercial bills). Advances are lending to the private sector. Thus it follows that a change in deposits must be matched by the net change in lending to the public and private sectors. Thus we may now write:

Δ M3 = Δ notes and coin
         + Δ bank lending to the public sector
         + Δ bank lending to the non-bank private sector.

How, in practice, do the authorities try to control these lending flows? We will deal with lending to the public sector first and do it briefly since much of the detail is relevant to our discussion of the bond market in Chapter Six.

Notice that it is not public sector borrowing as such that leads to increases in M3, but only that part of it which is met by bank lending. Thus the authorities have tried, with considerable success, to meet their borrowing requirements from non-bank sources. In practice, this has meant borrowing substantially from the non-bank private sector. Borrowing from the non-bank private sector has no effect upon the money supply provided the funds borrowed are spent. Strictly, speaking, there is a fall in the measured money stock as debt is purchased because people draw on their bank deposits. When the government spends the funds, however, the money supply is restored. This does not mean, of course, that there are no monetary consequences of any kind. There may be interest rate implications if the public has to be persuaded to hold the debt. Notice too that there is an increase in total financial wealth, since the public now holds government debt in addition to the unchanged stock of deposits.

Control of bank lending to the public sector, therefore, consists of pursuing a fiscal policy which yields that scale of deficit which can be financed by debt sales to the non-bank private sector. Notice that unlike the control of the monetary base we discussed in 5.2, which sought to limit banks' ability to *supply* loans, control here focuses upon limiting the *demand*.

Control of bank lending to the non-bank private sector also concentrates upon the demand side. The authorities endeavour to limit the scale of private sector bank borrowing by adjusting the level of short-term interest rates. Raising interest rates, *ceteris paribus*, should reduce the demand for bank lending. In section 5.9 we shall see that there may once have been a secondary channel through which a rise in interest rates helped reduce the rate of monetary expansion, but that this is now probably absent. How are short-term interest rates determined and what is the role of the authorities? The practice we are about to describe dates strictly from August 1981 though it differs little from the approach that the authorities had *hoped* to introduce after 1971.

Firstly, envisage a bank's balance sheet like those we saw earlier. Secondly, bear in mind that on each working day, there are substantial flows of funds between the public and private sectors. On many occasions, the *net* flow will be towards the government. Thirdly, remember that the government banks with the Bank of England, not with the commercial banks. Thus, on such a day, it follows that banks will lose deposits equal to the net flow to the government and that their balances at the Bank of England will of course be debited by the same amount as funds are transferred to the government's accounts. If deposits and balances at the Bank fall by the same amount, however, the *ratio* of balances to deposits must fall since the balances were only a fraction to begin with.

We said at the beginning of this section that banks do not observe a rigid ratio of balances to deposits. What they do do, however, is decide continually upon the ratio that seems to them appropriate in the circumstances, having regard to the composition of deposits between sight and time, the opportunity cost of holding non-interest earning assets and so on. The ratio may not be rigid, nor even very stable, but it is not unintended. A flow of funds which disturbs this ratio, therefore, if nothing else changes, must cause banks to consider a revision of their asset portfolio. In practice the adjustment is likely to be complex but in its essentials it must involve at least a partial restoration of the ratio by a switch from other assets into balances at the Bank. Banks will sell securities. Prices will fall and yields will rise. More importantly, Banks will recall overnight lending from the discount market. This passes the shortage of funds immediately to those who had borrowed the funds, the discount houses.

We shall have more to say about the discount market in section 5.9 so we shall deal briefly here only with its relevance to monetary control. The discount houses, technically 'banks', are a group of highly specialised institutions whose business consists mainly of buying and selling treasury and commercial bills. Their principal source of funds is the retail banks to whom the advantage of the market is that they can deposit surplus funds for very short periods 'at call', and yet earn interest.

The houses also stand in a particular relationship to the Bank of England. They tender for the weekly issue of treasury bills and also guarantee to take up any surplus, thus ensuring that the authorities always have a ready source of funds. In return, the Bank guarantees to provide assistance should the discount houses be short of liquidity as a result of retail banks' withdrawal of funds. Two things make the discount market central to monetary control. Firstly, this is a unique facility, granted to no other financial institutions in the UK. Secondly, the assistance, although guaranteed, is at a rate of interest of the Bank's choosing.

Return now to the position we had above, wherein the houses are short of funds because of retail banks' withdrawal of call money. The options they face are limited. Since the shortage of funds is general they are unlikely to be able to borrow elsewhere except at interest rates higher than those currently prevailing, and the same consequences would follow. The only alternative source is the Bank of England which could lend directly to them or, more usually since 1981, could purchase bills from them for cash. In either case, the Bank has to make a decision about the rate of interest or, what amounts to the same thing, the price at which it buys the bills. Assistance could be provided at the going rate of interest. Alternatively, if the Bank were looking to reduce the growth of lending, the assistance could be at a higher or 'penal' rate. If this happened, then discount houses, faced with a loss on the sale of bills to the Bank, would minimise those sales by trying to borrow elsewhere and short-term rates would generally rise.

At last, what is apparent is that the Bank has the ability to force a rise in short-term interest rates. As far as retail banks are concerned, the relative yields on their portfolio of assets has changed. Money at call now yields more than it did and, if we maintain our assumption of initial portfolio equilibrium, there must be some adjustment away from other assets and towards money at call. As banks divert funds away from other assets, yields will also rise there. Crucially, as banks restrict their willingness to make advances to the public, the rate of interest will rise on bank lending. Depending on the interest-elasticity of demand, the flow of lending will be curtailed.

5.7 THE SUPPLY OF BILLS

Like the supply of money and, as we shall see, the supply of bonds and equities, the supply of bills is a *stock*. Normally when people trade in bills they are trading in the existing stock. However, over time the stock will expand as firms and the Treasury issue new bills partly to replace maturing bills but also to finance a high level of borrowing.

Other things being equal, we should expect the rate at which borrowing increases to vary inversely with the level of interest rates. This is because we should normally say that a borrower will borrow up to the point where the cost of further borrowing, having regard to interest, administrative and other costs, exceeds the marginal utility to be gained from the expenditure which the borrowing finances. Given the familiar assumption that the goods and services which borrowed funds are used to purchase are subject to diminishing marginal utility, we are driven to the conclusion that, *for a given cost of borrowing*, there is an optimum level of borrowing at which the marginal cost is equal to the benefits obtained. Further indebtedness will require a fall in borrowing costs; a rise in costs will reduce the optimum level of borrowing.

Given a decision to increase borrowing, however, a further decision is then required about the form of that borrowing. The decision to finance expenditure by bill sales involves comparison with other short-term sources of finance. For firms, this usually means bank overdrafts. For local authorities an alternative is to accept money on deposit. The decision involves more than just a comparison of interest rates. A bill provides its issuer with a sum of money for a fixed period and at a discount which corresponds to a fixed rate of interest. An overdraft, by contrast, carries a variable rate of interest. Thus, even if the rate of discount on new bills stands above current interest rates, bill-finance may be preferable if the borrower expects short-term interest rates to rise in future. On the other hand, bills have expenses associated with their issue. To make them widely attractive, firms may find it necessary to get them 'accepted' or guaranteed by banks specialising in this activity and the banks will demand a fee. The issue will also require publicity and some administration. By comparison, provided a borrower stays within his overdraft limit, the cost of additional borrowing is merely the rate of interest. The decision, therefore, involves a comparison of costs which extend beyond those simply of the prevailing interest/discount rate, and some judgement about the future.

5.8 THE DEMAND FOR BILLS

At the end of 1986 there were £11.5bn worth of bills outstanding. Of these, the overwhelming majority were held by banks, 'institutions comprising the monetary sector'. The only significant holders outside that category were building societies. Within the monetary sector, by far the largest holders were the discount houses with £6.5bn. The magnitude of their bill dealings and their importance to the market is further underlined if we set this 60 per cent holding of bills against the discount houses' own comparative size. Their assets comprise just 3.7 per cent of the whole of monetary sector assets. Bill holdings make up over half the assets of discount houses. No other group of financial institutions holds more than 2.5 per cent of its assets as bills. As we saw in 5.6, the houses agree always to accept the weekly issue of treasury bills; the Bank guarantees always to provide liquidity to the houses, albeit at rates of its own choosing.

The fact that bills are widely held throughout the monetary sector and, to a lesser degree by building societies, is explained by their liquidity. As we saw in 5.1.2, bills are short-term instruments. Even if held to redemption, their holders are guaranteed funds commonly within three months. In practice, of course, the bills can be sold at any time in order to raise funds. Like all marketable instruments, their price if sold before redemption is uncertain and depends upon the prevailing level of interest rates. However, being short-term instruments their price is less affected by interest-rate fluctuations than is the price of long-term assets. We discuss this point in more detail in 6.1.

This extreme liquidity, combined with the fact that they yield a return, makes bills attractive to all deposit-taking institutions. Hitherto, we have thought, quite correctly, of banks' reserves consisting of notes and coin and balances at the Bank of England. These, we noted, were non-interest earning and were held as a very small fraction of outstanding deposit liabilities. Such first-line reserves can be held in such small quantities partly because bills are such close substitutes. Indeed, there have been times in the past when bills were regarded officially as liquid reserve assets.

5.9 THE DISCOUNT MARKET

The discount market is the oldest of a number of markets collectively referred to as 'money markets'. This is because the instruments traded within them are short-term and can be thought of as enabling their issuers to borrow 'money' rather than long-term 'capital'. The other markets within the category are those for interbank deposits, certificates of deposit and local authority deposits.

From an economic point of view, the importance of the discount market lies in the fact that it is here that the authorities conduct those operations which they hope will determine interest rates and the rate of monetary growth in the economy. As we saw in 5.6, the flow of funds through the discount market gives the Bank the potential to influence interest rates through its lender of last resort role. We can look at this again in more detail and more formally.

Fig. 5.2 has two quadrants. In the RH quadrant we have a demand curve for bank lending (D1), negatively sloped with respect to the rate of interest. For simplicity, we have assumed in the diagram that the rate charged on bank lending is identical to the rate of interest set by the Bank's bill-market operations, though in practice the lending rate is determined by a mark-up on money market rates. The LH quadrant shows the discount houses willing to sell bills, their willingness (Sb) increasing as interest rates fall i.e. as the discount on the bills

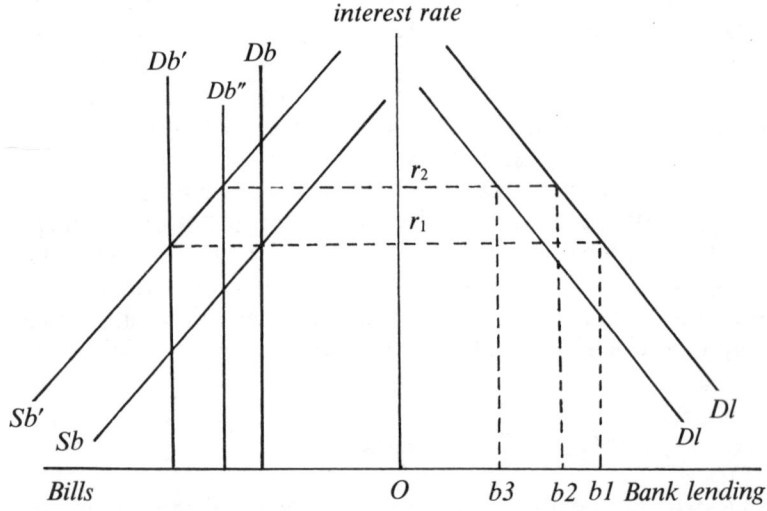

Figure 5.2

gets smaller. The bank of England is shown in the LH quadrant as a monopoly buyer of bills (Db), currently prepared to buy that quantity of bills which the houses wish to sell at r1. At r1, the flow of new bank lending is at b1 which is consistent with the authorities' money supply growth target.

Now imagine the case we met in 5.6 where there is a net flow of funds towards the government. The retail banks withdraw money at call from the discount houses, who are obliged to sell bills. The supply curve of bills shifts out to Sb'. The Bank can do one of two things. It could decide to buy the increased number of bills that the discount houses now wish to sell. If it does this, then Db shifts to Db' and everything else remains the same. However, if, as we supposed above, the Bank wants to take advantage of the shortage to raise interest rates and slow bank lending, it will signify its willingness to assist only if interest rates rise. It increases its demand for bills only to Db' and the houses are left to bid for this assistance by offering bills at greater discounts. Interest rates rise to r2 and, given the elasticity of demand for bank lending, the flow of new bank lending falls to b2.

We said at the opening of 5.6, stocks change because of the relative strengths of flows. Therefore, the effect of this reduction on the flow of new bank lending, *ceteris peribus*, should be to reduce the rate of growth of money stock. In fact, in certain circumstances, it is possible that raising short-term interest rates could reduce the flow of new bank lending via a second, supplementary route. Imagine that bank deposits and therefore the whole of the money stock is non-interest bearing. A rise in short-term interest rates is therefore a rise in the yield on non-money assets relative to money. As an asset, money becomes less attractive and people will want to hold less than was previously the case, as outlined in 5.4. This might well mean that the *stock* of money is expanding at a rate (determined by the *flow* of new bank lending, remember) which exceeds people's willingness to hold it. How is the flow of bank lending to be made consistent with people's willingness to hold the consequent stock of money? The answer lies in 5.4. Excess holdings of money will be used to purchase other financial assets, government or company securities, or National Savings instruments, for example. In effect, the excess money balances will be lent. The consequence of this is that the supply of *non-bank* lending increases. Since this is a substitute for bank lending the demand for bank lending will fall and the curve, Dl in fig. 5.2 will shift to the left. The flow of new bank lending will fall until it becomes consistent with the growth rate of desired money balances. In these circumstances therefore, a rise in interest rates has had a twofold effect. It has moved us up the demand for bank lending curve and it has pushed the curve towards the origin.

The distinguishing feature of these circumstances, however, is that money is non-interest bearing. A rise in interest rates imposes a penalty on holding money. Since the 1970s, however, banks have had to compete for deposits; firstly, against non-bank institutions but more recently between themselves. This process of 'liability management' has meant that bank deposits have come increasingly to bear interest. Now, when interest rates rise, there is no marked increase in the cost of holding money. This explains two points which we have earlier touched upon. Firstly, it explains why the demand for money is less interest–elastic than Keynes took it to be. Also it explains why variations in short term interest rates have only a small effect upon the growth of the money stock. A rise in interest rates no longer produces a leftward shift of the demand curve for bank lending. If a rise in interest rates leads to a reduction in the flow of new bank lending, it is now solely because of a movement *along* the curve. Monetary control has become crucially dependent upon the interest-elasticity of demand for bank lending, and this may be rather low.

Whatever the ability of interest rate changes to influence bank lending and monetary growth may be, however, there is no doubt that the authorities have considerable power to determine interest rates. But since 1981 it has been commonly said, and positively emphasised by the authorities themselves, that interest rates in the UK economy are largely 'market determined'. In the remainder of this section we shall look at what this means and just how true it is. The second and third case studies in this chapter examine two recent incidents which also shed some light on this issue.

The authorities' case is based upon a number of detailed changes made in 1981, to the way in which they operate in the discount market. Firstly, the Bank of England ceased to announce in advance the rate at which it would be prepared to deal in bills. Previously, a 'Minimum Lending Rate' had been continuously posted. The ability to reintroduce a MLR in extreme conditions was, however, retained and this in fact happened for just one day on 14th January, 1985. Secondly, the Bank gave notice that it would make its own forecasts of daily flows in the market so as to be ready to provide assistance but that when the need arose the houses would have to offer bills for sale to the bank at prices of *their* own choosing. This contrasted in two ways with previous practice. Previously, the Bank had been willing to *lend* to the houses, leaving their bill holdings intact; also, of course, the houses knew the lending rate they would have to pay. Under the new arrangements each house would have to offer bills at a price which the Bank hoped would reflect the degree of difficulty it was in. Thirdly, the stock of outstanding bills was divided into four bands according to maturity as follows:

band 1   0–14 days
band 2   15–33 days
band 3   34–63 days
band 4   64–91 days

and the Bank announced its intention to deal only in bands 1 and 2. Thus, it was argued, whatever effect upon the market the authorities might have, it would be confined to a very narrow spectrum of assets and interest rates. Elsewhere, it would be market forces that determined prices and interest rates.

CASE STUDY 5.1: THE LONDON MONEY MARKET

In the week beginning 19th October 1987 stock exchanges around the world saw the biggest falls in equity prices since 1929. The selling of shares which caused the collapse was matched by an increase in the purchase of fixed-interest securities which caused a rise in their price and a fall in yields. On 22nd October, as the report indicates, this process was reinforced by an additional demand for UK bonds and bills because cuts in US interest rates gave UK securities a higher relative yield. Three month interbank fell marginally to 10 per cent and the Bank of England indicated its acceptance of the position by providing assistance at $9\frac{7}{8}$ per cent.

Notice that total assistance amounted to £521 m. and was provided mainly through the purchase of 'band 1' bills. The flow of funds which gave rise to this need for assistance arose from bills already in the Bank's possession maturing and the issuers of the bills having to make corresponding payments to the Bank, and a further reduction in banks' balances as they drew extra notes of £60 m. Against this shortage (of £583 m.) other Exchequer transactions provided extra liquidity of £40 m. and it was estimated that the banks began the day with balances of £10 m. above target.

Source: Financial Times, 23 October 1987.

MONEY MARKETS

London reacts to lower US rates

INTEREST RATES eased on the London money market, as funds seeking a safe haven from the vagaries of the equity market, were encouraged into Government debt, in the form of bills and bonds.

The downward trend in rates was further reinforced by news that US banks were cutting their prime lending rates, and also by early intervention by the Federal Reserve, adding liqidity to the New York banking system.

UK clearing bank base lending rate 10 per cent since August 7

In London trading was relatively quiet and calm. Three-month interbank fell to 10⅛-10 per cent, from $10\frac{3}{16}$-$10\frac{1}{16}$ per cent. Sentiment was helped by sterling's steady performance on the foreign exchanges.

The Bank of England initially forecast a money market shortage of £550m, but revised this to £600m at noon. Total help of £521m was provided.

Before lunch the authorities bought £50m bank bills in band 1 at 9⅞ per cent.

In the afternoon another £291m bills were purchased, by way of £284m bank bills in band 1 at 9⅞ per cent and £7m bank bills in band 2 at 9⅞ per cent.

Late assistance of £180m was also provided.

Bills maturing in official hands, repayment of late assistance and a take-up of Treasury bills drained £523m, with a rise in the note circulation absorbing £60m. These outweighed Exchequer transactions adding £40m to liquidity and bank balances above target of £10m.

In New York banks reduced their prime lending rates to 9 per cent from 9¼ per cent. The Federal Reserve moved to calm financial markets, shaken by another sharp fall in stock prices on Wall Street. The authorities intervened an hour earlier than usual to supply liquidity to the banking system. The Fed offered four-day system repurchase agreements, when Federal funds were trading at $6\frac{15}{16}$ per cent, compared with an average of 6.47 per cent on Wednesday. After this direct injection of temporary reserves the rate fell to 6⅞ per cent.

In Berlin the West German Bundesbank left its credit policies unchanged at the regular central bank council meeting. The discount rates remains at 3 per cent and the Lombard emergency financing rate at 5 per cent. Mr Gerhard Stoltenberg, West German Finance Minister attended the meeting.

FT LONDON INTERBANK FIXING

(11.00 a.m. Oct. 22) 3 months U.S. dollars		6 months U.S. dollars	
bid 8	offer $8\frac{1}{8}$	bid $8\frac{1}{16}$	offer $8\frac{3}{16}$

The fixing rates are the arithmetic means, rounded to the nearest one-sixteenth, of the bid and offered rates for $10m quoted by the market to five reference banks at 11.00 a.m. each working day. The banks are National Westminster Bank, Bank of Tokyo, Deutsche Bank, Banque Nationale de Paris and Morgan Guaranty Trust.

MONEY RATES

NEW YORK (4pm)

		Treasury Bills and Bonds			
		One month	4.19	Three year	8.13
		Two month	5.28	Four year	8.44
Prime rate	$9\text{-}9\frac{1}{4}$	Three month	5.50	Five year	8.53
Broker loan rate	$8\text{-}8\frac{1}{4}$	Six month	6.34	Seven year	8.84
Fed. funds	$7\frac{1}{2}$	One year	6.89	10 year	8.97
Fed funds at intervention	$6\frac{15}{16}$	Two year	7.79	30 year	9.13

October 22	Overnight	One Month	Two Months	Three Months	Six Months	Lombard Intervention
Frankfurt	3.60-3.70	3.80-3.95	3.85-4.00	4.65-4.80	4.75-4.95	5.0
Paris	$7\frac{5}{8}\text{-}7\frac{3}{4}$	$7\frac{3}{4}\text{-}7\frac{7}{8}$	$7\frac{7}{8}\text{-}8$	$8\frac{3}{16}\text{-}8\frac{5}{16}$	$8\frac{9}{16}\text{-}8\frac{11}{16}$	$7\frac{1}{2}$
Zurich	$\frac{7}{8}\text{-}1\frac{1}{8}$	$2\frac{7}{8}\text{-}3\frac{1}{8}$	—	$4\text{-}4\frac{1}{4}$	—	—
Amsterdam	$5\frac{3}{16}\text{-}5\frac{5}{16}$	$5\frac{1}{4}\text{-}5\frac{3}{8}$	—	$5\frac{5}{8}\text{-}5\frac{3}{4}$	—	—
Tokyo	3.34375	3.84375	—	—	—	—
Milan	$10\frac{5}{8}\text{-}11\frac{1}{8}$	$11\frac{3}{8}\text{-}11\frac{7}{8}$	—	$12\text{-}12\frac{1}{2}$	—	—
Brussels	7.50	$6\frac{5}{8}\text{-}6\frac{3}{4}$	—	$6\frac{15}{16}\text{-}7\frac{1}{16}$	—	—
Dublin	$8\text{-}8\frac{1}{4}$	$8\frac{3}{4}\text{-}9$	$9\text{-}9\frac{1}{4}$	$9\frac{1}{4}\text{-}9\frac{1}{2}$	$9\frac{5}{8}\text{-}9\frac{7}{8}$	—

LONDON MONEY RATES

October 22	Over-night	7 days notice	Month	Three Months	Six Months	One Year
Interbank	$10\frac{1}{2}\text{-}6$	$9\frac{13}{16}\text{-}9\frac{3}{4}$	$9\frac{15}{16}\text{-}9\frac{13}{16}$	$10\frac{3}{16}\text{-}10$	$10\frac{5}{16}\text{-}10$	$10\frac{1}{2}\text{-}10\frac{3}{16}$
Sterling CDs.	—	—	$9\frac{7}{8}\text{-}9\frac{25}{32}$	$10\frac{1}{32}\text{-}9\frac{15}{16}$	$10\frac{3}{16}\text{-}10\frac{1}{16}$	$10\frac{1}{4}\text{-}10\frac{1}{8}$
Local Auth'rity Deps.	$9\frac{5}{8}$	$9\frac{13}{16}$	$9\frac{13}{16}$	$10\frac{1}{8}$	$10\frac{5}{16}$	$10\frac{3}{8}$
Local Authority Bonds	—	—	$10\frac{1}{4}$	$10\frac{3}{8}$	$10\frac{9}{16}$	$10\frac{5}{8}$
Discount Mkt Deps.	$10\text{-}9\frac{3}{4}$	$9\frac{3}{4}$	$9\frac{3}{4}$	$9\frac{3}{4}$	—	—
Company Deposits	—	10	$10\text{-}9\frac{15}{16}$	$10\frac{1}{4}$	$10\frac{1}{4}$	$10\frac{1}{2}$
Finance House Deposits	—	—	$9\frac{7}{8}$	$10\frac{1}{4}$	$10\frac{3}{8}$	$10\frac{1}{2}$
Treasury Bills (Buy)	—	—	$9\frac{13}{16}$	$9\frac{3}{4}$	—	—
Bank Bills (Buy)	—	—	$9\frac{27}{32}$	$9\frac{13}{16}$	$9\frac{27}{32}$	—
Fine Trade Bills (Buy)	—	—	$10\frac{13}{32}$	$10\frac{7}{16}$	$10\frac{13}{32}$	—
Dollar CDs	—	—	7.25-7.20	7.70-7.65	7.85-7.80	8.50-8.45
SDR Linked Deposits	—	—	$6\frac{5}{16}\text{-}6\frac{1}{16}$	$7\frac{1}{8}\text{-}6\frac{7}{8}$	$7\frac{3}{16}\text{-}6\frac{15}{16}$	$7\frac{7}{16}\text{-}7\frac{3}{16}$
ECU Linked Deposits	—	—	$6\frac{7}{8}\text{-}6\frac{3}{4}$	$7\frac{11}{16}\text{-}7\frac{9}{16}$	$7\frac{13}{16}\text{-}7\frac{11}{16}$	$8\frac{1}{16}\text{-}7\frac{13}{16}$

Treasury Bills (sell); one-month $9\frac{3}{4}$per cent; three-months $9\frac{9}{16}$per cent; Bank Bills (sell); one-month $9\frac{27}{32}$ per cent; three months $9\frac{25}{32}$ per cent; Treasury Bills; Average tender rate of discount 9.7858 p.c. ECGD Fixed Rate Sterling Export Finance. Make up day September 30, 1987. Agreed rates for period October 26 to November 24 1987, Scheme I: 11.42 p.c., Schemes II & III: 11.47 p.c. Reference rate for period August 29 to September 30, 1987, Scheme IV: 10.219p.c. Local Authority and Finance Houses seven days' notice, others seven days' fixed. Finance Houses Base Rate $10\frac{1}{2}$ per cent from October 1, 1987: Bank Deposit Rates for sums at seven days' notice $3\text{-}3\frac{1}{2}$ per cent. Certificates of Tax Deposit (Series 6); Deposit £100,000 and over held under one month 8 per cent; one-three months $8\frac{1}{4}$ per cent; three-six months 10 per cent; six-nine months $10\frac{1}{4}$ per cent; nine-12 months $10\frac{3}{8}$ per cent; Under £100,000 8 per cent from September 15, Deposits withdrawn for cash 5 per cent.

Source: *Financial Times*, 23 October 1987.

Bank imposes penal interest to hold line on base lending rate

BY JANET BUSH

THE BANK of England moved decisively yesterday against mounting pressure in UK financial markets for a cut in base lending rates.

As sterling continued to surge on foreign exchanges and UK Government bonds rode high on overseas buying, the Bank again lent money to the domestic money market at a penal rate to underline its desire to hold the line on interest rates for the time being.

Yesterday's operations in the money market were seen as the most aggressive stand against lower interest rates yet. The Bank of England has lent funds to the market at interest rates well above 11 per cent, the current level of base rates, on four occasions since February 19 but yesterday's rate of 11¾ per cent was the highest yet and dealt an expensive blow to discount houses pushing for a quick fall in base rates.

Much of the reluctance to allow base rates to fall now can be traced to the Government's desire to delay a cut until around the Budget on March 17 and maximise the favourable response expected to greet the Chancellor's package.

Mr Tony Blair, the Labour Party's Treasury spokesman yesterday said the Government's attempts to stop interest rates falling until the Budget was a "continuing scandal" and accused the Government of taking a political

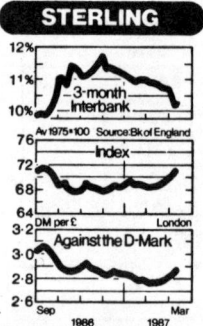

gamble with public money.

He calculated that, in a month, a 1 percentage point reduction in base lending rates would save homeowners £90m and industry £37m.

Some of sterling's rise has been on genuine optimism about prospects for the UK economy. However, the pound has also been helped by caution about trading other major currencies actively for fear of central bank intervention following the Paris agreement on stabilising currencies. Since the accord, sterling has risen by more than 3 per cent against a basket of currencies.

The Bank of England is likely to adopt a cautious approach towards lowering interest rates, as so often before, until it is sure that sterling's rise recently is soundly-based and not simply the result of the post-Paris environment or a bandwagon of pre-Budget optimism.

On balance, financial markets believe the authorities can resist cutting rates until they are ready. In January 1986, the Bank of England raised base rates by 1 percentage point and staved off another increase in spite of formidable market pressure.

A measure of current confidence in sterling was the market's ability to shrug off yesterday's publication of figures showing a £1bn current account deficit in 1986, three times larger than previously reported.

In London, sterling closed yesterday at $1.5775 compared with Wednesday's closing $1.5650 and surged to DM 2.8900 after DM 2.8750. In New York it ended the day at $1.584. The Bank's trade weighted sterling index closed at 71.4, up from Wednesday's closing 70.9.

UK government bond prices built on Wednesday's substantial gains to end up around ⁷⁄₁₆ of a point higher. Meanwhile some money market interest rates ended lower despite the Bank's determined signals but the key three-month inter-bank sterling rate, used as a guide to the level of base rates, ended little changed.

Editorial Comment, Page 28; Money markets, Page 41; UK trade worse, Back Page

Source: Financial Times, 6 March 1987.

CASE STUDY 5.2

In the early months of 1987 the pound sterling increased in value against a trade-weighted index of other currencies. Markets began to anticipate a cut in interest rates for three reasons. Firstly, it was thought that the value was approaching the top of a range previously agreed by finance ministers from the major economies; secondly, by raising the price of exports it was threatening the recent recovery of UK manufacturing industry; thirdly, the rising value of sterling combined with existing interest rates was making the UK bond market attractive to overseas investors, bond prices were rising and bond yields falling. This last point meant that long-term interest rates were already beginning to fall because firms found they could issue *new* bonds with lower yields.

Furthermore, the fact that sterling was being purchased by overseas investors in order to buy UK securities meant that the sterling was 'new' sterling, an addition to the money supply. When received by the sellers of securities, it would be deposited with banks raising both sterling bank deposits (in M3) and banks' balances at the Bank of England by equal amounts. This in turn would raise banks' liquidity and they would look to restore their earlier portfolio equlibrium by rearranging assets: amongst other things, they too would buy securities, pushing prices up and yields down. This was an additional source of pressure on long-term interest rates.

So long as banks maintain an asset portfolio approximating to equlibrium we know that there will be days when their deposits at the Bank of England will be seriously depleted by payments to the government. They will then recall funds from the discount markets and money markets will be said to need assistance. This happened on 5th March and the Bank then had to make a decision on the rate at which to provide it, knowing that its decision would be taken as an indication of its willingness to see *short*-term interest rates fall. As we know, it chose to assist at a rate higher than those generally existing at the time and temporarily at least base rates stayed as they were.

Does all this amount to a truthful statement that short-term interest rates are market determined? Plainly it does not in the usual sense in which textbooks present markets as producing an equlibrium price and quantity. The market in which short-run rates are being determined is one in which there is a monopoly supplier of liquidity (the Bank) and nine buyers (the discount houses). Case studies 5.2 and 5.3 both show that for a time at least the Bank as monopoly supplier can charge any rate it chooses. Case study 5.2 shows the Bank holding out against the market; case study 5.3 shows it imposing a new rate when 'market wisdom' was unprepared. More than that, it can if it wishes deliberately engineer a shortage such that the market has to seek assistance. By selling government debt to the public in exchange for funds which the government does not intend to spend, a process known as 'overfunding', the authorities can force a drain of funds from the monetary sector. In fig. 5.2, we know that this will result in an outward shift of the curve Sb as the discount houses face a liquidity shortage. The supply of bills curve, Sb, is in effect a curve showing the demand for liquidity and the Bank's demand for bills curve, Db, is a liquidity supply curve. In terms of a conventional supply and demand diagram, therefore, the situation we have just described is one which we have not only a monopoly supplier but that monopolist is able to influence the position of the demand curve.

Competition amongst bill holders, whether they are buying or selling, can also be overstated. The Bank offers to deal twice each day. The rates at which it has dealt, therefore, become quickly known in a market with comparatively few practitioners who are in continuous contact with each other. Even outsiders have the crucial information within twenty-four hours via the *Financial Times* money market report, reproduced in case study 5.1. However 'competitive' the discount houses offer to sell bills to the Bank may look superficially, we can be certain the houses will not make offers which are very far from either the price the Bank desires or from each other.

Indeed, the setting of money market interest rates often appears to happen by convention with no visible sign of the intermediate stages we have described. This is because the

CASE STUDY 5.3

As we saw in Case Study 5.2, sterling appreciated significantly against other currencies in early 1987, so much so that it was thought to have reached the top of its unpublished target range. This had led markets to anticipate a fall in interest rates a week earlier. On that occasion, however, the Bank had 'imposed a penal rate' to prevent short-term rates from falling. On 9th March, as the report shows, it 'signalled that it was ready to see borrowing costs fall' and this signal came as a surprise to financial markets.

Bank sanctions cut in base rates to 10½%

BY PHILIP STEPHENS AND JANET BUSH

BRITAIN'S LEADING banks cut their base lending rates yesterday by ½ percentage point to 10½ per cent after the Bank of England signalled that it was ready to see borrowing costs fall in response to the recent strength of the pound.

The reduction, which came as sterling registered further substantial gains, surprised financial markets. The Bank had strongly resisted market pressure for a cut over the past two weeks, creating the impression that it wanted no change until after next Tuesday's Budget.

Yesterday's move marked the first tangible evidence of a significant shift in government policy towards sterling since finance ministers of leading industrial countries agreed in Paris last month to seek a period of stability on foreign exchange markets.

Mr Nigel Lawson, the Chancellor, suggested then that he would react to a sharp rise in the pound's value by lowering borrowing costs. The Bank's tactics over the past two weeks were dictated by concern to ensure that sterling's gains were not simply the result of a pre-Budget speculative flurry.

A further rise of 0.6 points to 72.4 in the sterling index in the

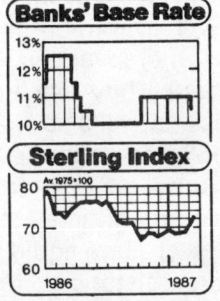

first few hours of trading yesterday apparently provided sufficient assurance, prompting the Bank to cut its money market dealing rates.

National Westminster Bank quickly responded by lowering its base rate to 10½ per cent and the other leading banks followed throughout the afternoon.

The authorities made clear that they were not ready to accept any further reduction in borrowing costs before next Tuesday, but did little to damp speculation that another ½ point cut might follow the Budget.

Mr Lawson is expected to announce simultaneous reductions in income tax and in public borrowing in his Budget speech, a strategy which most City economists expect will generate pressure for still lower interest rates. That sentiment was reinforced by sterling's ability to shrug off yesterday's move.

Another ½-point reduction in bank base rates might also persuade the building societies to cut mortgage rates, which in turn would ease upward pressure on inflation during the summer.

It is now clear that the Treasury has had an implicit target range for the pound's value since the Paris agreement. At that meeting, Mr Lawson said he did not want to see sterling fall further, nor did he want to see a "substantial rise." In the two weeks since then the pound has appreciated by nearly 5 per cent.

Officials insisted that the decision to cut rates yesterday did not suggest that the ceiling for the pound's' value had been

Continued on Back Page
Small companies' Budget call, Page 9; Producer prices, Page 10; Money markets, Page 35; Tax, Back Page; French interest rates, Back Page

Source: *Financial Times*, 10 March 1987.

Given the earlier resistance, why did the Bank change its position? The report suggests that the explanation lies in the strength of sterling. The exchange rate had continued to appreciate, making more acute all the problems we discussed in 5.2 and driving the pound to the top of its implicit target range. In effect, the action admitted that in future monetary policy was to be determined by the behaviour of the exchange rate.

What does this incident shed upon our earlier discussion of the way short-term interest rates are determined? Obviously in 'signalling' its acceptance of a reduction and in its ability to suprise the markets the Bank's influence is overwhelming. However, there is a sense in which this action may be said to have recognised and endorsed existing market forces. We know that markets had earlier been expecting a fall. One of the consequences of an appreciating exchange rate is an increase in the domestic money supply and in the liquidity of the banking system which inevitably causes medium and long term interest rates to fall as banks re-arrange their assets by buying securities. This change in the structure of yields will eventually cause banks to switch more assets into bills and advances whose yields are comparatively high. As banks buy bills and increase advances the yields on these assets will also fall.

For a time, the Bank can continue to use days of money market shortage to impose the short-term rate of its own choosing, but in the meantime the monetary sector's position will become ever more liquid with the consequence that the days on which assistance is required will diminish. It is conceivable, if the Bank continued for long enough to resist market pressure for a fall in interest rates, that its position would become irrelevant. To re-establish a position of influence over monetary conditions would then require a new set of rules and relationships and possibly major structural changes within the monetary sector.

market and its practitioners know the sequence very well and also because profit can be made (or losses minimised) by *anticipating* events. For example, markets will always have a view about the government's policy on monetary growth. Against this, they will be making continuous assessments of the scale of current bank lending. Suppose the feeling is that current bank lending figures are 'high' in relation to targets. This will be widely discussed in the financial press and by market practitioners. Some people will take the view that a rise in interest rates is at least probable. They will sell at least some of their bill holdings to avoid an anticipated capital loss. This selling will cause bill rates to 'edge-up'. The *Financial Times* money markets daily report will carry this information. Nervousness will grow. More selling and a further marginal increase in rates may occur. The question then becomes one of the Bank's view of this 'pressure for a rise in interest rates'. At what rate of interest will the Bank provide assistance when next it is asked? It may raise its rate, thereby 'sanctioning' the market's anticipation or it may resist the rise by continuing assistance at the original rate.

Furthermore, when it comes to the diffusion of short-term interest rate changes through the rest of the financial system, convention and administrative rules appear again. Recall that the authorities may have an interest in seeing interest rates rise in order to discourage bank lending and monetary growth. Plainly such action is only relevant to the objective if the rise in rates is passed on to would-be borrowers in the commercial and personal sectors. The interest rates charged by banks to their customers are determined by applying a set of administrative rules to a base rate of interest. Thus, a favoured commercial organisation, doing large business with a bank might be charged interest at '1 per cent over base' while an individual client might be paying 4 or 5 per cent over base for an overdraft. Changes in the level of interest rates charged on borrowing, therefore, depend almost wholly upon movements in the base rate. Clearly, if 'market' interest rates move up (as in our example), there will come a point at which banks will have to pay more for their deposits and, with the marginal cost of funds rising, they will eventually have to raise the rates charged to clients. However, although base rates move roughly in line with money market rates, the changes to base rates are both less frequent and, when they occur, larger. As case study 5.2 shows, banks are reluctant to follow movements in market interest rates unless and until the authorities have confirmed that they wish to see a change. Indeed, this reluctance has been so marked that on occasions, as in 1985, it was said to produce 'round-tripping'. This becomes possible when money market rates edge above banks' base rates enabling favoured customers, paying very little over base rate, to borrow from banks and then to lend the funds in the money markets.

Except that their role is more obscure to the public eye, the authorities' influence over short-term interest rates is not very different from what it used to be when they announced a Minimum Lending Rate each week and expected institutions to comply.

6 The Market for Bonds

In this chapter we examine the market for long-term, fixed interest securities. Because they yield a fixed rate of interest there are some respects in which bonds resemble bills, but the contrasts are much more significant. Bonds are issued by the government (gilt edge stock), by local authorities, and by firms.

6.1 CHARACTERISTICS

Notice firstly that bonds are issued with much longer terms to maturity than bills. Bonds with an initial maturity of less than five years are unusual. Many bonds are issued to mature in ten or even twenty years' time and there are some government bonds in existence which will never be redeemed. Obviously, as time passes the residual maturity of any bond shortens. It is common to classify bonds by their residual maturity. Bonds with lives up to five years are called 'shorts'; from five to fifteen are 'mediums'; over fifteen are 'longs'.

Secondly, the denomination of bonds, normally at £100 each, is much smaller than for bills. This makes it possible for individuals to deal in bonds, and many do. The market, however, is dominated by large institutions.

Thirdly, the return to bondholders is in the form of a conventional interest payment, rather than a discount to the maturity value. This interest payment is known as the 'coupon'. Consider the case of the government bond known as 'Treasury 13% 2000'. Its title tells us that it will be redeemed in the year 2000 and that until then it will pay £6.50 every six months to whoever is the registered owner. Thus someone buying such a bond for £100 at the time of issue, intending to hold it to redemption, is quaranteed a return of 13 per cent per annum.

Fourthly, because the coupon is fixed at the outset bond prices must fluctuate inversely with market interest rates. The reasoning is the same as with bills: if market rates rise, bonds with various coupons will be willingly held only if their price has fallen to the point where the coupon expressed as a percentage of the current price approximates the market rate. Let us look at this more closely, taking the case of 'Consols 2.5%'. These are irredeemable bonds which pay a fixed 'coupon' of £2.50 a year and will never be redeemed. Let us suppose that market interest rates are 10 per cent. Why should anyone hold an asset paying £2.50? The answer of course is that there will be buyers for the bond if its price is sufficiently low that £2.50 approximates the market rate.

We can see this more clearly if we think of the purchase of a fixed-interest bond as the purchase of a fixed stream of future income, the stream lasting until the bond matures. The present value, or price, of that bond is therefore the value that the market places upon the total stream of income. What determines this valuation? One obvious element is the size of each payment (given by the coupon). However, all but the first of these payments will occur at some distant time in the future. Their value will be influenced by both the length of time that one has to wait for them and by the prevailing rate of interest which indicates the opportunity cost of not having the payment available now. The present value of a coupon payment in a year's time is given by

$$C \cdot \frac{1}{1+r}$$

where C is the coupon and r is the rate of interest. The value of the same payment in two years time is

$$C \cdot \frac{1}{(1+r)^2}$$

Thus it follows that the value of the whole stream of payments is the sum of this progression. If P is the present value or price of the bond, then

$$P = \sum_{t=1}^{n} C \cdot \frac{1}{(1+r)^t}$$

Since our example is an irredeemable bond, the payments go on for ever and the value of t eventually becomes infinity. This means that the series

$$C \cdot \frac{1}{(1+r)^t}$$

is converging on zero and the present value P of the sum of the series can be more conveniently written as

$$P = C/r$$

From this it is easy to calculate that with interest rates at 10 per cent (r = 0.1) Consols 2.5% will trade at £25. If interest rates fall to 5 per cent, P will rise to £50.

However, most government bonds will in fact mature. In this case the buyer is acquiring a future stream of income which will terminate at a fixed point, together with the return of the £100 maturity value of the bond. The present value has therefore to incorporate both the income stream and the value of £100 at some years hence. In this case P is found as follows:[1]

$$P = \sum_{t=1}^{n} C \cdot \frac{1}{(1+r)^t} + M \cdot \frac{1}{(1+r)^n}$$

where M is the maturity value of the bond. Take the earlier case, Treasury 13% 2000. Its present value will be made up first of all of the present value of a £13 annuity paid for 13 years (from 1987) when interest rates are 10 per cent. From annuity tables we know this to be £92.3442. To this we have to add the present value of £100 receivable in 13 years time. This is £28.97, giving a value for P of £121.31.

Notice carefully the effect of making the bond redeemable at a particular date. On our earlier (irredeemable) formula, we should expect the price of Treasury 13% to be £130 in order for it to yield 10 per cent. However, it will be redeemed eventually for only £100 and buyers at £130 would make a capital loss of £30. By contrast, if interest rates rose to 15 per cent, the formula for irredeemables would value the bond at £86.66. On redemption, in thirteen years time today's buyers would have the additional reward of a capital gain of £13.34. In practice the effect of these capital gains/losses is to make the price of redeemable bonds less sensitive to interest rate changes than is the case with irredeemable bonds. With a 10 per cent interest rate, there will be a capital loss on redemption which has to be offset against the value of the coupon payments. Taking this into account the bond will be worth less than £130. As we saw its value will be c.£121. On the other hand, if interest rates rise to 15 per cent the capital gain on redemption will make the bond worth more than the £86.66 which results from the coupon payment alone. In fact, if we revalue the bond for interest rates at 15 per cent we find it is worth £72.58 plus £16.25 or £88.83. As interest rates vary between 10 and 15 per cent, the value of a 13 per cent bond varies between £130 and £86.66 if it is irredeemable. If it is redeemable in 13 years, its price will range more narrowly – between £121.31 and £88.53.

Let us repeat: for a given change in interest rates, all bond prices will vary inversely but the price of redeemable bonds will vary less than the price of irredeemable bonds. In fact, what we have stumbled across is one example of a very general principle. In changing a bond from irredeemable to redeemable we have in effect shortened its maturity. If *within* the category of redeemable bonds we compare the behaviour of bonds with a given coupon but different maturities we shall find that the price of short-dated bonds will always vary less than the price of long-dated bonds. A glance at the second formula shows why. Part of the present value of a redeemable bond is the value of M, the £100 paid on maturity. As the expression shows, the present value of M is determined by the rate of interest, r and the number of years to maturity, n. For a *given* value of r therefore, the present value is determined by n. Notice that with r positive, the expression within the brackets has a value greater than one. Thus, as we raise it to the power n it gets larger and the larger is n the larger this denominator will get. As n approaches infinity, the value of the redemption payment approaches zero. All that is left is the stream of annual payments. Table 6.1 illustrates the effect of the length of time to maturity on the price variability of four 13 per cent bonds.

Table 6.1: *The effect of maturity on price variability of bonds*

Period (years) to maturity of 13% bond	£ Present value when interest rate is 10%	15%
∞	130	86.66
13	121.31	88.83
7	114.63	91.67
2	105.13	97.80

Incidentally, the table also illustrates why economics texts always choose the (less common) undated bonds in order to illustrate the proposition that bond prices vary inversely with interest rates. The relationship is simpler and the calculations are much easier for irredeemable bonds!

Fifthly, we need to note that the yield on bonds can be expressed and is commonly published in two forms: the redemption yield and the running or interest yield. The redemption yield we have discussed above. It is the annualised yield on a bond held to redemption, taking account of both coupon payments and capital gain/loss on redemption. As we have indicated, market forces tend to push redemption yields on all bonds towards equality with current interest rates. However, as we also noticed, this means that the market price of bonds of the same coupon will differ depending on their residual maturity. Thus, someone buying a bond with the intention of selling before maturity, and thus being interested only in the coupon payment, will find that the return on bonds of the same coupon will vary. In our example, the price of the irredeemable 13 per cent bond was £86.66 and its holder will have paid £86.66 in order to get a return of £13 p.a. Buying the thirteen year bond, the purchaser will have to lay out more than £88.83 for the same reward and for the short-dated bond, will have to pay approaching £100. The coupon alone

150 *Understanding Markets*

expressed in relation to the price of the bond gives us the running or interest yield:

$$\text{running yield} = C/P$$

Clearly, if redemption yields tend to equality causing differences in the price of bonds with the same coupon, running yields will vary considerably.

6.2 THE SUPPLY OF BONDS

As with money and bills and equities, there exists at any time a *stock* of bonds. The trading of bonds therefore involves the trading of the existing stock. The willingness to sell is a willingness to sell from the existing stock. This contrasts with our normal ideal of supply being a *flow* over time of something newly created.

While it is true that the 'supply' of bonds at any particular time is limited to the existing stock, the stock of bonds, like the stock of other financial assets, expands over time as new bonds

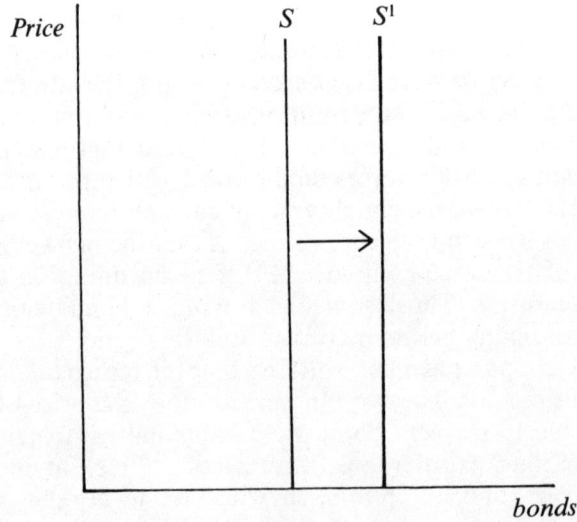

Figure 6.1

are issued to finance additional borrowing. This is shown by a rightward shift of the curve S, to S^1, in figure 6.1.

What influences decisions to issue *new* bonds? Bonds are a source of long-term finance to their issuers. Corporate bonds may take the form of *loan stock* or *debentures*, the latter usually being secured on specific assets of the company issuing the bond. Foreign institutions also issue bonds denominated in sterling. Sometimes the purpose is to raise funds for the purchase of equipment from the UK or to exchange for foreign currency, speculating on a later fall in sterling which will make subsequent repayments cheaper. Sterling bonds issued by foreign institutions are known as 'bulldog' bonds.

As we established in 6.1, the rate of interest paid on bonds is normally fixed for the lifetime of the bond, although variable rate and index-linked bonds do exist. In deciding on the appropriate method of finance, therefore, firms have to take into account not just the current level of interest rates, but also what they think is likely to happen to interest rates in future. If interest rates are high at the moment, for example, but firms expect them to fall in future, they will be reluctant to enter long-term commitments to pay high rates and will look to other sources of finance. In 1979–82 unprecedentedly high interest rates encouraged just such a view and led to a drying up of new issues of corporate bonds.

In recent years, it is the government that has been the main source of new bond issues. This sale of 'marketable debt', as government bonds are also known, is the direct consequence

Table 6.2: Government bond sales and PSBR 1980–1986 (£M)

Year	Sales of marketable debt	PSBR
1980	11,245	11,817
1981	7,488	10,587
1982	5,909	4,953
1983	8,184	11,591
1984	8,953	10,047
1985	9,232	7,622
1986	7,169	4,035

Source: CSO *Financial Statistics* (various issues), tables 3.5, 11.5 and 11.6.

of the public sector's annual borrowing requirement. You will recall that we said in 5.6 that controlling the growth of the money supply requires limiting the growth of bank lending to the public as well as the private sector. Thus governments have had to fund their budget deficits specifically by selling debt, including bonds, to the non-bank private sector. Table 6.2 shows both the annual sale of bonds and the corresponding Public Sector Borrowing Requirement since 1980. In most years, the sale of bonds has covered more than 80 per cent of the PSBR. The remainder has been met by the sale of 'non-marketable debt', i.e. National Savings instruments. Thus it can be seen that very little public sector borrowing has been financed by the 'residual' device of selling treasury bills.

Notice that bond sales were particularly large in 1984 and 1985. When sales of non-marketable debt are added it will be found that the PSBR was 'overfunded': the government borrowed more than it needed. This is an illustration of what we said earlier in 5.9, namely, that for monetary control purposes the authorities can always, if they wish, force a reduction in bank deposits by taking in funds from the private sector which they do not intend to spend.

Financing additional borrowing, government borrowing included, by bond sales inevitably raises questions about the effects on the level and structure of long-term interest rates. If, for example, the demand curve for bonds slopes downwards with respect to price, then a rightward shift in the supply curve in figure 6.1 should lead us *ceteris paribus* to expect a fall in bond prices and a rise in yields or interest rates. To answer such questions we need to consider the demand for fixed-interest bonds.

6.3 THE DEMAND FOR BONDS

Bonds are held both for the future stream of income which accrues to their holders and because speculating correctly on interest rate movements will yield capital gains.

The major holders of fixed-interest securities are pension funds, and life insurance companies. As we shall see in 6.4, deals in fixed-interest securities are normally very large, much larger than in equities for example. On the demand side, therefore, trading is dominated by large units trading in large quantities. Such institutions have comparatively long-term liabilities and the maturing of those liabilities in any particular year can be predicted by actuarial means with some degree of confidence. Since bonds held to maturity provide a guaranteed return they provide a core of guaranteed income which reduces the risk in setting the premiums and benefit rates while still leaving the companies free to invest aggressively in other assets to achieve high 'bonus' rates.

Unit and investment trusts are also significant holders of fixed-interest securities, some unit trusts with an emphasis upon generating income rather than capital gain devoting a high proportion of their portfolios to bonds. More usually, however, the bonds are held as a potential source of capital gain and therefore the proportion of the portfolio devoted to fixed-interest assets varies as the managers speculate on future interest rate movements.

Banks and building societies also hold significant quantities of gilts, but because they hold them as liquid assets they prefer

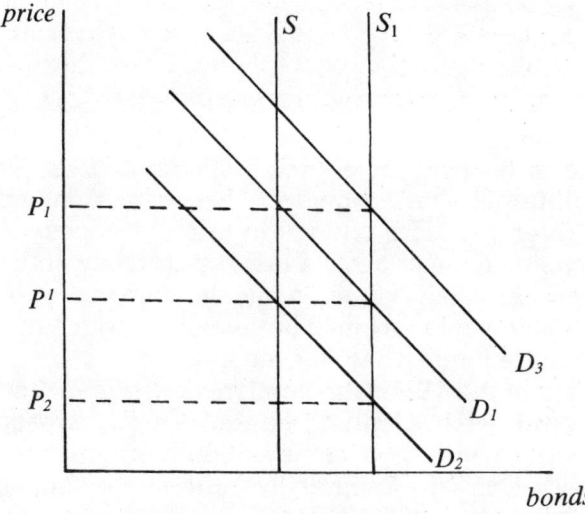

Figure 6.2

short-dated stock where the interest-risk is minimised. In fact, as bond prices have become more volatile over the last twenty years, banks and building societies have reduced the importance of gilts in their portfolios as well as shortening the maturity of their holdings.

6.3.1 The level of interest rates

Other things being equal, one would expect the demand for newly issued bonds to be positively related to their yield, or, which amounts to the same thing, inversely related to their price. Figure 6.2 shows a demand curve for bonds downward sloping and a supply curve drawn vertically. This is something of a simplification but only a small one.

At price P1, and its corresponding yield, the existing supply of bonds, S, is what investors are just willing to hold.

Assuming 'other things equal', however, is more than usually misleading here. We know that the return on fixed-interest stock not held to redemption consists of its current yield plus the capital gain or loss at the time of sale. This latter will be determined by interest rate movements *after* the date of purchase. What this means is that the demand for bonds is sensitive not just to current interest rates but also to expected *future* rates.

CASE STUDY 6.1: BOND PRICES IN 1987

The price of bonds is determined, *ceteris paribus*, by the level of interest rates. However, because a change in interest rates causes a change in price, it is possible to make a capital gain, or avoid a loss, by correctly anticipating interest changes. Consequently, the demand for bonds shifts in response to any incident which might itself foreshadow future interest rate movements.

For much of the 1980s the bond market was very sensitive to monthly bank lending figures. This was because governments had stated money supply targets and because, as we saw in Chapter five, the money supply *ex post*, incorporates *ex ante* lending plans. An 'excessive' growth in lending led to expectations of higher interest rates, intended by the authorities (again as in Chapter five) to restrict the flow of new lending.

In 1987 this sensitivity of bond prices to bank lending figures was still apparent. When June's large bank lending figures were published, for example, bond and share prices fell sharply. However, since the Chancellor's Mansion House speech in October 1986 reaffirming the importance of the exchange rate in the interpretation of monetary conditions, movements in the sterling exchange rate index have also provoked bond price movements. In the case studies in Chapter five we saw the Bank firstly resisting and then accepting the need for an interest rate reduction because sterling was at the top of its unpublished band. Bond prices had been rising in the weeks preceding the cut, in anticipation, and fell slightly when the cut was announced as bond holders took their capital gains.

Shortly afterwards, bond prices received another boost, when the Chancellor in his budget speech announced the possibility of a PSBR for 1987/88 of less than £4 billion., i.e. of less than 1 per cent of GDP. As we saw in this chapter, that implied a fall in the future ratio of government debt to GDP and acted once again as a pointer in the direction of future interest rate cuts.

After the setback of the large Bank lending figures of June, some poor trade figures in July and an *actual* rise in interest rates in August, bond prices received a very sharp boost in October, following the stock market crashes of the third week. This reflected partly a defensive inflow of funds from the equity market as the equity market suddenly looked very risky but it also reflected a belief, which turned out to be justified, that the authorities would have to lower interest rates in order both to support the dollar and also to indicate willingness to provide liquidity to financial institutions which might be in some difficulty after the crash.

Look again at figure 6.2. If the government wishes to sell more bonds, the existing demand curve tells us that the equilibrium price must fall, say to P1' (the yield of course rising). This is the first and the simple case.

However, there is a second possibility. Suppose that buyers, seeing the fall in price/rise in yield took the view that this was the beginning of a longer-term price fall. Thinking now of the prospect of *future* capital loss, the *existing* rise in yields is no longer sufficient to induce them to buy the additional stock. Demand has fallen and in the figure 6.2 the demand curve moves from D1 to D2. To achieve a new equilibrium, at P2, a much larger fall in price/rise in yields is necessary than might have been thought.

The opposite is a third possibility. Suppose that investors have a view that there is a 'normal' level of yield on fixed-interest bonds. In this case the increase in supply will push down prices, raising yields, as we move down the demand curve D1 as we did in the normal case. However, seeing this fall in price, 'norm' believers must expect a future rise as yields return to their previous level. They will anticipate a capital gain and be more willing to buy stock. The demand curve moves out to D3 and the yield and price will return to their original level.

In the 1950s and 1960s the authorities, on the basis of little firm evidence, believed that the demand for fixed-interest stock was dominated by the second category of investor. Such investors were said to hold 'extrapolative' expectations of prices and to be 'risk averse'. This view of the market had profound implications for the way in which the authorities acted. Briefly, it meant that they were committed to preventing large movements in bond prices. This in turn meant having to counteract spontaneous price trends by buying stock on a falling market and selling on a rising one, a practice referred to as 'leaning into the wind'. Most importantly, it meant that debt sales/purchases could not be used to fund the PSBR in a non-residual manner. Given that debt sales were aimed at smoothing interest rates, the money supply grew at (approximately) the rate dictated by the unfunded PSBR. This was a clear illustration of the textbook maxim that the authorities cannot control interest rates and the money supply at the same time.

Figure 6.2 shows increases in the stock of bonds occurring

over time as new stock is issued. Once we introduce time in order to shift the supply curve, however, we must accept that the demand curve is likely to shift also. After all, income and saving will both increase and therefore, with interest rates given, the demand for new debt will increase. In fig. 6.2 the demand curve shifts outward.

Remembering that *ceteris* are not always *paribus*, i.e. that the demand curve shifts outward over time, is not always easy. In the early 1980s, the Treasury repeatedly expressed the worry that annual debt sales, by steadily increasing the stock of debt, would require a steady rise in interest rates. However, with income increasing, the total stock of debt can expand while becoming either smaller or larger or staying unchanged *in proportion to income*. What happens in practice obviously depends upon the relative size of key magnitudes. In a steady state:

$$D/GDP = 1/g \times PSBR/GDP$$

where D is the existing stock of outstanding debt, GDP is national income at current prices and g is the rate of growth of nominal GDP. Using 1987 figures we have:

$$D/GDP = 0.40$$
$$1/g = 12.5$$
$$PSBR/GDP = 0.0025$$

But $12.5 \times 0.0025 = c.0.032$ which is a lot less than the 0.40 current ratio of debt to GDP. The obvious conclusion is that the current level of PSBR, given the rate at which nominal GDP is expanding, is insufficient to maintain the existing debt/income ratio. In the immediate future the stock of debt in relation to income will fall. Thus, even though the stock of debt is growing, *ceteris paribus*, we should expect bond interest rates if anything to fall.

6.3.2 The structure of interest rates

The effect of bond sales on the *level* of interest rates is one issue; the effect upon the *structure* of rates is another. It is normally assumed in the discussion of any market that the good being traded is *homogeneous*. This is plainly not true of bonds. The redemption yield on low-coupon stocks consists largely of capital appreciation. There may be tax advantages in this for some people. For others, high-coupon stocks may be preferable. Some bonds have a long-period to maturity, others a short-period. If they are not strictly homogeneous, then increasing the supply of any one particular type must be presumed to change its price/yield relative to other types. Our interest here lies with the issue of bonds of particular maturities. If borrowers choose to issue bonds mainly in one maturity category, what effect does this have upon interest rates?

It is normally assumed that lenders, *ceteris paribus*, prefer to lend short and that, therefore, a 'liquidity premium' will have to be paid to persuade them to lend long. We should then expect medium-dated bonds to have a yield below that on long-dated bonds but above that on short-dated ones. The dotted line in figure 6.3 is a *time-yield curve* and shows the pattern of yield with respect to time that we might expect. Suppose now that more medium term bonds are issued. This will tend to lower the price and raise the yield on medium-dated bonds both absolutely and in relation to the yields on short and long-term bonds. However, this relative rise should attract more lenders from the long and the short ends. This would tend to offset the rise in medium yields and to raise rates at the outer ends of the spectrum. The end result should be a restoration of the original relativities but at a higher absolute level of interest rates. The whole curve may move up, but we would not expect a change in its shape.

Experience tells us, however, that this does not happen. The solid line in figure 6.3 shows the yield curve on government bonds in August 1987. The 'hump' at 7–9 years lies in the maturity range in which the authorities have sold the greater volume of new issues in recent years.

This invites the explanation that the increased supply of medium-dated stock has depressed prices and raised yields and this in turn suggests a degree of market segmentation. What this means is that lenders generally have a very strong preference for debt of a particular maturity. Indeed, they may know little about the existence and characteristics of the alternatives. Therefore, only a few lenders are likely to be attracted from their preferred maturities and then only if yields

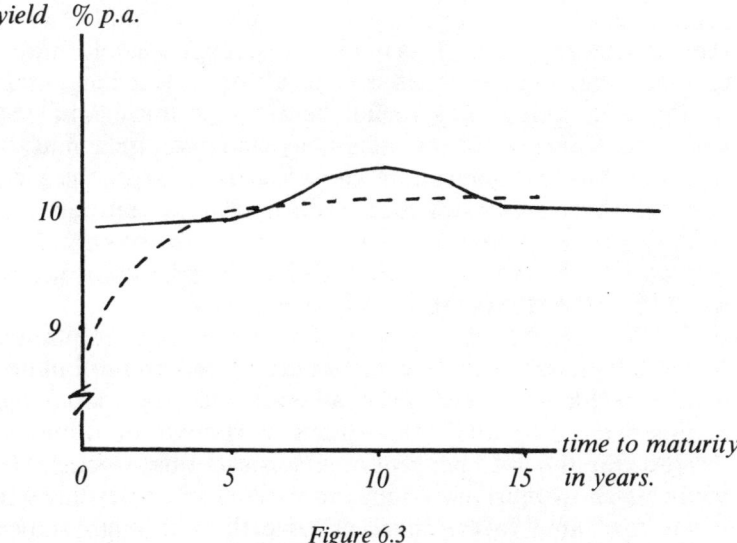

Figure 6.3

rise significantly. This explanation is reinforced by what we know of the holders of bonds. Life assurance and pension funds hold long-dated stock, closely matched to their long-term liabilities; banks and building societies prefer the liquidity of short-dated stock.

Market segmentation is just one reason why the yield curve may depart from the 'normal' shape shown by the dotted line in figure 6.3. Expectations of future interest rate movements will also affect the shape of the curve. Imagine that we begin with a normal pattern of yields. People will be holding bonds which give them a desired combination of return and maturity. Suppose now that we introduce the expectation that interest rates in future will fall. In these circumstances all bondholders will be expecting that when their holdings mature in future, they will be able to replace them only with lower-yielding bonds. There is thus some advantage to be gained by holding current bonds with a long-maturity since this enables today's interest rates to be enjoyed or 'locked-in' for a longer period. In choosing their preferred combination of yield and maturity people will feel that the normal disadvantage of long maturity has marginally declined. There will be a general shift in preference towards longer-dated bonds as people shuffle along the maturity spectrum. This redistribution of demand towards the long end causes prices to rise above what they would normally be, and yields to fall below their normal relative level. The tendency is to 'flatten' the yield curve. Indeed, if the expected fall in interest rates is sufficiently large, the yield curve can even slope downward over part of its length.

6.4 THE TRADING OF BONDS

In the UK, fixed interest securities are traded on the London Stock Exchange. Table 6.3 is a report of Stock Exchange business for July 1987 and shows a number of things of interest. Firstly, at 55 per cent of all transactions, measured by value, it shows just how important fixed-interest trading is when compared to the more newsworthy deals in equities. Secondly, by showing that such trading accounts for only 5.2 per cent of the number of deals it indicates that those deals are typically very large. Their average value in July 1987 was £996,000.

We already know that the principal holders of bonds are financial institutions and that the dominant supplier of new bonds is the government. The flow of buying and selling orders is received by 'market-makers'.

Table 6.3: Selected Stock Exchange Transactions, July 1987

	Total	British government securities	Fixed interest, preferred shares	Ordinary shares
Number (000s)	1,792	94	39	1,649
Percentage of total		5.2	2.1	92.0
Value (£m)	170,359	93,583	2,357	69,394
Percentage of total		55	1.3	41
Ave. bargain, size (£000s)		996	60	42

Source: Adapted from CSO, *Financial Statistics*, Oct. 1987, table 12.3.

Prior to the October 1986 changes to the London Stock Exchange, the market for gilts was made by just three specialist jobbers. After 'Big Bang' the market-making function was expanded to twenty-seven firms who were mainly specialist divisions of large (sometimes multinational) financial corporations. A market in corporate bonds is maintained by branches of those firms who also make markets in equities and we shall discuss their activities in more detail in the next chapter. The gilts market-makers also deal in other securities, commonly in Eurobonds for example, but their gilts business distinguishes them from other market-makers because it requires them to be 'recognised' by the Bank of England in order to deal with the Bank as the issuer of government bonds. Furthermore, the Bank's recognition requires certain standards of capital holdings and also that recognised firms 'undertake to make continuous two-way prices in the stocks they hold'. They must, in other words, always be willing to deal with buyers and sellers. The expansion of market-making to originally twenty-seven firms caused doubts to be expressed that enough profitable business would be available. Commissions on gilts' deals have always been lower than on equities, reflecting the economies to be had from the large average size of each deal. Since 'Big Bang', however, gilts' commissions have been virtually eliminated and market-makers rely for their profit on the 'spread' of bid/offer prices. This, and the withdrawal of Lloyds Bank from gilts market-making in June 1987 and Orion Bank in October (reducing the number to twenty-five), because they could not earn an adequate return on the capital employed, may partially confirm those doubts.

In these institutional arrangements there is clearly yet another departure from the popular conception of how markets work. The institutional arrangements for the setting of prices and for the exchanging of bonds is subject to considerable regulation. Even so, as we shall see in the next chapter the regulation has not always been sufficient to guarantee that prices respond spontaneously to offers to buy and sell.

Not only do the authorities have a regulatory role: they dominate the supply side of the market. The behaviour of prices and yields, therefore, depend both upon the authorities' objectives and upon their expectation of how the market will react. In the 1950s and 60s, for example, we saw that the authorities' view of the demand for bonds led to a policy of stabilising interest rates and relinquishing control of the money supply. In the 1970s, as commitment to monetary control and eventually to monetary targets increased, the stabilisation of interest rates was no longer possible. It became essential for governments to fund the PSBR by non-monetary means and this meant selling whatever quantity of gilts was required by the size of the deficit. This has had a number of consequences for the marketing of government bonds.

Firstly, in the 1960s and 1970s, it gave rise to the 'Duke of York' strategy in which, prior to an issue of government bonds, the authorities would announce an increase in minimum lending rate (MLR). This would depress the price of existing stock but it would lead potential buyers to expect a future fall in interest rates and therefore a capital gain. Once the stock had been sold, interest rates would be 'marched down' again and buyers took their profits. Obviously, this sort of market manipulation changes the nature of gilt edged investment. As price movements become more frequent and dramatic the risks and rewards increase. This accounts for the practice we noted in 6.3 of banks and building societies concentrating their giltholdings at the less volatile short end of the market.

Secondly, it has led the authorities consciously to exploit the capital gains attraction of gilts. Since 1980 it has been the practice to issue short-dated, low-coupon stock. Being low-coupon, of course, the stock can only be sold by offering it at a substantial discount to its redemption value, guaranteeing a short-term capital gain. The need to compete with official bond sales has produced similar developments in the corporate bond market where 'deep discount' bonds are now common.

Thirdly, it has led the authorities to develop new ways of issuing stock. Until 1979 the practice had been to announce the issue of a new stock at a fixed price and in a fixed amount. As much stock would then be sold as the market wished to take, the balance being taken up by the issue department of the Bank of England. The balance would then become a 'tap' issue, being offered for sale at intervals as market conditions seemed appropriate. For monetary control purposes this had the disadvantage that the funding of the PSBR was wholly at the mercy of market conditions. If an issue was wrongly priced or wrongly timed, the Bank would have to take up the unsold stock and the government would have to resort to residual financing.

An obvious alternative would be a tender or auction system of issue. Under such a system the authorities would be sure of selling all the stock they wished and so the PSBR would always be funded. The mechanism which ensured this, of course, would be the price. As a tentative step in this direction since 1979 it has become common to issue stock via a 'partial tender' mechanism. This enables buyers to bid for an issue but subject to a minimum price. The bids are ranked in descending order of price and that number of bids is accepted which just clears the issue. All bidders then pay the price of the lowest acceptable bid, the 'striking price'. If it is found that there are insufficient bids to clear the issue, the balance is taken up by the Bank and becomes, in effect, a traditional tap issue.

Although clearly a step towards letting the market determine bond yields and prices, the partial-tender system betrays a reluctance to go the whole way. The setting of a minimum price shows that the authorities are still worried about the consequences of selling debt on a falling market, driving yields to very high levels and causing large capital losses for investors. The fear is that unrestricted tenders might simply lead to a trade-off between the short and the long-run maximisation of debt sales. Allowing completely free price adjustment might guarantee clearing the market of each new issue, but the consequent volatility might drive some investors out of the market altogether leading in the long run to a contraction of the market for fixed-interest stock. Since 1987 the Bank has experimented with auctions of gilts. Under this arrangement, buyers pay what they bid (not a 'striking' price). Even so a great deal of caution is evident. Auctions take place for only a very small proportion of total new issues, concentrated at the short end of the maturity spectrum where, as we saw, the nearness of redemption has a stabilising effect on prices. In addition, buyers are further reassured by undertakings not to issue further stock of a similar kind for specified periods. In this, as in other markets, the intervention of the authorities is very clear.

NOTES

1. This and the preceding formulae assume that interest on the bond is paid annually. For bonds on which interest is paid at six-monthly intervals the value is found by

$$P = \sum_{t=1}^{2n} \frac{C}{2} \cdot \frac{1}{(1+r/2)^t} + M \cdot \frac{1}{(1+r/2)^{2n}}$$

7 Equities

In this chapter we examine the market for ordinary shares or equities. Firms issue ordinary shares in order to raise long-term capital rather than short-term 'money'. In this respect equities have some similarity with bonds. In the UK bonds and equities are both traded on the London Stock Exchange. But the differences are more important than the similarities. Firstly, as financial instruments, equities and bonds have quite different characteristics; secondly, because of these differences traders tend to specialise in either the bond market or the equity market; thirdly, because the government does not issue equities to finance its own expenditure, the authorities do not dominate the market in the way that they do the market for bonds.

7.1 CHARACTERISTICS

'Equities', we have just said, is an alternative name for ordinary shares. These shares are 'ordinary' in the sense that they carry no preferential rights. The owners of equities have a claim on the profits of the firm, on its assets in the event of liquidation, and they have a right to vote on specified issues concerning the operation of the company. Their claims and votes are in proportion to the proportion of a firm's ordinary share capital which they own. However, the holders of preference shares and debentures have prior claims on both profits and assets. That is to say that they are entitled to a guaranteed income payment from each year's profits and if a company is wound up they must, where possible, be repaid the value of their original investment before any claim can be made by ordinary shareholders.

Clearly, by comparison, ordinary shareholders are exposed to much greater risk. If the firm does badly, there may be little profit left for distribution after preferential claims have been met. On the other hand, if the firm does well the preferential claimants will still get only their guaranteed return and a substantial surplus will remain for distribution to ordinary shareholders. The difficulties involved in predicting this strictly uncertain flow of future income is one important reason for fluctuations in the market price of shares.

Buying a claim to a future income stream is, however, only one reason for holding shares. Remember that ownership of a share, unlike the ownership of a bond, entails part ownership of the firm itself, that is of the assets which comprise the firm. With time, we should expect a firm to add to its assets by a programme of capital investment. In consequence the income stream generated by those assets will grow and they will themselves become more valuable. Since each share denotes a part-claim on those assets, each share should also increase in value. Thus the reward to shareholders over any but the shortest period should consist of two elements, a rising stream of income payments plus capital appreciation. The fact that both elements are present crucially affects the way in which share performance is reported and analysed.

Imagine a firm whose issued capital consists entirely of 10 million ordinary shares. Suppose that its post-tax profits in the last financial year amounted to £1 million, and that its directors decided to distribute half of that profit to shareholders and to retain or 'plough-back' the remaining 50 per cent into further capital investment in the firm. Lastly, let us imagine that the current market price of the shares is £3. We now have the following information about the firm, expressed in the language of the equities market:

Shares in issue	= 10m	Dividend	= 5p
Share price	= £3	Dividend yield	= 1.667%
Market capitalisation	= £30m	Earnings yield	= 3.33%
Earnings	= £1m	Price/earnings or	
Distributed profit	= £500,000	PE ratio	= 30

The number of shares in issue and their market price need no explanation. The market capitalisation is found by multiplying the shares in issue by their market price and could be said to express the value that the market places upon the company. In recent years it has become common for some newspapers to report sharp rises or falls in the general price of equities in terms of a change in the total market valuation of firms whose shares are quoted. Clearly, the numbers are always likely to be large but they do not mean very much unless we know the total valuation of all quoted firms at the outset. Most people do not and therefore headlines like '£20bn. wiped off share prices!' are worthless.

Earnings are profits. They may be quoted pre-tax or, as here, post-tax. Frequently the figure for post-tax earnings has to be an estimate since analysts will not know enough about the firm to know exactly what its tax position is. The rate of corporation tax will be known but the firm may have various allowance or offsets available which mean that the rate is applied to less than the whole of pre-tax profits.

Profits can be used in a number of ways. We have assumed here that the firm is pursuing a policy of retaining half its earnings for future investment. Its immediate effect is to reduce profits for distribution to shareholders to £500,000. When this figure is divided by the number of shares in issue, we can see that the dividend per share will be 5p.

The ability to make comparisons between financial assets is of paramount importance. We know that the cost of buying the entitlement to 5p per share is £3 but to make comparisons we need to turn this into some widely comparable unit and the simplest way of doing this is to think of the 5p as a percentage rate of return on an outlay of £3. The resulting quotient is known as the *dividend yield* and in this case is 1.667 per cent. Notice that for a given dividend a rise in the market price of a share will lower the dividend yield and a fall in the price will cause a rise in the yield. Notice too that we cannot judge a share to be cheap or expensive by simply look at its price. A 25p share may be dear if its dividend is so small that the resulting yield is also very small in relation to yields on other shares; a share at £10 may be cheap if its dividend is very large.

Return now to the earnings which were not distributed.

These are to be used to finance further expansion. If they are wisely used, the firm will expand. The value of its capital assets will grow and the future income stream should also increase. Plainly the retained earnings are far from being lost to shareholders but are being put to use on their behalf for future benefits. This point was recognised years ago by labour representatives who objected to prices and incomes policies on the grounds that 'dividend restraint' did not involve the same sacrifice as 'wage restraint'. Withholding dividends simply meant that the firm grew faster and shareholders still got their rewards but in the form of capital appreciation. If retained earnings were always ignored, treated in effect purely as a loss of dividend income, then a firm adopting a policy of ploughing back most of its profits and expanding rapidly would be valued much more lowly than a firm distributing everything and thinking nothing about the future. One way of overcoming this problem is to devise a measure which is based upon earnings as a whole, treating retained earnings as just as important to shareholders (albeit in future) as dividends paid out now. Doing that in this case involves dividing £1m by 10m to give 10p per share and dividing by the share price to give an earnings yield of 3.33 per cent.

Although it conveys exactly the same information as the earnings yield, the price/earnings ratio is often preferred for its ease of expression avoiding percentages. It is calculated as the reciprocal of the earnings yield, in this case, 1/0.033, its value is almost exactly 30.

Notice the use to which earnings yield and P/E ratios can be put for comparative purposes. If a firm has a very high P/E ratio this means that the market values it highly for some reason other than current earnings. It is valued highly because of what its future earnings are expected to be. Naturally, the scope for increase in future earnings varies between sectors of the economy. Food retailing, for example, we should expect to grow more slowly than leisure facilities. Thus it is normal to compare firms' P/E ratios only within a particular sector. Typically, analysts will recommend a share as 'cheap' if its P/E ratio is low by comparison with the sector average and if they can see no reason why its earnings should grow less rapidly than its rivals.

7.2 THE SUPPLY OF EQUITIES

As markets are normally presented, the 'supply' of a good or service refers to a *flow* of something newly created over a period of time. This view of supply is not easily applied to the market for equities. Most of the time what is being bought and sold is part of an *existing stock* of shares. The first point to recognise, therefore, is that if we try to analyse the behaviour of the equity market in terms of a supply of shares and a demand for them we have firstly to distinguish between a *stock* of existing shares and a *flow* of newly-issued ones. The stock of existing shares is the total of all those shares issued by companies in the past while the flow is whatever new issues of shares firms may currently be making in order to raise new capital. Inevitably the stock is vastly greater than the flow and therefore when people buy and sell shares they are usually trading in the existing stock and it is trading in the existing

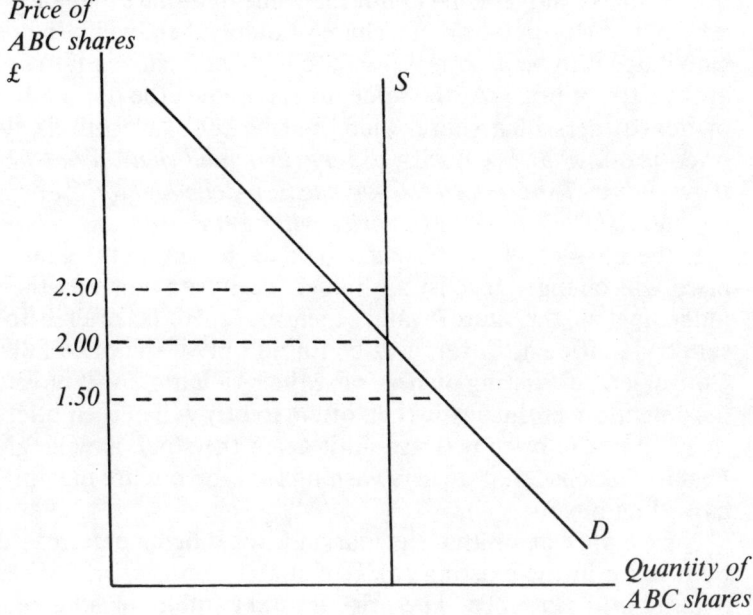

Figure 7.1

stock which consequently determines prices and yields. As we shall see in 7.4.1, this has important consequences for the firms wishing to raise new capital by the issue of shares. If we assume for the moment, however, that no issues are currently taking place then the 'supply' of shares is limited to the current stock. This is shown in figure 7.1 where S is the quantity of shares in ABC plc currently in existence.

Clearly, the existing stock of shares must all be held by someone. If the price of ABC shares is stable we must assume that the shares are willingly held, i.e. that their holders do not wish to sell them. Equally, it must be the case that potential buyers of the shares do not wish to buy them at the going price.

However, this gives the impression that when a share's price is stable there is no trading taking place in that share. Keen students of the *Financial Times* will know though that some of a firm's shares will change hands every day even when the price is stable. This is because, for reasons we shall see later, people have to make judgements about the value of a share and at any time out of a population of a share's holders there will be some who judge it to be in some sense 'too high' and *will* want to sell at the current price. At the same time, amongst the population of non-owners of a share, there will be those who think its price 'too low' and will wish to buy. *Provided that on balance the number of shares offered for sale is matched by the number people wish to buy, then the price will be stable.*

If the balance of judgements changes, however, the share's price will change. If existing holders revise downwards their judgement of the share's value, then more will be offered for sale and sufficient buyers will be found only if the price falls. Conversely, if existing owners raise their valuation or if buyers become more enthusiastic then offers to buy will exceed offers to sell and the price will rise until again the stock is willingly held in the sense that owners wishing to trade out are matched by willing buyers.

Notice once again that the market price is being determined by trading in the existing *stock* of shares. No new shares are coming into existence. The price is either stable, or adjusting until the existing stock is willingly held in the sense we have described.

We have now discovered a second contrast with markets as normally conceived. Normally a shift in demand would cause *both* a change in price *and* a *change in the quantity supplied*. As we have just described the behaviour of supply, there is no quantity change. Adjustments in equity markets involve only demand and price. Thus most of the interesting things to say about equity market behaviour stem from the analysis of demand. These interesting points we shall take up in 7.4.2.

7.3 THE DEMAND FOR EQUITIES

As we saw in the last section, when a share's price is stable the stock of shares to which it belongs is willingly held. There may be people at the margin willing to sell their holdings of the stock but these are just matched by people wishing to buy. In the aggregate, there is agreement that the current market price represents the correct value for the share. But what does this mean? What leads the market to agree that one particular price is appropriate?

In theory, the price of a share, like that of a bond, is determined by the value that the market places upon a future stream of income. But this in turn begs the question of how that value is arrived at.

Firstly, and again like bonds, there is the size of the income payments. Unlike bonds, however, the income payments will vary depending upon the success of the firm and its dividend policy. Thus the income payments, though they may be expected to rise in the long-term, are strictly uncertain.

Secondly, again like bonds, the value of the future payments has to be discounted because they lie in the future. If we had the payments now we could reinvest them at any one of various rates of interest. The rate at which we choose to discount the future earnings will also therefore have an effect on the present value of shares.

Mathematically, we can express the present value of a share as follows:

$$P = \frac{D1}{1+k} + \frac{D2}{(1+k)^2} + \frac{D3}{(1+k)^3} + \ldots + \frac{Dn}{(1+k)^n}$$

where D1 ... Dn are the dividend payments in each year and k is the chosen rate at which the future payments are discounted and P is the present value of the *expected* future income stream. If we rewrite this as:

$$P = \sum_{t=1}^{n} D \cdot \frac{1}{(1+k)^t}$$

then the expression is clearly identical to the one that we had for the valuation of an irredeemable bond except that D, the dividend, replaces C the coupon.

However, as we said above, unlike a coupon payment each dividend payment is uncertain though in the long-run it may be expected to grow. We cannot, therefore, act as though D were fixed. In the first of the two expressions above we could imagine the series D1 ... Dn to be a series of variable dividends. The critical question of course is how do we estimate their individual likely values? Undoubtedly the simplest solution would be to assume a steady rate of increase of dividends. Doing this the value becomes:

$$P = \frac{D1}{(1+k)} + \frac{D1(1+g)}{(1+k)^2} + \frac{D1(1+g)k^2}{(1+k)^3} + \ldots + \frac{D1(1+g)^{n-1}}{(1+r)^n}$$

Simplfying, this gives

$$P = \frac{D1(1+g)}{k-g}$$

or,

$$P = \frac{D2}{k-g}$$

Assuming dividends to grow at a constant rate is plainly a simplification but the expression is useful in that it draws our attention immediately to the variables which will determine the market's valuation of a share.

First of all there is the term g. Failing any better information this might be taken to approximate the long-run rate of growth of nominal national income but we might set it slightly higher or slightly lower depending upon the view that we take of the likely future performance of the sector to which this firm belongs and of the firm itself.

The rate at which we discount future earnings, k, is also subject to change. k is composed of two elements. Firstly it contains the going risk-free rate of return. This indicates that we require a rate of return at least in excess of that currently available on risk-free assets such as long-dated government bonds. Equities are far from risk-free, however, and so k contains a second element, namely a premium for the risk believed to be associated with that share. Thus now we can see that k will rise or fall with variations in interest rates and also with changes in the perceived risk attached to the share.

Given the expression above, a risk in k will lead to a bigger discounting of future earnings and therefore to a lower value for the share. A fall in k will lead to a rise in the share's value.

If we agree for the moment that people calculate the present value of a share in the manner that we have just indicated, what does that enable us to say about the demand for a share with respect to its price? What can we say about the demand curve for a particular share? Remember that the calculation requires a large amount of judgement: about the future growth of dividends, about the appropriate risk premium and about future interest rates. It is most unlikely that everyone will make exactly the same judgements. Thus at any time, in the population of potential holders of a given share there will be those who think its current price just right, some who think it too low and some who think it too high. If we vary the price, we shall vary the proportion of potential holders of the share who will fall into these categories. As the price rises, there will be a steady decrease in the number who think it undervalued. If we lower the price there will be an increase in the number who think it undervalued. If we now add the rather obvious point that a person will buy the share only if she thinks its present value exceeds or is just equal to its market price, then we can see that the number of buyers will vary inversely with the actual price.

In figure 7.1, the demand curve for ABC plc shares is drawn downward sloping. Figure 7.1 also shows that the equilibrium price is £2. We are now in a position to understand what that equilibrium means. The existing stock of ABC shares is shown (as before) by the curve S. For an equilibrium price, the stock must be willingly held in the sense we explained above. There are some people for whom £2 exceeds their estimate of the share's present value but equally there are some people for whom £2 seems an underestimate. The offers for sale are just matched by offers to purchase at the current price.

Imagine, by contrast, that the price were £2.50. At that price, the number of people who feel the share to be overvalued will increase and the number feeling it to be undervalued will fall. Offers to sell will exceed offers to buy. The opposite imbalance would occur if the price were lower at, say, £1.50. Only at £2.00 will the entire stock be willingly held by someone.

In the UK, shares are held overwhelmingly by what are called 'the institutions'. These are life assurance companies, pension funds, unit and investment trusts. Since the end of the First World War until the early 1980s, the personal sector either was neutral or a net seller of equities. With a steady flow of new issues year by year this meant, of course, a steady decline in the proportion of equities held by the personal sector. Since 1982, the *number* of private shareholders has risen, from 4m to 9m by 1987, partly in response to government inducements to buy ex-public sector firms and also by a prolonged stock market boom. However, their holdings of shares are very small, making no significant difference to the proportion of total equities held by the personal sector.

The important point to remember, therefore, is that when we talk about willing holders of the existing stock of equities, or about traders of marginal quantities of the existing stock, we are talking about decisions being made by large institutions. Indeed, when we talk about movements in the prices of *individual* shares (though not when we refer to a *general* movement in share prices) we are probably talking about the decisions of a very few large institutions.

In markets as conventionally analysed, the supply and

demand curves represent the preferences of a very large number of individual decision makers. A change in the preferences of any one buyer and seller cannot affect the market, only the combined preferences matter. Plainly this is not true for the equities market where one or two decisions to buy and sell can have a significant effect upon price.

7.4 THE BEHAVIOUR OF SHARE PRICES

Share prices fluctuate for the same reason that the prices of other assets fluctuate: in response to shifts in supply and demand. In the case of shares, however, because we are dealing with a stock that changes only slowly over time, fluctuations in price occur mainly because of shifts in demand. These in turn result from changes in people's valuation of an expected future stream of income from the share. We want now to look in more detail at the sorts of circumstances that give rise to these shifts.

7.4.1 Changes in supply

In section 7.2 we said that the market price of a share resulted from trading in the existing *stock* of that share because the stock was assumed to be fixed. This is indeed generally the case. However, there are some occasions when the stock of shares expands and we shall see that there are in fact a number of possible consequences of this expansion, mainly because changes in supply may themselves cause changes in demand. The market price of the share may fall, which is what we might expect, or it may not. Whatever happens to the price, however, the new price will always be closely related to that established by trading in the existing stock.

Imagine that ABC plc decides to expand by issuing new share capital. The stock of ABC shares is about to expand. In figure 7.1 the curve S is going to shift to the right.

If ABC is to find ready buyers for its new shares it knows it has to sell them at a price approximating the market's valuation. In fact, new issues will normally be made at a discount to the price of existing shares and the market price subsequently established for the whole of the issues will lie between the original and the new issue price. The reason for the discount are twofold. Firstly, it is assumed that the demand curve for ABC shares is negatively sloped. Thus if an enlarged stock is to be willingly held, it will only be at a lower price. Part of the discount therefore is an attempt to estimate the elasticity of the demand curve. Secondly, firms and their advisors find it embarrassing if new issues are not bought by the public and they fear that it might be difficult to raise new capital in future if they gain a reputation for new issue 'flops'. The tendency is to err on the side of caution by pricing the new issue even below that required by their estimate of the demand elasticity.

The effect of a new issue of shares is normally to depress the price of the share concerned. However, since one share is in some degree a substitute for another it follows that a sufficiently large flow of new issues could cause a fall in share prices generally. For this reason the Bank of England operates a queueing system for large new issues such as those involved in the government's privatisation programme in the 1980s. This does not of course guarantee that any individual issue will be a success. In October 1987, for example, the government's sale of its remaining shares in BP, together with some additional shares newly issued by BP, coincided with a crash in stockmarket prices. Very few shares were sold and the government had to launch an unprecedented operation to support the shares' underwriters by guaranteeing to repurchase the shares if their price fell below a given level. When its turn comes round, a new issue must take its chance but the queueing systems helps to prevent general fluctuations in market prices resulting solely from sharp increases in the supply of shares.

A small fall in a share's price may be thought of as the normal case with new issues. However, it occasionally happens that an increase in the stock of shares has no effect upon price or may even be associated with a rise. Because this is unusual firms will not rely upon it and will still price the new issue at a discount. In these circumstances, purchasers of the newly issued shares will make a profit equal to the difference between the market and the issue price. Such a situation comes about when the purpose of the new issue seems likely to increase future profits by more than is necessary to maintain the existing yield on the enlarged share capital.

In the case we have just looked at, the rightward shift of the supply curve has been accompanied by a rightward shift of the demand curve. It is also possible for shifts in demand to cause changes in supply. Imagine that over time, ABC shares become very popular. The demand curve is in effect moving to the right, their price is rising and the yield falling. The high price of ABC shares cheapens the cost of raising new capital by issuing new shares. ABC needs to issue fewer shares now in order to raise a given amount of capital than it did when their price was low. The fewer shares it issues, the smaller will be the dividend claims on future profits.

We have now arrived at the important point we anticipated in 7.2. Trading in the existing stock of shares establishes a level of prices and yields. In effect, therefore, trading in the existing stock is determining the cost of raising *new* capital through the equity market. When demand for shares increases, their rising prices and falling yields cheapens the cost of raising new capital. Falling share prices and rising yields mean the cost of capital is rising. Assume now that the yield on *real* capital, that is on plant, machinery and so on, is given and exceeds the current yield on equities. One would expect profit maximising firms to issue more equity in order to purchase more real capital equipment. In figure 7.1, the supply curve would shift to the right as the stock of equities expanded, prices would fall and yields would rise until raising finance in this way matched the return on real capital that firms could expect. In other words, one would expect equity prices and yields to match the return on real capital.

In the next section, and in case study 7.1, however, we shall see that the demand for equities behaves so erratically that prices and yields can be pushed a long way from the return on real capital and for long periods. In a 'bear' market, for example, yields may be pushed way above the prospective return on real capital making it impossible for firms to raise capital for real investment. This is one of several channels through which the behaviour of financial markets can have a serious impact upon the real economy.

7.4.2 Changes in demand

In section 7.3 we observed that the demand for a share depended in theory upon the value people placed upon the expected future income stream associated with it. In this section we want to examine the circumstances which might lead to changes in that valuation and therefore in the demand for and market price of the share. Some of these circumstances will affect the price of *individual* shares, others will cause shifts in the demand for shares *in general*.

Remember our expression for the present value of a future stream of dividends contained two terms, g and k, denoting respectively the rate of growth of those dividends and the rate at which we discounted them and remember also that they both require information which cannot be known with certainty.

About g we said that the simplest assumption we could make would be that it were a constant and that in practice we might take this to approximate the long-run rate of growth of nominal income. For a large and diversified portfolio of shares this is a reasonable assumption. However, for an individual share it is most unlikely in anything other than the very long run. The behaviour of dividends in the immediate future will in part be determined by the general state of the economy but it will also be influenced by the decisions and characteristics of the firm itself. It might be in a sector of the economy with high or low growth prospects. The firm might be diversifying from a slow growth into a high growth market. It may be a retail store whose pioneering of out of town shopping centres is about to pay off. It might be a drug company about to obtain a licence to manufacture for sale an AIDS-related treatment. All of these, and many more circumstances, will have a significant impact on the behaviour of future dividends.

Such things affect the projected earnings of individual firms and therefore the value of their corresponding shares. Many events, however, can affect the projected earnings of equities in general and if this changes the attractiveness of equities *relative* to other financial assets for which they are close substitutes then share prices as a whole will change. One obvious source of such circumstances is government policy. If it is expected that in future the government is likely to restrain the growth in demand in the economy, it will generally be expected that earnings will grow more slowly. The precise manner of demand restraint may affect some classes of shares more than others. A rise in direct taxes might cause shares in retail stores to fall more than shares in banks, for example, but the general movement will be downward. For this reason, a fall in share prices can be sparked off by figures showing a balance of payments deficit. Alternatively, a reported increase in the rate of inflation may cause a fall, if it is believed that the government is bound to take deflationary action.

The term k we said, incorporated the going risk-free rate of interest and a premium which it was felt expressed the riskiness attached to the company's future dividend stream. The value of k may change, therefore, because of circumstances attaching to a particular firm. A firm's diversification into new activity, as we said earlier, might be successful in raising the growth of dividends. But at the same time it may increase the variability of dividends. In this case both g and k increase and the effect on the market valuation of the share will depend upon the relative strength of the two developments. In a more straightforward case, a firm with a steady record of dividends from activity overseas may find that the country in which it operates is sliding towards civil unrest. Its dividends may remain unchanged but the market valuation will fall because of the increased risk thought to attach to them. Much more commonly, firms will find their share prices fluctuating as a result of changes in exchange rate risk. Many large UK companies with interests in the United States found their share prices depressed in the summer of 1987 because of uncertainties about the future behaviour of the dollar.

A change in the general level of interest rates will obviously affect the valuation of all equities. If interest rates rise, the value of k will increase and the value of the future income stream for all equities will fall. Thus share prices may react to rapid bank lending figures if the market believes that the government will raise interest rates in order to reduce monetary growth. In addition, as we saw in the last chapter, a rise in interest rates will cause a fall in bond prices and a rise in their (risk-free) yield. Since bonds are partial substitutes for equities, there will be some switching from equities to bonds reinforcing the fall in equity prices. Since a rise in interest rates has the effect of raising the cost of credit, it will be expected to slow the growth of demand, and of company earnings, and will reduce the value of g.

The terms g and k are sometimes referred to as the *fundamentals* of a share's value. Accordingly, changes in the values attached to g and k are referred to as changes in a share's fundamentals. Notice though, as we have said many times, that the fundamentals are not known with certainty. The values of g and k are estimates. Clearly, therefore it is changes in those estimates which are responsible for changes in the market's valuation of a share. A change in estimates may turn out, *ex post*, to have been entirely unwarranted, but the change will still cause a change in the price.

Since a change in estimates causes a change in price, it is obviously important to be first with the estimate. By being first, a capital gain may be made or a capital loss avoided. This is why, as we saw above, new balance of payments, or bank lending, or inflation figures appear instantly to have an effect on share prices. There is not time to wait for the balance of trade, or bank lending or inflation to have an *actual* effect upon the fundamentals.

The fact that it is changes in *estimated* fundamental values which cause changes in market valuations, introduces two issues of overwhelming importance to our understanding of the behaviour of the demand for equities. The first is that because people are uncertain about future values they are open to persuasion. Case study 7.1 looks at the marketing of equities and related financial products and at the efforts to control the generally recognised abuses. The second issue which we deal with here, is that because changes in estimates cause changes in prices, profit can be made from anticipating the estimates. Estimating other people's estimates could indeed be more profitable than estimating the fundamentals.

Estimating future share price movements, based upon both estimates of fundamentals and estimates of other people's estimates is the work of share analysts. These are people who work for large institutions which either hold shares as a major part of their assets or act as 'market-makers' in shares. Typically analysts specialise in thirty to forty shares, usually in a particular sector and work along the lines we have already described. They might begin with an estimate of g based upon the long-run prospects for the economy but then make marginal adjustments to it on the basis of research into those variables which might bear particularly upon their sector. In the retail sector, for example, these might be trends in consumer spending and saving. Further adjustments would then be made on the basis of research into individual companies and lastly a judgement made about the market view of similar shares.

In chapter 12 of his *General Theory of Employment, Interest and Money*, published in 1936, the English economist John Maynard Keynes, described the basis of successful share analysis. He began with some remarks about analysts or, as he called them the 'expert professionals'.

> Most of these persons are, in fact, largely concerned, not with making superior long-term forecasts of the probable yield of an investment over its whole life, but with foreseeing changes in the conventional basis of valuation a short time ahead of the general public. They are concerned, not with what an investment is really worth ... but with what the market will value it at, under the influence of mass psychology, three months or a year ahead.... For it is not sensible to pay 25 for an investment of which you believe the prospective yield to justify a value of 30, if you also believe that the market will value it at 20 three months hence.... The actual, private object of the most skilled investment today is "to beat the gun", ... to outwit the crowd and to pass the bad, or depreciating, half-crown to the other fellow. (pp. 154–5)

Keynes continued by comparing share evaluation to a competition.

> Professional investment may be likened to those newspaper competitions in which the competitors have to pick out the six prettiest faces from a hundred photographs, the prize being awarded to the competitor whose choice most nearly corresponds to the average preferences of the competitors as a whole; ... It is not a case of choosing those which, to the best of one's judgement, are really the prettiest, nor even those which average opinion genuinely thinks the prettiest. We have reached the third degree where we devote our intelligences to anticipating what average opinion expects the average opinion to be. And there are some, I believe, who practise the fourth, fifth and higher degrees. (p. 156)

What case study 7.1 shows, is that anticipating what average opinion expects average opinion to be can sometimes have devastating effects.

CASE STUDY 7.1; SHARE PRICES IN 1987

On 16 July 1987, the FT-SE 100 index touched its highest point of 2443. During August, in response to poor trade figures and a rise in interest rates it fell to 2200 where it stayed nervously until the middle of October. During this period an index movement of 30 points in one day was considered large.

On 19 October, as we note in 7.5, market-makers marked down prices by 5 per cent before trading began. Even so, prices fell dramatically in the morning and the index had lost 300 by midday. By the end of the week it had fallen 400 points to 1800. After two more weeks in which daily swings of in excess of 100 points became commonplace, it closed on 6 November at 1621, a fall of nearly 30 per cent in three weeks. Why did it happen and what does it illustrate of our description of how equity markets work?

The US budget and balance of payments had both been in serious deficit for several years and those deficits had been funded by lending from abroad. Important in foreign investors' willingness was to lend was an assurance that they were not going to be repaid in future in badly depreciated dollars. During 1987 this assurance had been provided by international agreement to support the dollar, but worsening trade figures and ambiguous comments by government representatives in the week ending 16 October suddenly reopened the possibility that the dollar might seriously fall in value. This in turn implied that future deficits could be funded only by very large interest rate inducements. Shares in New York fell sharply on 15 October, followed by other markets very soon afterwards.

In terms of the fundamentals, the reasoning seems to have been as follows. With higher interest rates, the rate of return on risk-free equity-substitutes such as bonds would rise (k rises). Higher interest rates would reduce investment and consumer spending and the future rate of growth of profits (g falls). Higher interest rates, leading to lower asset prices, cause people's wealth to fall which might have a further effect upon consumer spending (g falls further). In short, one fear was an interest rate induced recession.

The alternative, it was reasoned, involved preventing the slide in the dollar by eliminating the original US deficits. This might have been helped by Japan and W. Germany expanding their economies to boost US exports, but given their unwillingness to do this, the adjustment would have to be made by large cuts in US spending. This threatened recession via another route (with a fall in g) but from the markets' point of view this was probably preferable since it avoided the additional effect on asset prices of higher interest rates (and higher k).

Notice firstly that when share prices collapsed nothing had actually *happened* to change fundamentals. This prompted the UK Chancellor of the Exchequer to say in the following week that 'nothing had changed', 'markets had over-reacted', 'the UK economy was as strong as ever'. What it illustrates, is the point we made in 7.4.2 about markets working on estimates or anticipations of changes in fundamentals. After three weeks, long-term interest rates had not risen, they had in fact fallen as investors sought refuge in bonds. Short-term interest rates had also fallen as a result of central bank interventions to increase liquidity. Prices remained depressed because the markets still *foresaw* the dangers developing.

Notice secondly that the fall in prices had the effect of raising the average level of yields, from 3.5 per cent to almost 4.5 per cent. No one was suggesting that the productivity of real capital had changed over the course of ten days in October but the cost of raising the funds to buy it had risen by a whole point.

What the episode also reveals is Keynes's point about success requiring the anticipation of what other people are going to do. This was apparent even on Black Monday. No one was calculating the anticipated fundamentals as prices went down that morning. People were selling on the Monday because markets had never seen anything like it before and if they really were going into unknown territory the only sensible thing was to get out. Anticipating the actions of others was most clearly revealed, however, in the actions of market-makers who continued to adjust their opening prices in the light solely of *how other exchanges had behaved overnight.*

Lastly, the episode shows that governments accept a responsibility for what happens in equity markets much as they do in others. Throughout the period the UK authorities took every opportunity to insist that markets had overreacted to objective events. However, by the second week it was clear that verbal reassurance was not going to solve two rapidly developing problems. The first was the sale of BP shares, trading in which was due to begin on the second Friday; the second was the possibility of widespread defaults and conceivable bankruptcy in financial markets as people found they could not settle outstanding accounts.

As we saw in 7.4.1 the 'solution' to the BP problem amounted to an offer to buy back the shares if the shares fell below 70p. This in itself is an illustration that the authorities recognise the importance of 'competitive anticipation' in financial markets.

The authorities' response to the liquidity shortage was to cut interest rates and to create a climate of anticipation of further cuts if necessary. This was as much a signal of willingness to help, as help in itself. Genuine increases in liquidity came from the Bank of England's foreign exchange operations. Its continuing support for the dollar meant that the domestic money supply was expanding. Normally, this would have been offset by gilt sales. This was not done.

How does this analysis of the demand for equities compare with the way in which we normally think about the demand for a good? Clearly there is no difficulty in thinking of the present value of a future stream of earnings as corresponding to the 'utility' of a good. As markets are normally supposed to operate the demand for a good, and thus its equilibrium price, would change as income or tastes change. Neither of these are normally presented as volatile. In the case of equities, however, demand clearly shifts frequently. This happens, firstly, because buyers can only estimate the 'utility' they are going to receive.

This is because the flow of earnings and the risk associated with the flow (the fundamentals) lie in the future and are affected by many factors which do happen to change frequently.
But this is not the whole of the explanation. The 'utility' of a holding of equities lies not just in the flow of future income but also in the appreciation in value of the shares. Changes in the market value of shares may originate in changing estimates of the fundamentals but since it is changes in estimates (rather than in the fundamentals themselves) which cause changes in price traders will act on estimates. In many markets, as we have already seen, the quality of information available to traders falls far short of the level commonly assumed in economic theory.

CASE STUDY 7.2: THE REGULATION OF FINANCIAL MARKETS

It is often claimed that financial markets come closest to the textbook ideal of how markets should work. We now know that that is an exaggeration. Financial markets are dominated by large firms, governments have a large role, products are not homogeneous, supply and demand conditions are not stable, above all relevant information is poor.

So far, the poverty of information we have discussed has affected all market participants to a greater or lesser degree because it has resulted from a need to predict both the future and people's anticipation of the future, and no one is able to do this with consistent success. There are other respects, however, in which information is defective and some of these give rise to *inequalities* of information.

One of these gives rise to the phenomenon of 'insider trading'. Insider trading means trading to one's own advantage using information which is available by virtue of a position of trust and is not available to others. Since 'Big Bang' the possibilities for insider trading have undoubtedly increased. With the market-making and equity-broking functions being carried out by departments of the same organisations that are advising firms on new issues, mergers, takeovers etc., the scope for crucial information becoming available to the privileged few is plainly considerable. For the moment, it is hoped that two things will deter people in the same organisation from divulging sensitive information to colleagues. The first is professional honour, known more colourfully as 'Chinese Walls'; the second is the electronic recording of all equity deals which should enable significant trading immediately prior to the publication of information to be observed. The conviction of several persons during 1987 suggests perhaps that the second is more effective than the first.

Another respect in which information is sufficiently defective to cause concern arises in the marketing of financial products. In an ideal world, as we know, people buy a product at a price which corresponds to their subjective evaluation of its marginal utility. We already know that establishing the 'utility' of equities is difficult, even for professionals. It is very much harder for amateurs, the small savers. This makes it tempting for firms selling equities and equity-related products like unit trusts, traded options and so on to persuade potential purchasers of their merits. One of the easiest forms of persuasion lies in the selective use of information. Common examples in recent years have been the quoting of unit trust performance measuring from the 'bid' (lower) price at the start of the period to the 'offer' (higher) price at the end; the choice of 'favourable' years over which to carry out the measurement; ignoring the effects of inflation; understating the risk associated with some financial products.

Amongst the most aggressively marketed products in recent years have been the shares in privatised companies. In addition to the lavish advertising, the shares were also priced at a discount and the two practices together created many first time shareholders whose previous knowledge of equity markets one must assume was limited. In the October 1987 share crash, the price of existing BP shares fell way below the equivalent of the newly issued 120p shares days before the offer for sale closed. In fact, the indications were that the 120p shares would trade at about 80p. Even so,

270,000 people applied for the shares at 120p.

The Financial Services Act of 1986, when fully implemented, will endeavour to end many abuses by establishing 'self-regulatory organisations' to enforce standards in all financial markets. It is doubtful, however, that it will prevent governments from abusing their information advantage.

7.5 THE BUYING AND SELLING OF EQUITIES

The institutional arrangements whereby desires to sell and to buy are coordinated do not normally feature in discussions of how markets work. This may not matter very much in the case of most markets. At least, for those markets which fall short of the ideal their shortcomings may have little to do with the precise manner in which buyers and sellers exchange information. This is not true, however, of the market for equities.

We know that the existing stock of equities must always be held by someone. By far the greater part will be held by people or institutions loosely referred to as 'investors'. However, an active market requires that an additional pool of shares should be maintained in the hands of people willing always to buy and sell. Before October 1986, in the UK such people were known as 'jobbers'. They are now referred to as 'market-makers' and are often subsidiaries of very large, sometimes multinational, financial conglomerates. Their function is, in the jargon, 'to quote continuous two-way prices' for shares in which they have chosen to make a market and, in theory, they risk their membership of the Stock Exchange if they fail to do so. Consequently, their interest in the shares is not normally in their income or capital appreciation but in the profits to be made from dealing. These come from a 'spread', the difference in the prices at which market-makers are prepared to buy and sell a share. If offers to sell a share outweigh offers to buy, the market-makers must accept the offers to sell but they will lower both the buying and selling prices, hoping of course to discourage sellers and to encourage buyers. When newspapers quote the prices of shares it is usually the average price taken from a number of market-makers. Equally, the continuous calculation of share price indices uses prices taken from market-makers.

So far there is nothing exceptional in this. Provided that market-makers *do* quote 'continuous two-way prices', provided that they *are* always ready to deal at the quoted price, provided that they adjust their prices *solely* in response to actual flows of offers to sell and offers to buy, then they are simply the institutional means by which this particular market clears.

However, there are already serious doubts that this is what always happens. In the second week of August 1987 equity prices fell sharply in response to a rise in interest rates and figures showing a large increase in bank lending in July. With prices falling sharply, accusations were first heard of market-makers being slow, if not actually unwilling, 'to answer the phone'. The same allegations followed the much more dramatic collapse in share prices on Black Monday, 19 October 1987. In such circumstances, we no longer have an equilibrium price. A quoted price exists and at that price people are very anxious to sell, but they cannot. What is more, the temporary inability of the market to clear, in the case of equities, is likely to have an effect upon the price at which the market does eventually settle. Remember what we have said about estimating other people's estimates. In the circumstances described it is quickly known, or at least strongly suspected, that other people are selling and that the price ought to be falling. This reinforces the desire to sell. The longer the desire to sell is frustrated, the greater the willingness to sell when the opportunity presents. If it is difficult to sell and prices are falling it is important to sell now while one can. More selling takes place and the price falls further.

Another practice which suggests that the market-making process falls short of the ideal whereby prices respond passively to desires to buy and sell is the adjustment of prices by market-makers *in anticipation* of flows of orders. On the morning of Black Monday BBC news broadcasts were announcing before trading began that prices 'would open five per cent lower'. In the course of that dramatic week there were further early-morning announcements of market-makers 'marking prices lower' or (more rarely) higher, in anticipation of trading, and radio correspondents were offering their own recalculation of share price indices *at the opening* of trading. There is nothing irrational, even less improper, about this. At the opening of London trading, market-makers have near-perfect information about trading in many of the same shares in Tokyo or Hong Kong to within an hour previously. It is a perfectly reasonable supposition that what is happening to ICI or Glaxo shares in one country is going to happen in another. But it is a big contrast with the way in which markets are supposed to function. As we have just described events, the auctioneer calls a price which is below the initial market-clearing price. However, since the object of the game is to anticipate average opinion and average opinion is based in part on the movement in the auctioneer's price, it may be wise to sell. As Keynes might have said, 'It is not sensible to hold at 25 an investment of which you think the prospective yield to justify a value of 30, if you also think the market will value it at 20 by lunchtime.'

8 Foreign Exchange Markets

An exchange rate is the price of a country's currency expressed in terms of another currency. Each currency therefore has an exchange rate with every other currency. Many of these sets of exchange rates are determined in markets by the forces of demand and supply. This, however, begs two questions which we must consider later: (a) why are foreign currencies demanded and supplied? (b) who does the demanding and supplying?

But let us look firstly at the number of currencies which may be traded in markets. Every Tuesday the *Financial Times* provides a table giving the value of the pound sterling against all other currencies. This table includes approximately 200 countries with exchange rates for the pound quoted against around 150 currencies, ranging from the Afghani to the Zimbabwe Dollar, via the Pataca, the Colon, and the New Dong.

Thus most countries have their own currency for internal purposes. There is also an international demand for all currencies to allow the purchase by foreigners of domestic goods and services. Equally, people in all countries wish to buy foreign goods and services and to travel abroad and hence need to supply their own currency in exchange for foreign currencies. This provides the potential for a set of market-determined exchange rates for each currency.

We can show this on a standard demand and supply diagram but we need to be careful in labelling the axes. Figure 8.1 shows the demand for and supply of a foreign currency ($US) in terms of the domestic currency (£sterling).

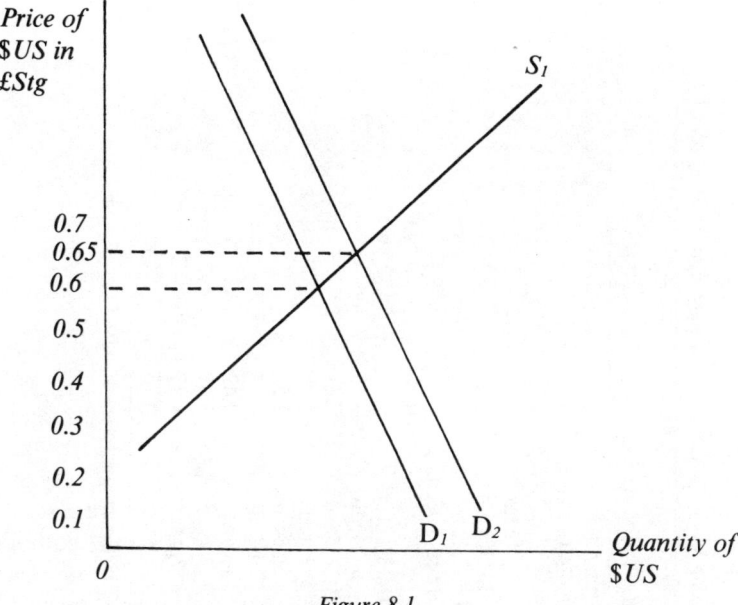

Figure 8.1

On the horizontal axis we have the quantity of dollars. On the vertical axis we have the price of a $US in terms of sterling, for instance £0.60 = $1. Suppose now that because British citizens wish to buy more American goods than previously there is an increase in the demand for dollars. The demand curve moves out from D_1 to D_2. In our diagram the price of a dollar has increased to £0.65. In other words, the value of the pound has fallen in relation to the dollar.

In practice, there is very little international demand for most currencies. Foreign citizens and firms are unwilling to accept them in settlement of debt, and other governments will not hold them in their international reserves. They are not then part of international liquidity.

Currencies of a few industrial countries (hard currencies) are willingly held by other governments and are part of the international trading system. A few of these (key currencies) are freely used in transactions not involving the issuing country. The most important is the American dollar which makes up such a large part of total international liquidity that

Table 8.1: Pound spot–forward against the pound

Nov. 10	Day's spread	Close	One month	% p.a.	Three months	% p.a.
US	1.7855–1.8005	1.7855–1.7865	0.33–0.30cpm	2.12	0.60–0.55pm	1.29
Canada	2.3580–2.3752	2.3580–2.3590	0.08dis–0.03cpm			
				–0.13	0.03–0.18dis	–0.18
Netherlands ...	3.33¾–3.34¾	3.33¾–3.34¾	1⅛–1cpm	3.81	3⅛–2⅞pm	3.59
Belgium	61.75–62.43	61.75–61.85	13–10cpm	2.23	31–26pm	1.84
Denmark	11.44¾–11.49½	11.46¼–11.47¼	1⅛–2⅛oredis	–1.70	6½–7⅜dis	–2.42
Ireland	1.1160–1.1235	1.1190–1.1200	0.01pm–0.06cdis			
				–0.27	0.12–0.29dis	0.73
W. Germany ..	2.96¾–2.97¾	2.96¾–2.97¾	1⅜–1¼pfpm	5.30	3½–3⅜pm	4.63
Portugal	240.93–242.91	240.95–241.95	36–94cdis	–3.23	206–320dis	–4.36
Spain	199.47–200.64	199.75–200.05	102–158cdis	–7.81	298–391dis	–6.90
Italy	2187–2202	2189½–2190½	5–7liredis	–3.29	16–20 dis	–3.29
Norway	11.31–11.41¼	11.31–11.32	5–5¼oredis	–5.57	16⅛–16⅞dis	–5.83
France	10.09–10.12	10.09–10.10	⅝–1⅛cdis	–0.97	2⅜–3dis	–1.06
Sweden	10.75–10.80	10.75–10.76	⅛–⅝oredis	–0.42	1¾–2½dis	–0.79
Japan	239¼–240¾	239¾–240¾	1⅛–1ypm	5.31	2⅞–2⅝pm	4.58
Austria	20.90–20.97	20.94–20.97	8–7gropm	4.29	20¾–17⅝pm	3.66
Switzerland	2.43–2.45	2.43¼–2.44¼	1⅛–1cpm	5.23	3–2¾pm	4.72

Notes: Belgian rate is convertible francs. Financial franc 61.95–62.05. Six-month forward dollar 1.07–1.02cpm 12-month 1.50–1.40cpm.

Source: Financial Times 11th November 1987

its exchange rate and changes in it are of importance to everyone.

8.1 EXPRESSIONS OF EXCHANGE RATES

In fig. 8.1 we have used the normal form for the expression of an exchange rate—the direct quotation method. We have quoted the price of the foreign currency. That is, how much domestic currency is required to buy one unit of the foreign currency. For example, the exchange rate of sterling might be quoted as £0.002 = 1 Polish Zloty or £0.176 = 1 Mongolian Tugrik. An alternative method (indirect quotation) quotes the price of the domestic currency, for example: £1 = 4.248 Malaysian ringgits or £1 = 7.475 Nigerian nairas. The London foreign exchange market is the only major market to use this indirect form.

8.1.1 The presentation of spot rates of exchange

Towards the back of any copy the *Financial Times* you will find a page headed 'Currencies, Money & Capital Markets'. In table 8.1 we reproduce an example of the table headed 'Pound spot—forward against the pound'.

Look at the column 'close'. There you will see the spot exchange rate for the pound against sixteen other major trading currencies as at the close of the London foreign exchange market on the previous day on which trading occurred. The closing spot rate for the pound against the dollar is given as 1.7855-1.7865. The lower of these two figures is the buying rate—the rate at which dollars could be bought at the close (remember, British practice is to quote the price of the domestic currency, rather than the price of the foreign currency). The higher price is the selling rate—the rate at which dollars could be sold. Turning this into the more usual direct quotation form, we see that for every dollar we had wanted to buy we would have had to pay 56 pence; but for every dollar we had wanted to sell we would have received 55.96 pence.

If you wish to take a single figure for the exchange rate you should split the difference and take the figure £1 = $1.786. The column headed 'day's spread' gives the range over which the pound traded against the dollar over the course of the previous day. When you look at these figures, however, you should bear in mind that they are average figures taken by the *Financial Times* from major traders in the London market at about 5 p.m.. But foreign currency markets are twenty-four hour markets operated by telex, telephone and computer link. The New York market opens some hours before the London market closes and continues to operate through the European evening. When New York closes, the Tokyo market is already open. By the time the London market re-opens the following morning, actual rates may have changed considerably from those which applied at the previous evening's close.

Also, of course, tourist rates of exchange which ordinary citizens will obtain from exchange offices will be a good deal worse for both buyers and sellers of a currency and will have a

Table 8.2 Other currencies

Oct. 15	£	$
Argentina	5.8170–5.8540	3.4900–3.5100
Australia	2.2840–2.2870	1.3720–1.3730
Brazil	87.5785–86.0700	52.5430–52.8060
Finland	7.2235–7.2360	4.3405–4.3425
Greece	228.46–232.43	137.49–139.86
Hong Kong	12.9975–13.0100	7.8020–7.8040
Iran	118.10*	71.00*
Korea (Sth)	1329.20–1341.20	802.00–808.60
Kuwait	0.46620–0.46660	0.228010–0.28020
Luxembourg	62.45–62.55	62.85–62.95
Malaysia	4.2050–4.2160	2.5370–2.5380
Mexico	2678.38–2678.85	1607.00–1608.00
N. Zealand	2.5645–2.5720	1.5410–1.5445
Saudi Ar	6.2420–6.2470	3.7500–3.7510
Singapore	3.4845–3.4915	2.0910–2.0920
S. Af. (Cm)	3.4100–3.4230	2.0460–2.0505
S. Af. (Fn)	5.4610–5.6465	3.2785–3.3900
Taiwan	49.60–49.85	29.95–30.05
U.A.E.	6.1130–6.1800	3.6725–3.6735

Notes: *Selling rate.

Source: Financial Times 16th October 1987

much bigger spread between the buying and the selling rate. Can you see why this is so? The difference between the buying and selling rates (together with any commission charges) covers the costs of exchange offices and provides their profits. Because tourist transactions are on average small, the administrative costs of an exchange office in a shopping centre are high relative to its turnover. In addition, such an office holds currencies of several countries for the convenience of its customers and runs the risk that some of those currencies will lose value while it is holding them.

In table 8.2 we print an example of a column from the *Financial Times* headed 'other currencies'. This gives the closing rates for the pound against another eighteen less important currencies. Many of these currencies are subject to considerable amounts of official exchange rate control.

Notice that the closing spread between buying and selling rates differs from currency to currency. For example, the price of £s in terms of Canadian dollars is given (in table 8.1) as 2.3580-2.3590, a spread of only .042%. On the other hand, the spread for the Greek Drachma (in table 8.2) is 228.46-232.43—a very large spread of 1.723%.

These differences reflect the variability of a currency and hence the risk to banks in holding it. It stands to reason that the greater the risk, the greater the margin of profit which banks will seek in return for trading in the currency. The variability of the exchange rate of a currency is likely to be greater the less important a country is in international commerce and thus the smaller the amount of the currency which is traded. This is because the currency's value may be significantly changed by only one or two large transactions. Such markets are said to be 'thin'.

8.1.2 Exchange rate indexes

It is likely that at a particular time a currency's value will be increasing in relation to some currencies and falling in relation to others. Hence, to obtain a general view of its performance it is necessary to calculate an index, averaging the performance of the currency against a number of other currencies (a currency basket). Such an index is known as a country's effective exchange rate. Since some currencies will be more important to a country's trade than others, the index is weighted. The weights are usually based on exports and imports, taking into account the extent to which countries compete in third markets. Thus, although Japan and Italy do not trade much with each other, a change in the value of the yen affects Italian trade because the two countries compete with each other in other countries. For instance, Japanese and Italian cars are in competition in the British market.

For the UK, the effective exchange rate (the exchange rate index or ERI) is calculated by taking a weighted average of the value of sterling against seventeen other currencies ranging from the US$ to the Finnish mark. Table 8.3 shows the variation in the sterling index over a day's trading.

Table 8.3: Sterling index

		Nov. 13	Previous
8.30	am	75.3	75.1
9.00	am	75.3	75.2
10.00	am	75.4	75.2
11.00	am	75.3	75.1
Noon		75.2	75.2
1.00	pm	75.2	75.3
2.00	pm	75.1	75.2
3.00	pm	75.3	75.1
4.00	pm	75.3	75.3

Source: Financial Times 14th November 1987

The base of 100 for this index represents the average value of sterling in 1975. Thus the figure of 75.3 means that the weighted average value of sterling was 75.3 per cent of its 1975 level.

Another index sometimes calculated is the real exchange rate. This reflects the combined impact of changes in the exchange rate between two currencies and differences between the inflation rates in the countries concerned. Its aim is to allow the consideration of changes in a country's competitive position in international trade. Suppose that in foreign exchange markets we could buy £1 for US$1.75. Suppose, too, that a particular piece of textile machinery which is manufactured in both the US and the UK costs £10,000 in the

UK and will thus cost an American company US$17,500. Suppose next that the US version of the machine sells in the US for US$18,000 and that therefore the British product is very competitive.

We can see that there are two circumstances which will reduce the UK's competitive advantage. The price of the UK machine in sterling might rise due to inflation in the UK—if it rises to £11,000, it will cost an American company $18,375. Alternatively, the value of the pound against the dollar might rise—if it rises to £1 = $1.83, the £10,000 machine will cost $18,300 in the US. In both cases, American companies are likely to switch away from the British-made machine to the American product. A country's real exchange rate attempts to take into account both of these influences.

8.2 THE DEMAND FOR AND SUPPLY OF FOREIGN CURRENCIES

The basic reason for demanding the currencies of other countries is to buy goods and services produced in those countries. Equally, other countries will supply their currencies in exchange for the domestic currency in order to buy domestically produced goods and services. It follows that countries whose goods and services are much desired by foreigners should experience strong international demand for their currency.

Thus, any tendency for a country's balance of payments on current account to go into surplus (exports greater than imports) should be associated with a strong demand for and an increase in the value of its currency. This in turn should make its products more expensive for foreign buyers and lead to a fall in demand for them. In theory then exchange rates should change to maintain a balance in the value of each country's exports and imports.

Life is not, however, so simple. To begin with, there are very long time lags in international trade. A fall in a country's exchange rate is ultimately likely to lead to an increase in the international demand for its goods but this may take a very long time to come about. It takes time for the exchange rate change to feed through into product prices, for traders to notice the alteration, and for new contracts to be entered into. Indeed, it is likely that in the short run a fall in exchange rate will actually make a country's balance of payments worse before it gets better.

Consider again our case above with a British company producing a machine for £10,000 and selling it in the US for $17,500. (Question: why are these figures unreasonable? Answer: because they ignore transport costs to the US, marketing costs in the US and possible US tariffs.) Now suppose the value of the pound falls to $1.70 and the British company reduces the price of its machine in the US in line with this fall to $17,000. Initially, because of time lags, the company will not sell any more machines; but it will receive less foreign currency for each one it sells. The UK balance of trade worsens. Eventually, however, as the company does sell more machines (its trade improves in volume terms) the position begins to improve. This phenomenon is known as the J-curve.

Because of this it may very well be the case that to correct a balance of payments deficit, a country's exchange rate will need to fall much further initially than will eventually be the case. That is, exchange rates 'overshoot'.

Again, exchange rates are greatly influenced by international capital flows which have nothing to do with trade. A recent estimate for the world's leading thirty industrial nations concluded that over the first half of the 1980s turnover in the foreign exchange market had doubled to $150 billion per day whereas total world exports had grown by only $8\frac{1}{2}$ per cent. It has been estimated that perhaps 95 per cent of deals in the market are for speculative purposes. This means that exchange rates are much influenced by changes in international interest rates and above all by expectations of future interest rate and exchange rate changes.

If exchange rates were principally determined by trading performance, we would expect exchange rate relationships to change only slowly over time since trading performance depends on factors such as labour productivity and levels of investment which themselves change only gradually. In fact the experience of recent years has been of rapidly fluctuating exchange rates.

8.2.1 The importance to governments of exchange rates

We have already seen one major reason for a government to be very concerned about the international value of its currency—it has a considerable impact on the international competitiveness of the goods and services it produces. Despite the time lags which we noted above, it remains that a rise in the value of a country's currency makes its goods more expensive in foreign markets and makes it more difficult for its exporters to compete abroad. Equally, foreign goods become cheaper in domestic markets and locally produced import-competing goods find it more difficult to compete with them. From the point of view of trade, it would seem then that the lower the international value of a country's currency the better. But other factors need to be considered.

Above all, we must take account of the effect of exchange rate changes on inflation rates. Reversing our example above, we can see that a fall in the value of a country's currency makes imported goods more expensive and helps import-competing industries. However, the rise in the price of imported goods feeds through into the country's cost of living—not only do the prices of wholly imported products rise but so too do the prices of the many locally produced goods which use imported raw materials or intermediate goods. The initial rise in the cost of living may then lead to increases in wage demands and to the extent that these are met the cost of living rises further.

As the inflation rate rises the advantage of the fall in the currency's value begins to disappear (remember the real exchange rate notion above). Many governments also believe, of course, that high inflation rates have other undesirable effects—leading to greater uncertainty, lower investment and, in the long run, higher unemployment. Thus a government which regards the control of inflation as its major macroeconomic policy aim may wish to keep the international value of its currency relatively high. We can see that any government faces a major conflict of interests in deciding on the desirable level of the exchange rate of its currency.

8.2.2 The particular problem of developing countries

The problem of deciding on the 'correct' international value of a currency is, like almost all economic problems, particularly intense for developing countries. Take Zambia as an example. Its currency (the kwacha) is not acceptable in international trade. It has few exports. Its principal traded product is copper which is priced in international markets in US dollars. Thus a change in the kwacha/dollar relationship has no impact on the amount of copper which Zambia can sell or on its foreign exchange earnings. However, it does have an impact on the domestic prices of Zambia's imports.

In recent years (with the low price of world copper) Zambia's foreign currency earnings have fallen far short of what it has required to pay for the imports it has desired. A market solution would require a large fall in the value of the kwacha, increasing sharply the price of imports and reducing the demand for them. This, however, could have unfortunate results.

Firstly, some of Zambia's imports can be regarded as essential. The country does not grow enough food to feed itself and has to import basic foods (in particular maize meal). A sharp fall in the value of the kwacha pushes up food prices and the overall rate of inflation dramatically, may have serious consequences for the health of the people, and is very likely to cause severe political unrest. An economist might respond by saying that the increase in food prices would provide a strong incentive for Zambia to grow more food and to become less dependent on imports. But this may require major social and structural changes and may be very difficult even in the long run.

Another response from our economist might be that the country has to develop other industries in order to increase its export earnings. Yet this may require imported capital equipment and expertise and hence foreign exchange. We have a neat circle which it is very hard to break into. The situation becomes worse if international lending agencies such as the International Monetary Fund refuse to lend to the country until it reforms its economy and if a high proportion of the limited amount of foreign exchange available already goes to pay interest on past loans from abroad.

Secondly, the market solution may lead to the scarce foreign exchange being used in ways which do not appear to contribute most to the welfare of the country as a whole. The rich may still be able to afford to buy luxury goods, to pay for expensive foreign medical treatment and so on despite the high cost. Meanwhile, the low value of the domestic currency may make it too expensive for new import-competing firms to start operation and the poor may not be able to buy enough food. In these circumstances it is not surprising that many governments attempt to replace the foreign exchange market altogether, or to curtail severely the operation of the market mechanism.

8.3 GOVERNMENT INTERVENTION IN FOREIGN EXCHANGE MARKETS

We have seen several reasons why governments may wish to intervene in foreign exchange markets—to improve their trading position, to help control inflation, to avoid political and social disturbances, to influence the way in which scarce foreign exchange is used. But as in all markets there are varying degrees of government intervention.

8.3.1 Attempting to replace the market

Let us consider firstly the many countries which attempt to set and maintain official exchange rates which value the country's currency much more highly than a free market would do. Such rates can only be maintained if governments are able to control the foreign exchange market.

They try to do this by legislation which (a) limits the ability of people and firms to buy and sell the domestic currency and (b) requires that all foreign currency earned by exporters be sold directly at the official rate to the central bank. Only a few specially authorised agencies are allowed to sell the domestic currency within the country and its export is strictly limited so that it cannot be traded in markets outside the government's control.

Since governments cannot succeed fully in this, they need also to try to prevent the import of their own currencies. Such laws are supported by harsh penalties for transgressors. If you wish to have a cheap holiday in, say, Burma you can buy Burmese Kyats very cheaply from money changers in

Singapore and take them into Burma illegally. But your stay will become an unfortunately long one if you are found out.

If a government manages to control the foreign exchange market, it will need to ration the scarce foreign exchange by administrative rule. (Markets, remember, ration by price). Thus it may decided that foreign exchange will be available at the official price to importers of capital equipment and of basic foodstuffs but not to citizens wishing to travel, study, or invest abroad or to buy luxury consumer goods. There are three difficulties with such an approach.

Firstly, the government may make unwise decisions in the allocation of the scarce foreign exchange. It may, for example, use its powers for short-term political advantage; to maintain extravagant embassies abroad for the benefit of its members and officials; or to keep the armed forces happy by buying expensive military equipment.

Secondly, such arrangements themselves use resources and often lead to administrative inefficiencies and delays and to corruption. Inflexible rules may be established; companies may have to wait for long periods to find out if they can obtain foreign exchange and be unable to plan ahead; allocations may be made to friends and relatives or on the payment of bribes to officials.

Thirdly, the greater is the gap between the official price of the currency and the price which would result from a free market, the greater are the incentives for people to break the rules. Export earnings are understated; foreign currencies are exported illegally and kept in foreign bank accounts; black markets flourish.

8.3.2 Multiple exchange rates and foreign exchange auctions

An alternative approach is to allow the market a role but to act so as to influence strongly the outcome. A government may declare different official rates of exchange depending on the purpose for which the foreign exchange is desired. For instance, a high value may be placed on the local currency for the government's own uses of foreign exchange (paying back foreign loans, running embassies abroad, purchasing office equipment etc.). A rather worse exchange rate may be given to importers of capital equipment. And private citizens wishing to travel abroad or to buy imported consumer goods may face a much worse rate still.

Such a system operates in the same way as a tax and subsidy scheme. People who receive worse rates of exchange than they would be able to get in a free market are in effect being taxed on their use of foreign exchange. Those who obtain rates better than an unregulated market would provide are being subsidised. A redistribution of income is taking place in the economy.

Multiple exchange rate systems may involve all of the problems discussed in 8.3.1 but they do not, even in theory, give the government full control of how the foreign exchange will be used.

In recent years some governments (notably Nigeria and Zambia) have operated foreign exchange auctions. Here the government sets aside the amount of the available foreign exchange which it needs for its own purposes (valuing the domestic currency highly for budgetting purposes) and then auctions what is left to private firms and citizens. The effective exchange rate for the economy is then set in the auction. This method provides a major role for the market mechanism and is likely to lead to a sharp devaluation of the domestic currency. In Zambia foreign exchange auctions in the mid-1980s led to an 85 per cent devaluation of the kwacha against the $US. This then causes the same worries which we looked at in 8.2.2.

8.3.3 Buying and selling one's own currency

Another way in which a government can influence the exchange value of its currency is to enter foreign exchange markets to buy and sell its own currency. To be able to buy its own currency a country must have (or be able to borrow) international reserves—stocks of the currencies of other countries or of gold.

Sometimes a number of central banks will combine to buy and sell currencies in order to influence exchange rates. In the last few years several such operations have been mounted by the central banks of the Group of Five (the US, West Germany, Japan, France, and the UK) to try to influence the value of the dollar.

8.3.4 Changing domestic economic policy

Finally, a government may alter its domestic macroeconomic policy so as to have an impact on the demand for and supply of its currency. Most obviously, governments alter their interest rates for this purpose. For example, if the British government is worried that sterling is becoming too weak it will raise interest rates, making British financial assets more attractive to foreigners. They will then increase their demand for pounds, forcing the value of the pound up.

If a country is sufficiently large and powerful it may attempt to push another government into altering its domestic policies in order to affect exchange rates. The United States regularly attempts to persuade the governments of Japan and West Germany to change their domestic economic policies so as to help the US balance of trade.

8.3.5 Talking the exchange rate up or down

Uncertainty is so great in foreign exchange markets, and expectations so important that a government can try to influence its future exchange rate by playing on the fears of the market. Thus, if a government believes that its currency is presently too highly valued by the market, the head of the central bank may make a major speech indicating that in his view its value should fall.

This may lead the market to feel that the central banker knows something about the real state of the economy which the market does not yet know. Or, it may lead to the view that the government is soon going to intervene in the market to cause the value of its currency to fall. In either case, if market participants believe that the value of the currency will soon fall, they sell the currency in order to avoid a loss with the result that its value does indeed fall.

The practice of trying to talk the currency up or down has been much followed in the United States by the Chief Secretary to the Treasury and the Chairman of the Federal Reserve (the central bank of the US). Unfortunately for the effectiveness of the practice and for the sanity of the market, they have frequently been trying at the same time to talk the dollar in opposite directions. As an example of factors influencing the value of the currency we consider in case study 8.1 the experience of the US dollar in late 1987.

Foreign exchange markets 205

CASE STUDY 8.1: TALKING THE DOLLAR DOWN AND UP

The United States dollar has had an extraordinary history in the 1980s. From 1983 through to late 1985 it became progressively stronger against all currencies. This was despite the fact that the US had been running a very large balance of trade deficit. For a long time people had been predicting its fall, but it had not happened. The strength of the dollar came in part from high US interest rates which attracted flows of capital from abroad (especially from Japan) which more than offset the trade deficit. At a meeting at the Plaza Hotel in New York in September, 1985, the central banks of the Group of Five countries decided to intervene in the markets to sell dollars. Following this, the dollar began to fall and fell steadily.

By the beginning of 1987, it was, in the view of its major trading partners (in particular, Japan and West Germany), in danger of becoming too weak. At another Group of Five meeting, this time in Paris in February 1987, the Louvre Accord was reached, with central banks agreeing to act together to keep exchange rates within unannounced target ranges. This introduced stability into the market and rates remained relatively steady for much of the year. In mid-October, the dollar was trading at exchange rates around 142 yen and 1.80 Deutschemarks. The US was still, however, running a very large trade deficit.

Throughout 1987, the Chief Secretary of the US Treasury, James Baker, had been arguing that Japan and West Germany should expand their economies to allow the US to increase its exports to them and hence to overcome its trade deficit. West Germany in particular resisted, seeing the problem as being over-expansion of the American economy (through its large budget deficit). It was worried as always about inflation (although the West German inflation rate at the time was only just over 1 per cent).

In October, the German central bank (the Bundesbank) increased interest rates, tightening its economy and behaving in the opposite way to America's desire. A public argument followed and James Baker strongly implied that, faced with the unwillingness of the Germans to help, he would be prepared to see the value of the dollar fall considerably. This was talking the dollar down with a vengeance. The markets decided that the Louvre Accord was now dead and became worried both about the possibility of a large fall in the dollar and about the US's budget and trade deficits.

This all helped to damage investors' confidence and to produce the great stockmarket crash of 1987. Some days later the dollar began to fall steeply. On the 10th of November, the dollar reached record lows against the Deutschemark (1.6475) and the yen (133.1) as well as against the Swiss franc and the Dutch guilder. This was despite huge purchases of dollars by the Japanese central bank, in a vain attempt to halt the fall.

Then along came the cavalry in the form of President Reagan who was heard to say of the dollar's value: 'I don't look for a further decline. I don't want a further decline'. The dollar was now being talked up. And here certainly the talk was stronger than central bank intervention. By the end of trading in London on the 10th of November, the dollar had recovered to DM 1.665 and ¥ 134.5. Increased confidence in the next few days that the US was about to act to reduce its budget deficit led to a further rally.

This episode shows the importance of expectations in foreign exchange markets, the speed with which market sentiment can change, and the ability of US government spokesmen to influence that sentiment. On the other hand, it demonstrates that central bank intervention in the markets may have little or no effect when market sentiment is strongly in the opposite direction.

8.4 FOREIGN EXCHANGE ASSETS

So far we have been talking about foreign exchange transactions as if they involved the immediate exchange of one currency for another. Such transactions (spot transactions), which are settled within two business days of the date of the transaction, are important.

However, it is also possible to buy and sell foreign currencies

or delivery at some future date (forward transactions), the most common contracts being for one month or three months ahead of the transaction date. Forward exchange rates are usually quoted as being at a premium or a discount from the relevant spot rate.
To understand what this means, look again at table 8.1. Here we are told that the $US is selling three months forward at a premium of 0.60–0.55. This means that someone needing dollars in three months time can arrange the purchase now at an agreed price but will receive 0.60 cents less for each pound than if the deal was a spot one. That is, the three-month forward rate of exchange is £1 = $1.7795–1.7810. On the other hand, you will observe that the Italian lira is at a discount for three-month forward transactions. We shall consider later why people may wish to buy or sell currencies forward. However, forward transactions have come to play an increasingly important part in foreign exchange markets in recent years.

8.4.1 Roles in foreign exchange markets

The principal participants in foreign exchange markets are the large international banks. In their ordinary banking role they are the professional risk-takers, the 'market makers', although they also engage in speculation. Other participants include securities houses, multinational corporations, and commodities firms. As we have seen, governments also take part through their central banks.

To make a little more sense of operations in the market, we need to consider the extent to which the various participants take risks and the nature of those risks. First we must introduce a few terms.

Transactors are said to assume an exchange rate risk if they remain in an 'open' position in relation to their net current claims or net liabilities in a foreign market. That is, an open position is one where what is owed to them in foreign currencies (their claims) is different from what they owe in foreign currencies (their liabilities) and so their financial position can be affected by exchange rate changes.

Open positions can be of two types. A long position exists when net claims in foreign currencies are greater than liabilities. The risk which is being run in this case is a risk that the value of the foreign currencies involved may fall. To avoid this risk (that is, to move from an open to a closed position in the market) it is possible to sell anticipated foreign exchange receipts forward.

A short position is the reverse: claims are less than liabilities and the risk which is faced is that foreign currencies will rise in value. To eliminate this risk, foreign currency may be bought forward to meet anticipated payment obligations.

8.4.2 Exchange rate arbitrage

Exchange arbitrageurs seek to take advantage of differentials in the price of a currency in different markets at the same time—for example differences in the £/$ exchange rate in London and Paris. Such an operation, involving only two currencies and two markets, is known as 2-point arbitrage. Operations may be much more complex, involving more than two currencies and more than two markets. No matter how complex the operation, arbitrageurs do not need to take risks except during the very short periods of time which it takes to complete transactions—with modern technology and communications this need be no more than a minute or two and so there is virtually no risk. However, the returns are low in relation to the size of the transactions.

Let us construct a simple arbitrage example. Suppose we notice that in the London market the spot rates are £1 = $1.66 = 10 French francs, but that in the Paris market $1 is exchanging for 6.2 francs. Starting with £1000 we could buy $1660 in London and exchange them in Paris for 10,292 francs. Converting back to pounds in London we would finish up with £1,029.2. The effect of these deals would be to increase the demand for francs in Paris and increase the supply of them in London. The Paris $/franc rate would fall, the London rate would rise and the discrepancy would, through arbitrage, quickly disappear.

In practice an operation such as this would involve transactions costs and so arbitrage continues until the exchange rates in different markets are so close that any potential profit would be wiped out by transactions costs. Rates are then said to be 'transactions costs close'. The role of the arbitrageur is seen as vital in the geographic integration of exchange markets.

8.4.3 Interest rate arbitrage

Another type of arbitrage is possible—interest rate arbitrage. This aims to take advantage of international differences in interest rates on comparable assets and in so doing acts to integrate international financial markets. The arbitrageur avoids risk in this case by the use of forward exchange markets. The difference between spot and forward rates is then part of the cost of the interest-arbitrage operation and is said to represent an 'implicit interest rate' on the use of forward exchange. As long as this implicit interest rate is less than the actual interest rate differential there is an incentive to shift funds into the foreign currency concerned.

Consider two countries, the UK and the US, in which assets of similar risk and maturity bear different interest rates—higher in the UK than in the US. An investor in the US can choose between using dollars to buy US dollar securities and buying sterling spot in order to buy UK sterling securities. In the second case, the investor would be able to sell sterling forward so as to hold dollars again at the end of the period.

Let us take some figures. We start with $1 million and assume it could be invested in New York for three months at 9 per cent. This would produce interest of $22,500. Alternatively, suppose our $1 million could be exchanged for pounds at a spot rate of $1 = £0.60 and the resulting £600,000 be invested in London for three months at 12 per cent, producing interest of £18,000. Suppose further that at the time we exchanged our dollars for pounds spot, we could enter into a forward transaction to sell the £618,000 we would end up with in three months time at the same rate of $1 = £0.60. Then we would know that we would finish up with $1,030,000—we would be $7,500 better off than if we had kept our money in the US.

In such a case arbitrageurs would have a field day. They would purchase large quantities of pounds spot and use them to buy British securities, covering the risk of a fall in the value of sterling by selling pounds and buying dollars forward. The impact would be to drive up the price of British securities (and hence drive down British interest rates), push down the price of American securities (and push up American interest rates), push down the spot exchange rate of the dollar and push up its forward rate. This would continue until all possibility of profit had been removed. Any remaining difference in interest rates between the two countries would be offset because forward dollars would be trading at a premium. We would finish up with what is known as interest parity.

There is a general rule embedded here. The currencies of countries in which interest rates are higher than in the home country are very likely to be selling at a discount in relation to the home currency. The currencies of countries in which interest rates are lower than in the home country are very likely to be selling at a premium. You should check this by comparing the forward exchange rate premiums or discounts in the *Financial Times* with the interest rates in different countries. You will find these on the same page of the paper.

8.4.4 Speculation

Speculators try to profit by backing their own view of likely future exchange rates against that of the market. Their business in other words is exchange rate risk. Speculators may be divided into two groups: pure speculators whose only aim is to take advantage of changes in exchange rates; and merchant speculators, firms or banks which regularly use the forward exchange market for commercial purposes but who engage in speculative activity from time to time (for example by choosing not to cover future liabilities in foreign currencies or not to sell forward their anticipated foreign exchange earnings). As in other financial markets, speculators may be 'bulls' (taking a more optimistic view of a currency's prospects than the market) or 'bears'.

The forward market is especially susceptible to speculative activity. It is possible in spot markets, but is more expensive than in forward markets, since currency (on which interest is not paid) must be held. This therefore requires either interest to be paid on borrowed funds or interest to be foregone. A more usual speculative activity is selling forward foreign currency that the speculator does not have, in the hope that the foreign currency will fall in price before the end of the contract period (taking a short position); or purchasing forward foreign currency which the speculator does not need in the hope of a rise in the price of the foreign currency (taking a long position).

8.4.5 Firms and foreign exchange markets

We have already seen a major reason for the interest in the exchange rate of producers of traded goods (exports and import-competing goods)—the effect of changing rates on competitiveness. Producers of non-traded goods and services will also be interested if they use imports in production and to the extent that exchange rate changes influence the general rate of inflation in the economy.

We have also noted that firms engaged in international trade will frequently enter into contracts which will require them to make payments in foreign currency or provide them with receipts in foreign currency at dates in the future. But if a company is to assess accurately the profitability of a particular venture it needs to know what its expenses and receipts will be in its own domestic currency. Yet these will depend on what happens to exchange rates between the signing of the contract and the making or receiving of payments in foreign currency.

Again, a company which owns subsidiary companies abroad can be much affected by exchange rate changes. The profits of a subsidiary may seem quite satisfactory expressed in the currency of the country in which it is trading. But a sharp fall in the international value of that currency may play havoc with the parent company's financial position.

For all these reasons, it is clear that firms face exchange rate risk and that this risk increases the more variable are exchange rates. Most trading countries therefore would prefer stable exchange rate systems. In the absence of such a system, however, let us look at some ways in which firms may seek to protect themselves against exchange rate risk.

8.4.6 Protection against exchange rate risk—an example

Consider the case of a UK firm which produces a good in the UK at a cost of £75 a unit. It places a 33% mark-up on top and sells the good in the home market for £100. Now it contracts to sell 1000 units to a US firm, the goods to be supplied and paid for in three months' time. The contract is set out in dollars. The existing three-month forward exchange rate is $1.65 to the pound and so the agreement is for $165,000. The UK company then knows that it will receive $165,000 in 3 months' time but it will not realise its profit until that is converted into sterling.

The firm is in an 'open' position (it is subject to exchange risk) and it is 'long' in dollars (its claims in dollars are greater than its liabilities). The risk it runs is that the dollar will fall in value. For example, if it fell to a rate of £1 = $2.20, all the UK firm's profit would disappear.

How can it 'close' its position? Suppose there were no forward exchange market. Then, on the strength of its contract, the firm could hope to borrow $165,000 from a US or a Euro bank and convert it now into sterling at the existing rate of exchange. Then, when the dollar payment is received on the delivery of the goods, it could use the dollars to pay off the dollar loan. It would have avoided foreign exchange risk by matching its claims and liabilities in the foreign currency. It would also have had the funds available for an extra three months. However, it would have had to pay interest on the loan for three months, and it might have faced difficulties if it had not been able to deliver in time, or if its client was slow in paying.

What about with a forward market? In this case, at the time of signing the contract the firm could enter the forward foreign exchange market and agree to sell $165,000 in three months' time. It would then know the amount of sterling it would receive when the contract was fulfilled and would have protected its profit from foreign exchange risk, without having to pay interest on a loan. Of course, it could still be in difficulties if the payment for the goods was slow in coming.

This is an example of transactions exposure. It is easy to make out a similar case for, say, an importer. Then, the domestic firm would be short in the foreign currency and would run the risk of the value of the foreign currency rising. Can you see what actions it would need to take to avoid risk?

Firms, however, may deliberately choose not to protect themselves against risk, even when protection is available. In such cases, they will be keeping an open position and will be engaging in merchant speculation. Firms may add to their profits in this way if exchange rates move in favourable directions. But if exchange rates move in the wrong direction firms' profits can suffer badly.

8.5 MARKET CLEARING AND EXCHANGE RATE SYSTEMS

8.5.1 Fixed exchange rates and quantity adjustments

Between 1945 and 1973 a virtually fixed exchange rate system operated under the auspices of the International Monetary Fund (IMF). The US dollar was linked in value to gold and all other currencies of member countries of the IMF were linked to the dollar. A central rate (or par value) was declared for each currency in terms of dollars, and exchange rates were allowed to vary within a band of only 1 per cent up or down from those central rates. The central rates themselves could only be changed by significant amounts with IMF approval. In fact, there were very few major re-alignments of central rates, and so exchange rates were effectively fixed for quite long periods.

Governments were required to act to keep the value of their currencies within the agreed band either by buying or selling their own currencies (see 8.3.3) or altering domestic economic policy in order to change the demand for their currencies (see 8.3.4). They were also allowed to restrict capital flows but were not meant to maintain multiple exchange rate systems (see 8.3.2), although some countries did so.

In fixed exchange rate systems, foreign exchange markets clear by quantity adjustments rather than by price adjustments. Let us see how this might work.

In fig. 8.2 we have the demand and supply curves for US dollars in terms of pounds sterling. We start with an exchange rate of £0.60 = $1. Then we assume an increase in demand by British citizens for US produced goods, leading to a shift in the demand curve for dollars from D_1 to D_2.

If the British government were to take no action the value of the pound would fall to £0.65 = $1. Suppose, however, that the government had agreed to keep the rate at the original level. Then it could enter the market and buy back its own currency using the stock of American dollars it has in its international reserves. This would increase the supply of dollars on to the market, moving the supply curve down from S_1 to S_2. The exchange rate remains at its original level. The price of American dollars has not changed but the quantity of dollars traded has.

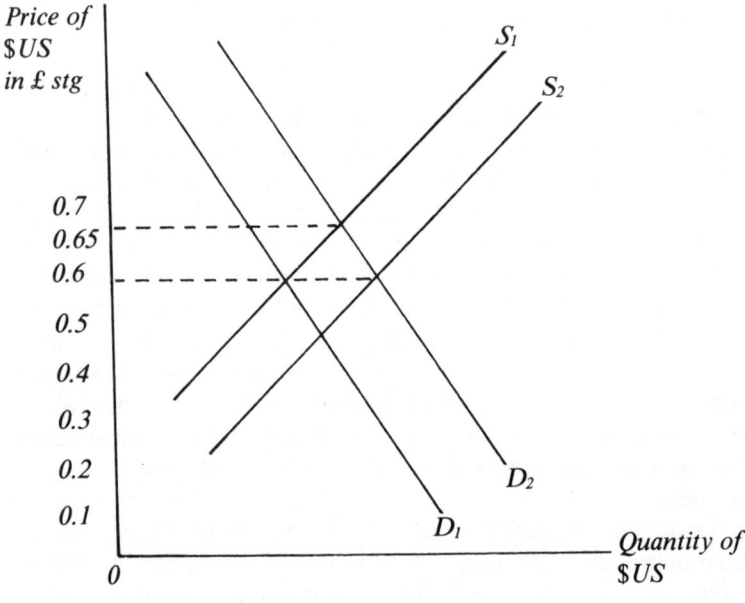

Figure 8.2

If US goods continued to remain attractive to UK residents and the private demand for US dollars remained high, the UK government would ultimately run out of dollars in its reserves. It may for a time borrow foreign currency from other central banks but sooner or later it would have to take other action. We have seen that it could increase its interest rates, attracting foreign purchases of UK financial assets. This would expand the UK's reserves and allow it to continue to support the pound in the market.

The rise in interest rates would also lead to lower domestic investment. Alternatively the government could increase tax rates or cut government expenditure. Either of these policies would be expected to deflate the UK economy and lower the UK's demand for imports. In this way the demand curve for dollars would be moved back from D_2 to D_1. Again, however, the market would clear only through quantity adjustments. Now the same quantity of dollars would be being traded as at the start but changes would have occurred in investment, consumption, employment, imports and other variables.

8.5.2 Managed floats and market adjustments

Following the break up of the IMF system in 1973 a mixed system took its place. Several important currencies floated against each other including the US dollar, the Canadian dollar, the Yen, and the pound. In 1979 the European Monetary system (EMS) was formed, linking the major European currencies (with the exception of the pound) in an exchange rate mechanism which is relatively fixed. Even though it allows considerably greater flexibility than the old IMF system did, demand is brought into line with supply within the EMS largely through quantity adjustments. The EMS currencies float together against the other major world currencies.

A market in which currencies floated freely would clear through price adjustments. However, no currency has been allowed to float freely. Central banks have intervened, not to maintain a fixed rate, but perhaps to keep the value of a currency within an unannounced target range; perhaps to slow down an unwanted rise or fall in the value of a currency; at the very least in an attempt to smooth out day-to-day fluctuations in a currency's value. In addition, governments have been very willing to use economic policy instruments to affect exchange rates. In the UK interest rates have been increased on several occasions specifically to protect the value of the pound. Thus even here market clearance is often brought about by quantity adjustment.

We have then in the foreign exchange market competition, large deals, continuous price fluctuations, relatively low transactions costs—much which apparently fits in with a view of free and competitive markets. Yet the market is heavily constrained by government action. There has always been much argument over whether governments can ultimately resist market forces in foreign exchange markets. Whatever one's view it remains that governments do intervene in an attempt to do so and they will continue to intervene. We seem indeed to be again entering a period of increased attempts to restrain foreign exchange markets and to limit the variability of exchange rates.

In case study 8.2, we consider the growth of the Eurodollar market to show that markets can develop and alter to overcome restrictions placed on market activity by the authorities.

CASE STUDY 8.2: THE EURODOLLAR MARKET

The Eurodollar market is a good example of a market developing to overcome restrictions placed on other markets.

A Eurodollar is a US dollar bank deposit held in a bank situated outside the United States and therefore not subject to the various controls which the US government exercises over banks located within the US. The first step in the creation of Eurodollars occurs when a foreign firm (say a UK company) sells goods to a US firm and is paid in US dollars. These dollars are placed by the British firm in an account in a US bank. The British firm then has three choices. It may leave the dollars in the US account and use them in future American operations. It may transfer the dollars to the UK and exchange them for pounds sterling. The dollars then finish up with the Bank of England as part of the British Government's foreign exchange reserves. Or, it may transfer the dollar deposit to a bank outside the US (an offshore bank). The offshore bank is then able to lend US dollars freely to firms and governments outside the US.

This dollar deposit in a bank outside the US is called a Eurodollar simply because initially dollar deposits were transferred to banks in Europe (above all in London). Often these offshore banks were foreign branches of American banks. This practice of creating Eurodollar deposits began in the late 1950s and grew very rapidly. Other Eurocurrencies have since been created. Thus, a Euroyen is a Japanese Yen bank deposit held in a bank outside Japan. There are also Eurosterling, Euromarks and many others. However, because the US dollar is the world's principal trading currency, Eurodollars have always been far greater in number and far more important than other Eurocurrencies. These days, Eurocurrency markets exist in Hong Kong, Singapore and several other countries outside of Europe.

But why did the Eurodollar market develop and grow rapidly? From the point of view of depositors, the fact that the banks involved were offshore and could not be controlled by the US government gave them two advantages. Firstly, bank deposits could not be frozen by the US government. Governments have occasionally in the past frozen the bank deposits of foreign citizens and firms for political reasons. During the height of the cold war in the 1950s, Eastern bloc countries needed to maintain dollar balances to allow them to trade, but they preferred to hold them outside the United States to remove the risk of the deposits being frozen.

More importantly, however, offshore banks were not subject to the various credit restrictions imposed by the US government on its banks in an attempt to control the United States money supply and to resist the downward pressures on the US dollar which were a regular feature of the 1960s and early 1970s. This meant that offshore banks were able to pay higher interest rates on dollar deposits than banks within the US could, and for this reason they became attractive to depositors.

As well as this willingness of people to make dollar deposits outside the US, there was also a large and growing demand by foreign companies and governments to borrow US dollars. This was partly simply because world trade was growing rapidly and dollars were needed for that purpose. The demand for dollar borrowings was added to by the growth of transnational corporations whose operations were largely carried out in dollars. Later, after the oil price rise at the end of 1973, governments of third world countries needed to borrow to meet their oil bills and to finance their development plans. But why could not these dollars which were wanted be supplied from the US?

The problem again was that the US, in trying to defend the international value of the dollar, imposed many restrictions on the outflow of capital from the country, and sought also to improve the country's balance of trade. Thus, firms and governments who wished to borrow in dollars found that they could only get them from the Eurodollar banks. Again, because there were no restrictions on them, Eurobanks were able to lend at favourable interest rates. The net result of all this was that the market grew rapidly.

In other words, an attempt by the US to control its own

money and capital markets led to the growth of a market outside US control. This ability of markets to change or to develop to overcome government regulation has been an important feature of all financial markets.

9 Commodity Markets

We deal here with the markets for major agricultural products and minerals, including oil. These are vital markets for the world economy. Changes in the prices of food and of raw materials such as copper, oil, tin, rubber and aluminium have large impacts on world inflation rates and rates of economic growth. As well, these products make up a high proportion of the exports of many countries, especially of developing countries. For example, 90 per cent of Uganda's foreign exchange earnings come from coffee exports.

A wide range of products are traded in organised commodities markets. In the principal commodities markets of London, New York, and Chicago up to fifteen minerals (ranging from aluminium to zinc) and twenty-five agricultural products (including grains, coffee, cocoa, sugar, cotton, pepper, frozen orange juice and pork bellies) are handled. These numbers underestimate the range of contracts traded since markets deal with several types of grain and grades of oil. In addition, futures—promises to buy or sell commodities at agreed prices at specified future dates—have always played an important role in commodities markets. The nature and role of commodity futures are treated in 9.6 below.

9.1 THE DEMAND FOR AND SUPPLY OF COMMODITIES

From the point of view of demand, commodities may be divided into two groups—raw materials and foods. The demand for most raw materials for manufacturing industry is price inelastic because they have few good substitutes, in the short run at least. Thus, small changes in their prices have little impact on the quantities demanded. In the longer run raw materials such as cotton and rubber face competition from synthetic products and demand for them becomes more price elastic.

Demand curves for these commodities may shift dramatically. Since the vast bulk of them is consumed in the rich, industrialised countries, the demand for them depends heavily on the level of income and the rates of economic growth in those countries. Thus the world recession in the early 1980s led to sharp reductions in demand for many commodities.

Because supply of these commodities is also price inelastic, these falls in demand are bound to lead to sharp falls in prices as shown in fig. 9.1

Here initial supply and demand conditions are shown by the demand curve D_1 and the supply curve S_1 with the market

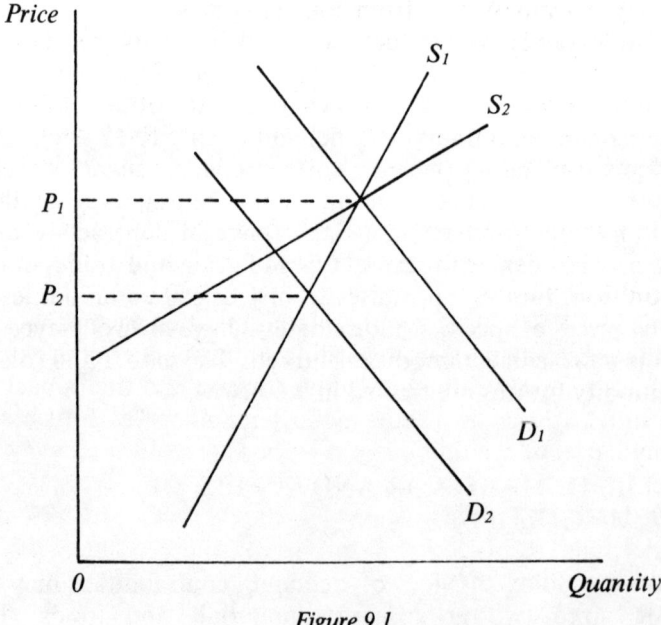

Figure 9.1

price at P_1. A recession occurs in industrial countries and the demand curve shifts down to D_2 Price falls sharply to P_2. Consider what would have happened had supply been much more price elastic (for example, as shown by the curve S_2).

The position is more complex with foods. The demand for them is more likely to be price elastic since different types of foods are often good substitutes for each other (beef versus sheep meat; butter versus margarine). On the other hand, they may well be less income elastic than raw materials since, as a group, they are essential products.

Supply of commodities is usually price inelastic because of the nature of the production processes. A large proportion of the total costs are fixed costs—costs arising from the ownership and preparation of the land, from the planting of long-living plants such as coffee or rubber trees, or from the sinking of a mine. These costs exist whether or not any of the good is produced in a particular year. As long as the price on offer is higher than the relatively low variable costs of production—those costs which are directly related to the size of the annual output—producers will wish to sell so as to obtain some return on their past capital expenditure.

However, as prices rise there is not much which they can do to increase production in the short run. A coffee tree takes at least five years to mature sufficiently to produce a commercial crop. Increasing production from a mine may require the opening up of a new seam or the introduction of new capital equipment which may take several years to obtain and put into use. In other words, most commodities have a long production cycle. The supply of a product will be less price elastic the longer its production cycle.

This low elasticity of supply of commodities means that the most interesting questions regarding supply concern the extent to which a supply curve may move around and the impact of such shifts. Just as with shifts in the demand curve, shifts in the supply curve of a commodity may produce sharp changes in price. In fig. 9.2, we begin at price P_1. An increase in supply shifts the supply curve down to S_2

Price falls steeply to P_2. This time you should consider what would have happened if demand had been much more price elastic—as given, say, by D_2.

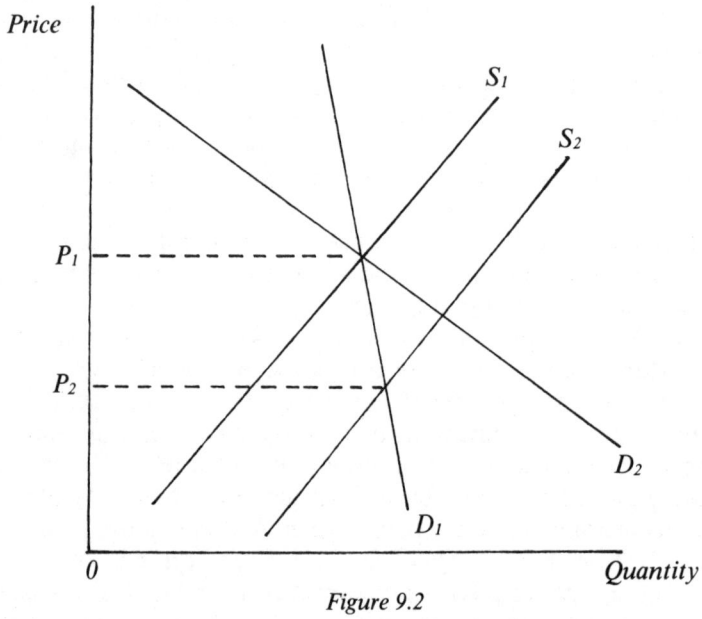

Figure 9.2

9.2 COMMODITY MARKET PROBLEMS

9.2.1 The problem of price fluctuations

It is easy to see then that world commodity prices may be subject to severe price fluctuations. These fluctuations might be caused by changes in either demand or supply conditions, although they are not equally important for all products. For example, because the demand for foods is income inelastic, demand curves may not shift much and the principal source of price movements is likely to be on the supply side of the market.

The possibility of sharp price fluctuations has led to much argument between commodity producing and consuming countries. But why might price changes be a problem? After all, the whole idea of a freely operating market is that prices should fluctuate and, indeed, should be able to change rapidly when required to equate demand and supply.

Producing countries dislike sharp price fluctuations because, as we have seen, it is difficult to adjust supply in the face of price movements. As well, price changes can lead to sudden changes in the level of prosperity of individual producers. The fact that many commodities are produced principally by poorer countries causes another problem. Most of these countries are heavily dependent on the export of one or two commodities for foreign exchange earnings and large price falls may lead to sharply lower earnings and a much reduced ability to import essential foreign goods. The difficulties associated with sudden changes in foreign exchange earnings increased markedly at the beginning of the 1980s with the onset of the international debt crisis because of the need of many developing countries to earn foreign exchange to pay high interest charges on past foreign borrowing.

Consuming countries also have a general preference for stable prices since manufacturing industries find it difficult to plan production and investment schedules when prices of important raw materials undergo frequent changes.

9.2.2 Fluctuating prices and cobwebs

Fluctuating prices can in turn lead to further instability in the relationship between demand and supply. Take the case of agricultural markets. In simple terms, we can say that the total amount of a crop grown in a season will depend on (a) the amount of land planted with the crop and (b) the weather during the growing and harvest seasons. A particular problem arises from the uncertainty of harvests. In an unregulated market, an unexpectedly good season will cause the supply curve to shift down producing a sharp fall in the price at which the product can be sold. On the other hand, bad weather during the growing season, sudden frosts just before harvest or prolonged droughts may result in small crops, a shift backwards in the supply curve to the left and a sudden increase in price.

But let us return to the question of the amount of land planted. Each year, growers must decide how much of their available land to plant or whether, indeed, to clear additional land to expand production. But they must make these decisions before they know the price they are going to get for their crop since that will depend on what all other growers do as well as on the weather and on the level of demand in the market.

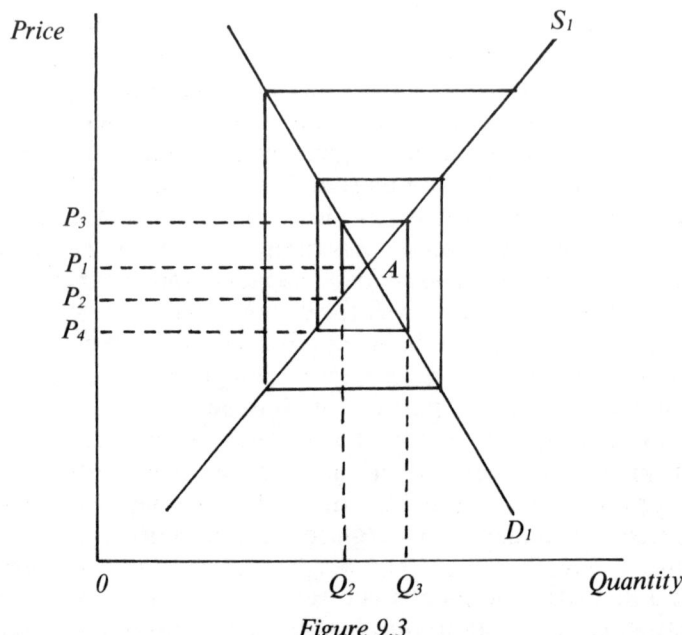

Figure 9.3

Thus there will be a strong tendency for growers to base their decisions on last year's prices for the crop. We have here a time lag—this year's output is a function of last year's price. Look now at fig. 9.3 and see what might result.

S_1 is the supply curve for the product. We have an equilibrium price established in the market at P_1 where demand and supply curves intersect. Suppose, however, that the previous year (as a result of unexpectedly good weather conditions) the price had been pushed down to P_2. Our growers have to decide how much land to plant this year. P_2 was such a low price that they decide that it will only be worthwhile to plant their best land with the crop. Other parts of their fields require more fertiliser and more care and attention and so the costs of production on them are higher—too high to make production profitable at low prices.

Suppose next that we have average weather conditions. Since all growers have planted only part of their available land, total supply will fall to Q_2 and price will shoot up to P_3. The following season growers will greatly expand their plantings on the assumption that the price will remain high. Supply will increase to Q_3 but this can only be sold at the extremely low price of P_4. Clearly, we can continue around the diagram producing a cobweb pattern.

As we have drawn the diagram, the price moves ever farther and farther away from our equilibrium price of P_1. We have constructed here an exploding cobweb and the equilibrium at A is what we referred to in Chapter one as an *unstable equilibrium*—that is, if we move away from the equilibrium position, there will be no tendency in the market to move back towards it. Indeed, quite the reverse occurs.

You should note, however, that the diagram can be drawn with different slopes of demand and supply curves to produce a gradual convergence on the equilibrium at A. In this case, the equilibrium would be *stable*. You should try drawing demand and supply curves with different slopes to see under what conditions divergent and convergent cobwebs will be produced. You will find that if the demand curve is more steeply sloped than the supply curve, you will produce a diagram with an unstable equilibrium. In the reverse case, the equilibrium will be stable. Thus, we should expect those agricultural products which face relatively elastic demand curves and have inelastic supply curves to have a stable equilibrium price. However, even with a convergent cobweb and a stable equilibrium it may take several years for a market to return to the equilibrium price and another temporary move from it may set up another cycle of disequilibrium.

No one suggests that actual growers are quite so simple-minded as this implies. No one would act only on last year's price. However, a run of high prices, for whatever reason, may persuade growers to increase plantings. And most primary commodities (as with coffee) take some years to mature and to produce a marketable crop. We have been talking of agricultural products here but the same argument can apply to minerals. High prices for several years may persuade companies to open new mines or to invest in additional capital equipment. Decisions such as these will lead to an increase in supply some years hence, by which time other market conditions may have changed.

In these circumstances markets may very well be

characterised by swings from gluts and very low prices, to shortages with very high prices and back again.

9.2.3 The problem of low average prices
For many commodities there is a strong long-run tendency for supply to outrun demand, forcing average prices to low levels. Since the second world war, commodity prices have fallen in real terms by an average of about 1 per cent a year. Primary producing countries have been especially worried in the 1980s. Between 1980 and 1985 commodity prices in US dollars averaged 7 per cent below the level of 1980 and 16 per cent below the average of 1960–80. Export earnings over this period for seventeen commodities fell from $121.3 billion to $94.5 billion. This in part was simply a reflection of the world-wide strength of the American dollar for much of this period, but commodity prices in dollars remained low as the dollar became progressively weaker during 1986 and 1987.

9.3 ATTEMPTS TO CONTROL SUPPLY

Everything we have so far said about agricultural markets has been assuming that agricultural products have to be sold at the time they are grown. In fact, they can be stored for substantial periods of time, opening up the possibility of controlling the supply of products onto the market after they have been grown. We therefore have three possible methods of control—limiting the amount of the crop planted; destroying part of the crop after it has been grown; and storing part of the crop produced.

9.3.1 Limiting supply to raise average price
Where the demand curve for a product is price inelastic, directly limiting supply can act both to raise the price level and to raise total revenue received by producers. Consider fig. 9.4.

A reduction in supply moves the supply curve up from S_1 to S_2 raising the price from P_1 to P_2, and increasing the total revenue earned by the suppliers—that is, the rectangle OP_2BQ_2 is larger than OP_1AQ_1.

The destruction of crops often seems to ordinary people to be both irrational and anti-social, especially when it is done in

Commodity markets 227

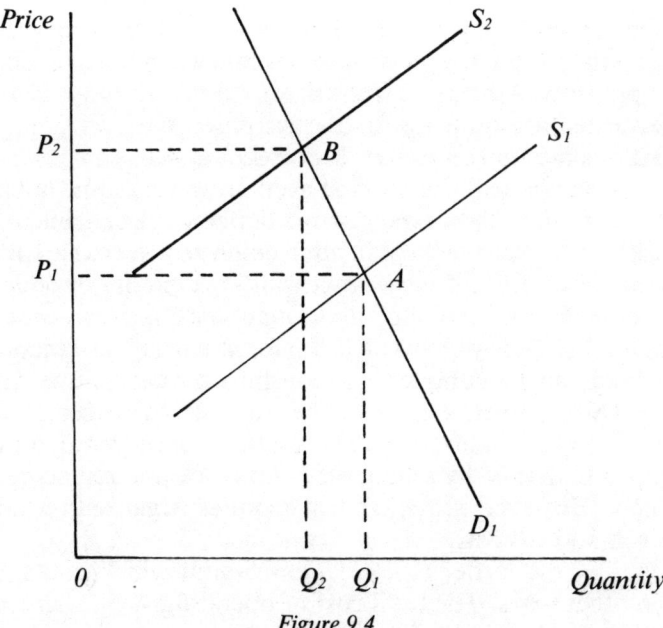

Figure 9.4

depressions when unemployment is high and many are hungry, or when there is starvation and malnutrition in other parts of the world. However, we now have a perfectly good explanation of why farmers might wish to do it.

There is another possible reason. Even if the demand curve for the product is price elastic, farmers may need to destroy part of their crop to prevent the price from falling to a level below their marketing and distribution costs. A year or two ago, for example, Israeli farmers were forced to destroy 23,000 tonnes of a bumber avocado crop to ensure that prices in Europe were sufficient to cover the costs of getting the avocadoes to the market and selling them.

We shall deal later with other attempts to limit supply and to raise market prices artificially.

9.3.2 Storage and buffer stocks
The ability to store commodities means that we may be able to reduce price fluctuations by stockpiling part of the crop in years in which large amounts are produced (thus preventing

the price from falling as low as it would otherwise do) and releasing the product from storage in years when the harvest is small, preventing the price from rising sharply in those years. Stocks which are built up for the purpose of reducing price fluctuations are known as buffer stocks.

Some disadvantages of storage need, however, to be noted. Firstly, storage is itself expensive. If buffer stock schemes are to work, stocks must be kept in good condition to enable them to be sold later. Even if the storage is of high quality, products do eventually deteriorate and may ultimately become unmarketable. As we saw in the labour market in Chapter four, there can be complex relationships between flows and stocks. Thus, sometimes it will be possible to preserve the quality of a commodity by increasing flows both into and out of the stock; that is, by selling off older stock and replacing it with new. However, stock control requires organisation and may itself add to costs.

Secondly, the buffer stock ties up capital which could be used in other ways. The total cost of operating such a scheme must therefore include a notional interest payment on that capital to reflect its opportunity cost—that is, to reflect the rate of return which could have been earned on the capital in the best alternative use for it. These storage costs and the cost of capital will need to be weighed up against the benefits of smaller price fluctuations.

Thus buffer stock schemes can only really work if there is a fairly regular pattern of good and bad years. This in turn means that buffer stock schemes are not suitable for attempting to raise the average price of an agricultural product. Consider fig. 9.5.

Suppose that in the first year, the supply curve is S_1 and the price is established at P_1 (we have drawn the supply curve vertical here on the assumption that once the product has been grown, it has either to be sold or stored). Now in the second year there is a bumper harvest and the supply curve moves out to S_2. If there were no intevention, the price would fall to P_2. In order to avoid this, Q_1Q_2 of the crop is stored, keeping the actual supply on to the market at the same level as the year before. The price remains at P_1. In year three, the harvest is poor and the supply curve moves back to S_3. We have drawn

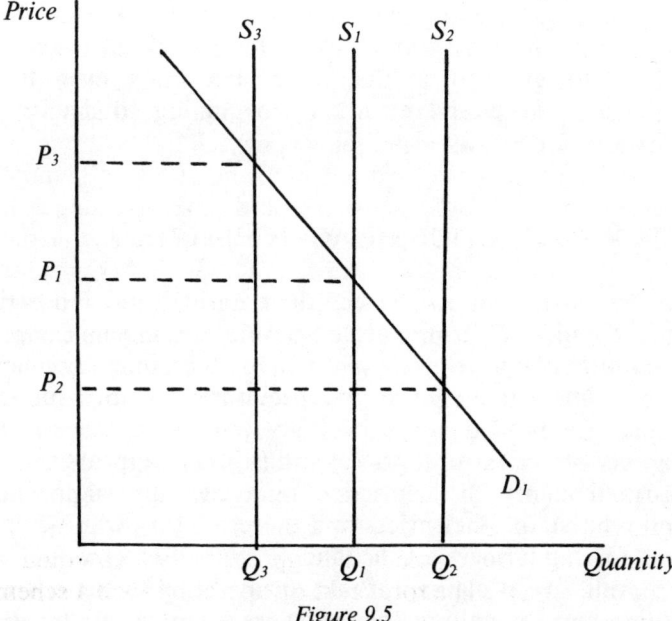

Figure 9.5

the diagram so that the shortfall in the harvest from the first year is exactly equal to Q_1Q_2. Clearly then we will be able to release the Q_1Q_2 of the product which we have stored and again supply the market with S_1.

The buffer stock scheme works perfectly. The price is kept at P_1 for all three years. Naturally, the net price to the grower is less than P_1 because of the existence of storage costs. In practice, one could never hope to fix a price at an exact level. Buffer stock schemes set a price band with a floor and a ceiling. When the price falls to the floor, the crop is bought and stored so that the price will not fall lower. The stock or part of it is sold if the price reaches the ceiling. Within this band, the price is allowed to fluctuate freely.

But what happens in our above example if we decide that the initial price P_1 is too low? Faced with the bumper crop in the second year, we choose to store more than Q_1Q_2. Suppose indeed that we store Q_3Q_2 and push the price up to P_2. Then if we are to maintain that price in the third year, we shall be unable to release any of the crop from our buffer stock. If we have an average or good crop the following year, we shall have to add even more to our stocks. Our stocks are likely to continue to grow over the years, becoming ever more expensive to keep and eventually beginning to decline in quality.

9.4 THE PROTECTION OF AGRICULTURE

Many countries act to protect their agricultural industries against competition from abroad. Several arguments are used for so doing. We have already seen some economic arguments for government intervention in agriculture: (a) price support schemes are needed to protect growers from the natural instability of agricultural prices; and (b) there appears to be a long-run tendency for the prices of many agricultural products to fall relative to other prices and therefore for farm incomes to fall, forcing farmers off the land.

As well, it is claimed that social benefits arise from maintaining a flourishing domestic agriculture. Thus we might add: (c) people are kept on the land instead of moving to already overcrowded cities in search of non-existent jobs; (d) to the extent that people should, in the long run, move from the land, the move should be slow and controlled; (e) a country with a healthy agriculture is less dependent on potential enemies for vital products and will be more able to be self-sufficient if the need arises during wartime; and, (f) farming preserves traditional ways of life which are in themselves desirable.

The problem is that many of these arguments are difficult to evaluate. Further, agricultural support has on some occasions given quite the wrong signals to producers and has led to unwanted expansion of food production. This has, on some occasions at least, involved social costs—for example, through the destruction of old rural landscapes and the natural habitats of birds and animals; soil erosion; pollution of water resulting from the heavy fertilisation of fields or from pest control.

The costs and benefits from the protection of agriculture are extremely difficult to quantify and are seldom carefully weighed up. In most cases it probably occurs not because it has economic advantages for the country as a whole but because it can be seen to be preserving jobs and because of the political power of farming communities. However, our interest here is not with the rights and wrongs of protection of agriculture but with the methods of protection used and their effects on agricultural markets.

Broadly, we can divide the methods of protecting agriculture into two: (a) those which allow prices to be determined freely in the market place but which pay subsidies or grants to domestic farmers (often called deficiency payments); (b) those which act to force market prices up above normal competitive levels. Let us consider what each of these involves.

9.4.1 The effects of subsidies

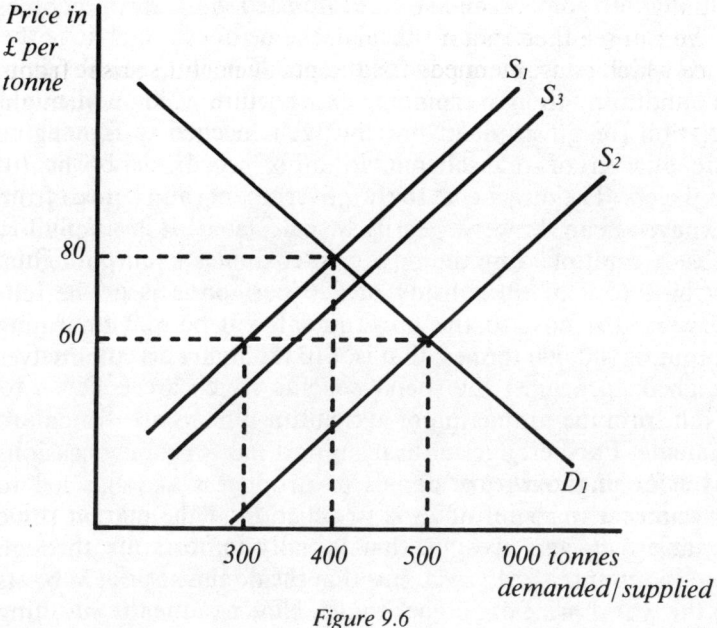

Figure 9.6

We assume that the supply conditions for the domestic wheat industry without government assistance are expressed by S_1 in fig. 9.6. Given the demand curve, D_1, we can see that if no imports were allowed, the price would settle at £80 per tonne. However, let us assume that the world price of wheat is £60 per tonne and that any amount of it can be imported at that price. We can see that at this price, people will demand 500,000 tonnes per year but that the domestic industry will supply only 300,000 tonnes. The remaining 200,000 tonnes will be imported.

Next, suppose that the home government pays domestic producers a subsidy of £20 on each tonne they produce. This effectively lowers their costs and shifts their supply curve down to S_2. Home producers are now able to supply all of the wheat demanded at a price of £60 per tonne. Imports disappear from the market. Of course, an intermediate policy would be possible. The government could pay a smaller subsidy, just enough, say, to move the domestic supply curve down to S_3. Then home producers would supply more wheat than they did initially, but some would still be imported.

We can see then that a subsidy scheme does not change the price which consumers pay for the product. But the subsidy is an addition to government expenditure and additional taxation (or government borrowing) is needed to finance it. The burden of the scheme, in other words, is borne by taxpayers. The direct cost to the government (and hence to the taxpayers) can, however, easily be calculated. It is simply the subsidy multiplied by the now greater domestic output. Thus in fig. 9.6, if a full subsidy of £20 per tonne is granted to growers, the cost to the government will be £20 times the output of 500,000 tonnes: that is, £10 million. This can then be weighed up against the social benefits which are believed to result from the protection of agriculture.

9.4.2 Raising market price

An alternative to subsidies is to act to raise the market price artificially. Again assume that initially imports are allowed into the country freely and thus that the domestic price is equal to the world price of £60 per tonne. Now assume that in some way the domestic price is raised to £80 per tonne. At that price the quantity demanded will be only 400,000 tonnes—all of which will be supplied by the domestic industry. Again, imports disappear from the market. As before, an intermediate position could be adopted—raising the price to something between £60 and £80 per tonne, reducing the quantity demanded to a smaller extent and leaving some room for imports.

The burden of the protection of agriculture is being borne here by the consumers. Obviously, they pay a higher price. To the extent that they continue to buy the product, they suffer a real income loss—their money incomes will now buy fewer goods in total. In addition, the increase in the price of the product relative to other products causes them to switch among products—a substitution effect which also lowers the total satisfaction received by consumers from their money incomes. The increase in price acts in the same way as a tax, but it is in effect a tax on consumers of the product rather than the tax on all taxpayers needed to finance a subsidy.

There is another aspect to the loss suffered by consumers as a consequence of the price increase. The nature of consumer demand is such that when a price is established in a market

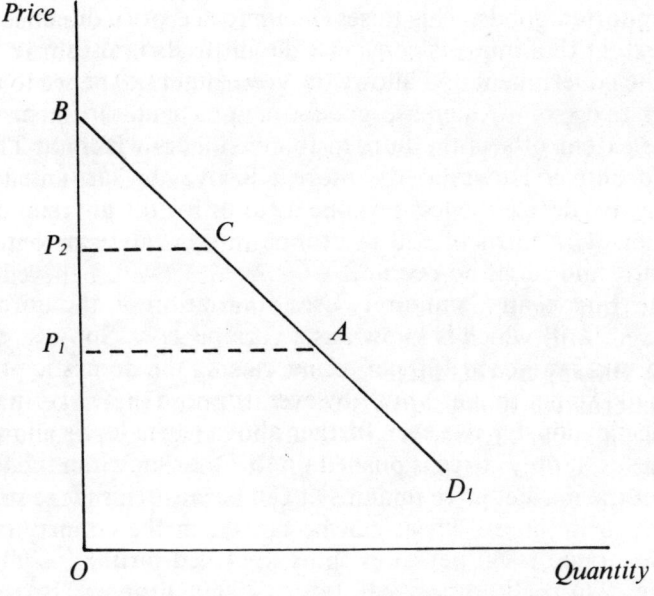

Figure 9.7

(say £60 per tonne), there will be some consumers who obtain the product at that price but who would have been willing to pay a higher price. These consumers are said to enjoy consumer surplus. The amount above the market price which a consumer would have been willing to pay is a measure of the surplus enjoyed at the existing market price. It follows that the higher the market price is for any given demand curve, the less consumer surplus there will be. We can illustrate this point in fig. 9.7.

At price P_1 consumer surplus is shown as the area of the triangle above the market price, P_1 (that is, P_1BA). An increase in price to P_2 reduces consumer surplus to the area P_2BC.

Because the cost of protection through raising the market price is borne by consumers in this way, it is not as clear exactly what the protection is costing the economy as it is when protection is through the payment of a subsidy to growers.

9.4.3 Tariffs and variable levies

The best known form of protection is the application of a tariff on imported goods. This raises the imported price directly. To the extent that imports continue, the tariff also raises revenue for the government and allows the government either to lower other taxes or to increase government expenditure. This to some extent offsets the burden to consumers which we have noted above. However, the more effective the tariff is as a protective device the less revenue it raises for the government. Obviously, a tariff of £20 per tonne in fig. 9.6 keeps out all imports and raises no revenue.

The European Community uses a variation on the normal or fixed tariff which is known as a variable levy. Suppose our fixed tariff is indeed £20 per tonne, raising the domestic price level to £80 per tonne. Now, however, suppose that costs in the domestic industry rise even further above world levels and the domestic supply curve is pushed up to S_4, as shown in fig. 9.8.

But the market price remains at £80 because this is the price at which imported wheat can be landed in the country (the world price of £60 per tonne plus the fixed tariff of £20 per tonne). Domestic supply will fall to 200,000 tonnes. Imports will be 200,000 tonnes. Suppose, however, that the government

Commodity markets 235

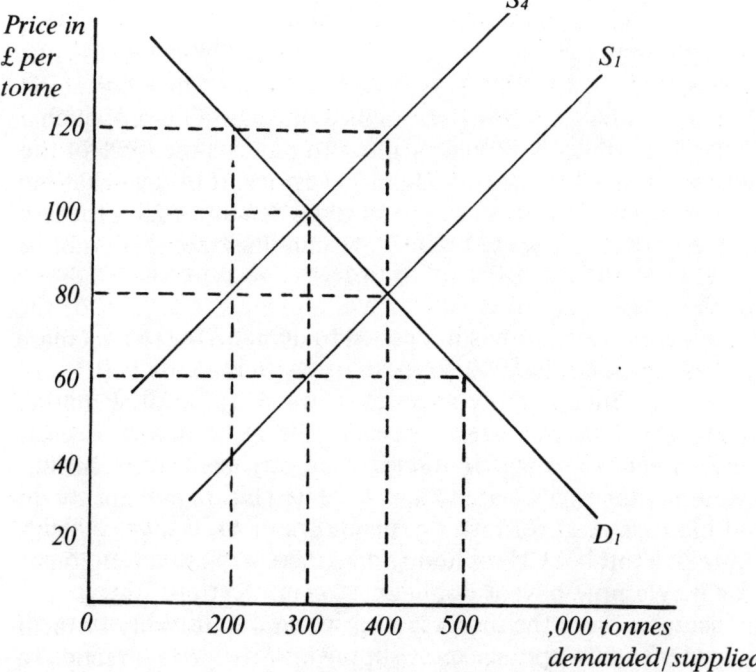

Figure 9.8

does not wish this to happen. Then it may act to increase the tariff automatically to £40 per tonne in order to keep imports out. In other words, the tariff (or levy) is varied to reflect the difference between domestic and foreign costs of production, irrespective of what that difference is. It follows that if foreign producers begin to produce more cheaply, pushing the world price below £60 per tonne, the levy will also be increased. In this way the variable levy completely detaches the domestic price from the going world price.

Can you see what extra problem results? With a fixed tariff, although the domestic industry receives protection, there remains an incentive for it to keep its costs down as close to the world level as possible. That is, there is an incentive for the industry to increase its efficiency. With a variable levy, this is no longer so. The domestic industry knows that it will continue to be protected no matter what the cost to the consumer.

9.4.4 Agricultural lakes and mountains

We can use fig. 9.8 to show another problem which sometimes arises while artificially increasing market price. Suppose that the government decides that domestic production should remain at 400,000 tonnes irrespective of what happens to domestic costs of production. As before, we assume that domestic costs have risen so that the domestic supply curve is S_4. In order to keep home production at its previous level, it must raise the tariff to £60 in order to push up the domestic price of £120 per tonne.

But see now what has happened to demand for the product. It has fallen to 200,000 tonnes. At the new market price of £120 per tonne, supply exceeds demand by 200,000 tonnes. The only way this high price can be sustained is for the government to engage in intervention buying. That is, it must itself buy the excess supply and store it. This, of course, means an increase in government expenditure of £120 times 200,000 tonnes, a total of £24 million and an increase in taxation to pay for it. We now have a double cost of protection—the cost to consumers from the increase in price *and* an increase in taxes in order to buy up the excess supply.

If a government continues to maintain such a high price for any period of time it will quickly build up large stores of the product—wine lakes, butter mountains and so on. We thus have here a simple representation of the problem which is at the heart of many of the arguments over the European Community's Common Agricultural Policy (CAP).

9.4.5 Export subsidies and dumping

But what can the government then do with these lakes and mountains? The usual answer is to attempt to export them. We have seen, however, that the act of protection has meant that domestic prices are higher than world prices. Thus, a government may buy excess production from its own farmers at high prices and then sell it at a loss on world markets. That is, the government provides a subsidy to its exporters and *dumps* the product on the world market.

In many cases, this will force down the world market price even further, providing hardship for growers in other countries. These countries will often, in turn, retaliate by subsidising their agriculture, causing a trade war among producing countries as each one battles to preserve its market share. A struggle of this kind has developed in recent years between the US and the EC, with both countries spending well in excess of $25 billion dollars a year in export subsidies. In case study 9.1 we provide an example of export subsidies in action through the EC sugar pricing regime.

CASE STUDY 9.1: THE EUROPEAN COMMUNITY AND WORLD SUGAR PRICES

We could take almost any aspect of the European Community's Common Agricultural Policy to illustrate agricultural protection and interference with the operation of markets. We have chosen the sugar regime, but it is worth collecting information about other Community programmes to support points made in the text.

The EC obtains its sugar from two sources. It is itself a grower of beet sugar. In addition, some member countries, in particular the UK, import cane sugar from the countries in the African, Caribbean and Pacific trading group. At one time the EC as a whole was a net importer of sugar. However, under the Common Agricultural Policy, the Community established a strongly protectionist policy which led to considerable growth in beet production.

Member countries were given production quotas. These quotas were of three types: 'A' quotas which were meant to be rough estimates of national demand; 'B' quotas which were for sugar grown above the country's needs but which were related to production levels over a fixed reference period; and 'C' quotas for extra sugar grown above 'A' and 'B' levels. High prices were guaranteed to growers for amounts within the 'A' and 'B' quotas. This led to a high price for sugar for consumers within the EC, often well above world sugar prices.

These high prices tended to slow down the growth of demand for sugar but encouraged producers to expand production to meet quotas and then to push for higher quotas. Production began to outstrip consumption and the

Community found itself with sugar to export. This sugar was dumped on the world market—that is, it was subsidised and sold for prices well below the cost of production.

By 1985, the EC was growing 13 million tonnes of sugar and continuing to import 1.3 million tonnes of cane sugar under the Lomé convention which was intended to assist developing countries linked to the EC. Against this, Community consumption was down to only 9.5 million tonnes. Community growers were guaranteed a price of £350 a metric tonne. If the world price was lower than this, the shortfall was intended to be made up from a fund derived from levies on producers. Thus the scheme was, from the point of view of the EC budget, meant to be self-financing, although in practice it was not. The high guaranteed price, however, encouraged production and export.

Between 1977 and 1985, the Community's exports rose from 1 per cent of Western countries' exports to 25 per cent, mostly going to the Soviet Union and to Arab countries. This vast increase in supply, together with increased protectionism in the US, drove the world price down catastrophically. In 1985 it fell to £62 a tonne, less than 20 per cent of the price guaranteed to EC growers and well below the cost of production of even the most efficient producers.

Once this position was reached it became politically difficult to persuade member countries to reduce their production, no matter how inefficient the production was in terms of resource use. The combination of high prices and quotas had led, as they are likely to do, to the preservation of inefficient production patterns and to a struggle by member countries to maximise their market shares.

The sufferers were Community consumers who were, in effect, paying a tax to subsidise Community growers, and the sugar industry in the rest of the world which had to try to cope with much lower world prices.

9.4.6 Non-tariff barriers to trade

Governments may also act directly to limit the import of foreign products through the application of import quotas. Importers must apply to the government for import licences and these licences restrict the amount of the product which can be brought in. The outcome from quotas is similar to that from tariffs. The quotas reduce total supply and push up prices, leaving the burden of protection to be borne by consumers.

The similarity is even greater if the government also raises revenue by selling (or auctioning) the import licences. Quotas are, however, a more certain protective device than tariffs since, with quotas, the same quantity of imports is allowed in irrespective of any change in the relative costs of the domestic and foreign industry. Their effects are thus very similar to those arising from the operation of a variable levy.

In both agricultural and manufacturing industries in recent years we have seen a large growth in so-called voluntary export restrictions (VERs). These are quotas under another name. Instead of the importing country imposing a quota on imports, the exporting country 'voluntarily' agrees to restrict its exports to the importing country. Here, of course, the importing country cannot raise revenue from the sale of import licences. The increase in price resulting from the application of a VER increases the profit margin of the exporting country. Thus, although they sell less than they would like, it is preferable for them to accept a VER than to have an import quota imposed on them by the importing country. New Zealand operates a VER limiting the export of lamb to the European Community.

Governments also act indirectly to restrict the number of imports and/or to cause the costs of imports to increase by the use of regulations and administrative practices. For example a government's health regulations may specify the way in which a product is to be produced or may require foreign suppliers of a product to be specially licensed before their products are allowed to enter the country. Such regulations may result from genuine health concerns. It remains that they can be and are used to protect domestic industry by making life more difficult for foreign producers.

Governments frequently slow down imports by increasing the administrative complexity associated with importing. This again increases costs to the importer and can lead to agricultural imports being spoiled.

9.5 INTERNATIONAL COMMODITY PRICES

In the previous section we have been talking about attempts by countries to raise domestic prices above world price levels in order to protect domestic industry. Here we are concerned with attempts to raise the world price of a commodity. We can distinguish two kinds of attempts to do this.

Firstly, supplying countries may combine in a cartel to limit supply and by so doing force up world price. The best known international cartel is OPEC (the Organisation of Petroleum Exporting Countries). We can use it to illustrate the problems facing cartels.

Secondly, sellers and buyers may get together and agree on measures to control the market and to regulate the world price. International Commodity Agreements which have operated in, for instance, the markets for coffee, cocoa and tin, are of this kind.

9.5.1 International cartels

For an international cartel to succeed it needs (a) to include most or all of the major producing countries; (b) to be able to agree on the desired price and hence the desired level of total supply; (c) to be able to agree on how that total supply is to be divided up amongst member countries; (d) to be able to enforce the agreed allocations. In recent years, OPEC has failed on all of these counts and so has had only a limited influence on the world price of oil.

Although the thirteen members of OPEC continue to produce around 40 per cent of world oil, important oil producers remain outside the organisation including Mexico, Bahrain and the UK. Sometimes, non-OPEC members have gone along with OPEC wishes to reduce supply, but the potential remains for non-members to frustrate OPEC policy by expanding their supply and hence taking a greater share of the total market.

There have been many policy disagreements among members. Some countries (in particular Iran and Iraq—it hardly helps a cartel to have a war being fought between two of its members!) have had a strong need for foreign exchange earnings and have wished to maximise these earnings, even if this has meant a lower oil price. Apart from such particular needs of countries, there is a strategic problem. Too strong a limit on supply, leading to a very sharp price increase acts to encourage consuming countries to reduce their dependence on oil and may damage future demand for the product. As well, it may lead to oil companies increasing their efforts to find new oil reserves outside the OPEC countries, thus undermining the long-term position of OPEC.

Further, a difficulty arises from the very nature of cartels—a variation of the free-rider problem which we considered in relation to public goods in 1.3.6. The problem here is that a member country may feel that it can increase its production beyond its agreed production quota without affecting the world price. Yet if all members attempt to do this, total production will increase significantly, world price will fall and all producers will be worse off. However, each country knows that if other members break the rules and produce and sell extra amounts but it does not, the price will fall and it will lose out both in terms of revenue and in terms of market share. Thus, there is an incentive to break the rules in case other members do so. It follows that the operation of a cartel such as OPEC requires considerable discipline among members.

The final difficulty is that the organisation has very little power to prevent individual members from breaking the rules. It is not much help to expel offending countries from the organisation since that merely leaves them free to undermine OPEC plans from outside. All it can do is to appeal for members to show a united front and to act in everyone's joint interest. At times OPEC has maintained its influence over world prices because Saudi Arabia, the largest producer, has been willing to act as a 'swing producer'. That is, when other countries have expanded their production beyond their agreed levels, Saudi Arabia has decreased its production in order to keep total OPEC production from rising. However, this necessarily means a loss of market share for Saudi Arabia and when it has tired of this role and sought to expand its own exports, world oil prices have been driven down.

9.5.2 International commodity agreements
There are two major advantages in having consuming and

producing countries working together to control the price of a commodity. The first is a practical one. The presence of consuming countries in the agreement should remove the possibility of the rules being broken by a producing country exporting amounts above its quota to a non-member country and having it shipped on from there to a consuming country. In fact, commodity agreements have been broken in this way, for example the International Coffee Agreement where coffee going through non-member countries on its way to its final destination is referred to as 'tourist coffee'. It remains that consumers can be asked to limit their purchases to supplies coming from member countries.

The second advantage is a theoretical one. Consuming countries have a natural interest in obtaining the commodity as cheaply as they can and hence have an interest in its being produced by the most efficient producers. Consuming countries should, therefore, be on the side of new, efficient producing countries which are trying to obtain a place in world markets. This also, however, does not work well in practice. Production quotas associated with ICA's often preserve past production patterns and make it difficult for new and efficient producers to increase their market share. This again has been a particular problem with coffee.

The problem of having consumers and producers both being party to an agreement on supplies and price is that their interests are so different that it is always extremely difficult for them to reach agreement. The history of international commodity agreements is one of long and often sterile negotiations and of agreements which break down or are not renewed when they expire. Consider case study 9.2 on the collapse of the International Tin Council.

CASE STUDY 9.2: THE COLLAPSE OF THE INTERNATIONAL TIN COUNCIL

The International Tin Council (ITC) was established in 1956 to stabilise the world price of tin, both by imposing quotas on producing countries and by operating a buffer stock scheme. The Council operated this scheme through metals brokers on the London Metals Exchange (LME), building up a stockpile of tin in the process.

In 1981, the sixth international tin agreement was signed, to run until 1988. By this time there were twenty-two member governments of the council—both producing and consuming countries. However, one of the world's biggest and cheapest producers, Brazil, was not a member, while companies in the third biggest producing country, Thailand, smuggled tin in order to circumvent quotas. Thus, world supply was exceeding demand at the Tin Council's target price. The world's biggest consuming nation, the United States, also did not participate in the agreement. Although conditions seemed to suggest that the time had come to sell stocks and to allow the tin price to fall, member governments could not agree on actions of this kind.

As a result, the ITC's stockpile grew steadily to an unstable level, reaching 85,000 tonnes (the equivalent of world demand for eight months) by October 1985. The member governments were unwilling to supply the ITC with sufficient funds to maintain the target price and, in any case, the Council had already bought up all the tin it was allowed to do under the 1981 agreement.

It tried to overcome its problem by operating on the LME's tin futures market—buying forward quantities of tin which it could not ultimately afford to take delivery of. These contracts had to be constantly rolled over, and the Council borrowed heavily from banks (using tin as collateral for its loans).

This process could not continue. Finally, in October 1985, the Council ran out of money and could not meet outstanding contracts. It defaulted on its contracts and loans to the tune of £900 million. The LME suspended trading in tin, the price at the time standing at $8,140 a tonne. After attempts to rescue the market had collapsed, the LME closed down all trading in tin in March 1986, ruling that all outstanding contracts should be settled at a price of $6,250 a tonne.

The losers were the banks, the metal brokers of the LME, and the tin-producing countries. With the ITC no longer intervening to support prices and with now a huge stockpile of tin in the hands of brokers and banks, the world price of tin quickly fell on secondary markets to below $4,000 a tonne—well below the cost of production of most tin producing countries. The biggest sufferers of all were the already-subsidised high cost producers in Cornwall (where the cost of production was £7,500 a tonne) and in Bolivia (where the cost of production was over £10,000 a tonne). Since tin exports had previously provided 40 per cent of its export revenues, the blow to Bolivia was devastating.

The tin episode provides an excellent example of trying to maintain too high a price for a commodity, especially where not all major producers and consumers are members of the agreements. It also provides an example of the poor use of futures markets. They can be used to protect countries and firms against future uncertainty. Here, they simply allowed an untenable position to be maintained for longer, with the result that the crash when it finally came was much bigger than it would otherwise have been.

Even if production quotas and target prices can be agreed between producers and consumers, it is very difficult for producers to keep to their production or export quotas. The international agreement has to be translated into domestic policy. A country may agree to reduce its output of a product, but then will need to adopt policies at home to encourage or to force suppliers to reduce production. In many cases this is extremely difficult to do for domestic political reasons. The problem is much worse for agricultural commodities because of the uncertainties about the size of harvests.

9.5.3 Side-effects of supply controls
Further, all of the many schemes that have been tried over the years in various countries to limit supply, especially of agricultural products, have had undesirable side-effects. For example, in Australia, production quotas of sugar are attached to holdings of land and all growers are guaranteed the same price for their quota, irrespective of their level of efficiency. This ossifies production patterns as well as distorting the market for land. In the United States at one time farmers were paid *not* to produce corn; this was so successful that there was

insufficient corn grown to feed the number of pigs being raised. Farmers were then paid not to raise pigs so that they wouldn't eat the corn which wasn't being grown!

'Set-aside' policies are being increasingly advocated for the EEC to overcome problems of over-supply. Payments are made to farmers for setting land aside—that is, for taking land out of production. However, this may lead to only the worst land being taken out of production while the best land is farmed even more intensively than before. Total production may not fall.

Finally, many policies aimed at limiting supply have a considerable impact on the distribution of income. In the last few years in the European Community, quotas have been placed on the number of dairy cattle which can be raised by farmers. Because these quotas had to be applied from a particular date, they inevitably affected farmers unevenly. Even if the overall limitations are justified, some farmers will experience great hardship.

9.6 FUTURES MARKETS IN COMMODITIES

An alternative way for consumers to attempt to protect themselves against uncertain future prices of vital commodities is to make use of futures markets. By so doing, traders are said to be hedging against the risk of future price changes. In the past twenty years futures markets have grown up within foreign exchange and equities markets. However, they have existed in commodities markets for a very long time.

Future markets in commodities operate in the same way as do forward markets in foreign exchange. A producer who knows that she will need a particular amount of cocoa in, say, six months' time but who is worried that the price of cocoa might rise substantially before then can protect herself by entering into a contract to purchase the cocoa in six months time at a price fixed at the time the contract is arranged. Futures contracts to sell commodities can also be entered into, allowing people to hedge against the risk of a falling price. Which groups of traders may wish to do this?

The operation of futures markets leads to prices being

Table 9.1

Sugar ($ per tonne)

Raw	Close	Previous	High/Low
Dec	158.80	161.00	161.00 159.20
Mar	164.80	167.20	168.00 164.00
May	166.00	168.40	169.00 166.00
Aug	167.80	170.00	170.00
Oct	169.00	171.20	171.60 169.00
Dec	173.00	174.00	
Mar	178.80	180.00	

White	Close	Previous	High/Low
Dec	190.50	193.50	193.50 190.50
Mar	196.60	199.00	200.00 196.40
May	200.00	205.00	203.80 203.50
Aug	203.00	207.00	207.50 203.00
Oct	204.00	210.00	208.50 204.50
Dec	205.00	211.50	209.20 209.20
Mar	208.00	217.50	---

Turnover: Raw 2226 (1992) lots of 50 tonnes.
White 1226 (1786)
Paris- White (FFr per tonne): Dec 1112, Mar 1148, May 1175, Aug 1210, Oct 1220 Dec 1231.

COCOA £/tonne

	Close	Previous	High/Low
Dec	1106	1114	1117 1104
Mar	1139	1147	1151 1137
May	1162	1169	1171 1160
Jly	1186	1190	1192 1183
Sep	1205	1210	1213 1203
Dec	1228	1235	1235 1227
Mar	1253	1259	1260 1252

Turnover: 3897 (3548) lots of 10 tonnes
ICCO indicator prices (SDRs per tonne). Daily price for November 3: 1430.67 (1440.78).10 day average for November 4: 1463.15 (1466.27).

COFFEE £/tonne

	Close	Previous	High/Low
Nov	1245	1250	1246 1240
Jan	1277	1285	1279 1274
Mar	1303	1310	1304 1297
May	1326	1338	1327 1321

Table 9.1 (continued)

COFFEE £/tonne

	Close	Previous	High/Low
Jly	1346	1365	1348 1341
Sep	1368	1390	1368
Nov	1400	1418	

Turnover: 2048 (5305) lots of 15 tonnes
ICO indicator prices (US cents per pound) for November 3: Comp. daily 113.30 (113.20).15 day average 111.89 (111.93).

Source: Financial Times 5th November, 1987

quoted for the delivery of commodities well into the future. Table 9.1, from the *Financial Times* of the 5th November, 1987 showed delivery prices for cocoa for more than fifteen months ahead.

In recent years, the trading of options contracts on commodities has increased considerably, giving their buyers the right to buy or sell a commodity at an agreed price at a future date but without imposing the obligation to do so.

9.6.1 Speculation in futures markets

Just as in the case of forward exchange markets, commodity futures provide opportunities for speculation. For example, a speculator who, on the 5th November, 1987 had thought that the price of cocoa in July would be less than the quoted price in our table of £1186 per tonne could have signed a futures contract agreeing to sell cocoa at that price in July. If she had been correct and the world cocoa price had fallen, she would have been able to enter the spot or physical market just before the expiry of the futures contract and buy at the current price (say of £1100 per tonne) and then close the futures contract by selling at the agreed price of £1186, thus making a profit. Of course, if the world price of cocoa had risen in the intervening six months, the speculator would have lost.

It is interesting to consider what effect speculation has on commodity prices. Some economists argue that speculation, by its nature, must necessarily be stabilising. If this is true, speculation should be helping to overcome the problem of fluctuating commodity prices which we discussed earlier. That should mean that we do not need government intervention or international arrangements to steady prices. Uncontrolled markets could be trusted to produce desirable outcomes.

The argument that speculation is stabilising is simple and persuasive. It assumes that speculators are professional risk-takers who are only trading in order to make a profit. If a speculator is to make a profit, she must buy when the market price is low (thus increasing demand at low prices and preventing the price from falling further) and sell when the price is high (increasing supply at high prices and preventing the price from rising further). Thus, speculation should act to cut off the peaks and troughs of fluctuating prices. If speculators do not do this, they will lose and will soon go out of business. Only successful speculators will remain and they will be acting to stabilise the market price.

Many economists, however, are sceptical about the effectiveness of this process. As with forward exchange markets, speculators include merchant speculators as well as pure speculators. These are companies which are actually going to make use of the physical commodity in production but who nonetheless try from time to time to make additional profits through speculation. We have mentioned an example of failed speculation of this kind by the chocolate makers, Rowntrees, in Chapter three.

Pure speculators also lose. In addition, from the point of view of speculation, commodity markets have become an extension of markets in financial assets. In the past, when equities markets slumped, commodities prices often rose as people withdrew their funds from equities markets and sought a different home for them. In the stockmarket collapse of 1987, commodities prices (other than gold) also suffered as people sold to meet losses sustained in other markets.

Certainly, the considerable price variations which continue to exist in both commodity and foreign exchange markets throw into great doubt the notion that speculation is stabilising. It is even possible that in thin markets, speculators can set out deliberately to destabilise a market in order to make a profit. To the extent that speculators can force up the price of a commodity or a currency by buying it and this price rise causes other people to enter the market also to buy, speculators will be able to sell out at a profit. Alternatively, they may try to depress the market price by selling, hoping to buy back in at a lower price.

We have seen that commodity agreements and other forms of intervention in commodities markets often either fail to work or produce undesirable and costly side effects. It remains, however that in many cases, markets left to themselves will also produce unfortunate results. There certainly seems to be little evidence that speculation acts to ensure that free markets produce satisfactory outcomes. In any case, as with all the other markets we have looked at in this book, governments and market participants themselves are unwilling to allow commodity markets to follow an untrammelled course.

Index

active balances, 119
added worker effect, 94
advertising, 34-8, 68, 72
agriculture, protection of, 230-40
Akerlof, George 45
arbitrage
 exchange rate, 208
 interest rate, 209-10

bandwagon effects, 41-2
Bank of England, 113, 115, 125, 127-9
 bill market operations, 131-44
bank credit multiplier, 117
bank lending
 and money supply, 125-7, 133
 control of, 127-9
 interest rates and demand for, 131-44
banks and money supply, 113-17, 123
'Big Bang', 161, 185
bills, 109-12
 supply of, 129-30
 demand for, 130-1
 holders of, 130
 issuers of, 129

maturity bands, 135
price and discount rate, 110-11
'Black Monday', 182-3, 188
bonds, 145-50
 auctions, 163
 coupons, 146
 demand for, 152-60
 government sales of, 156, 161-3
 holders of, 152-3
 interest rates, 154-9
 issuers of, 151
 market equilibrium, 153-4
 partial tenders, 163
 prices, 147-9, 154-5
 supply of, 150-2, 158
 trading in, 160-4
 valuation of, 147
 yields, 149-50
BP, 176, 184, 186
buffer stocks, 227-30, 242-4
'bulldog' bonds, 151

capital gains
 and demand for bonds, 153, 162
'Chinese walls', 186
Coase, Ronald, 6-7
commodities

cartels in, 240–1
controlling supply of,
  226–30
demand for and supply of,
  219–21
price fluctuations of, 222–6
Common Agricultural Policy,
  236–8, 245
competition
  perfect and imperfect, 54,
    57, 58
  policy 73–6
concentration ratio, 62
consumer surplus, 233–4
costs, fixed and variable, 221
cross-subsidisation, 70–2

debentures, 151, 165
debt/income ratio, 157
deficiency payments, 231–2
demand for money, 118–2
demand for money, 118–21
  and income, 119
  and interest rates, 120
  precautionary, 119
  speculative, 120
  transactions, 119
dependence effect, 35
discount market, 131–44
discount rate, 110–11
discouraged worker effect, 94
disequilibrium, 16, 223–6
'Duke of York' tactics, 162
dumping of exports, 236–8

economies of scale, 68, 72, 74,
  75
elasticities
  in commodities markets,
    220–2
  cross, 29
  income, 29–30, 221
  interest, 30

price, 13–16, 38, 43, 220–2
equilibrium, 16, 19, 45
  of bonds market, 153–4
  of equities market, 174
  of foreign exchange
    market, 190–1
  of labour market, 88–90, 92
  of money market, 121–2
  stable, 19, 225
  unstable, 20, 225
equities, 165–8
  demand for, 171–5, 178–81
  dividends, 167
  earnings, 167
  holders of, 174
  issues of, 176
  market equilibrium, 174
  p/e ratio, 168
  prices, 172–4, 178–84
  risk, 166
  supply of, 169–71, 175–7
  trading in, 187–9
  valuation of, 172–4
Eurodollars, 216–18
European Monetary System,
  215
exchange rates
  defined, 190
  and the demand for labour, 81
  and developing countries,
    200–1
  direct quotation of, 193
  effective, 195–6
  fixed, 213–14
  forward, 205–11
  importance to governments
    of, 199
  indirect quotation of, 193
  managed, 215–16
  multiple, 202–3, 213
  real, 196–7, 199
  spot, 193–5, 206
  tourist, 194–5

expectations, 10, 32–3, 34
  and share prices, 180–1, 182–4, 188
  and bond prices, 154–5, 156, 159
  and exchange rates, 198, 204, 206

Financial Times, xi, 62, 136–8, 141, 143, 170, 190, 192–6, 210, 246–7
fix-price markets, 16–18, 20
  and the labour market, 78, 103–5
  and the foreign exchange market, 213–16
flex-price markets, 18–19, 78
  and the labour market, 90–2
foreign currency
  auctions of, 203
  demand for and supply of, 197–201
  earnings of from commodities, 223
forward markets, 2, 10, 11, 205–12
'free riders', 5, 241
fundamentals, in share valuation, 180, 183
future markets, 11, 219, 243–4, 245–9

Galbraith, J. K., 35, 65
'gilts' – see bonds
government
  bond sales, 156, 158, 161–3
  and Eurodollar markets, 216–18,
  and interest rates, 131–44
  intervention in foreign exchange markets, 201–6, 213–16

and labour markets, 101–2
policy and share prices, 179–83
and privatisations, 23, 184, 186
and regulation of markets, 4, 7, 8, 45–53, 73–6, 176, 185–7
treasury bills, 110
Group of Five, 203, 205

human capital, 79, 98

idle balances, 120
income distribution, 33, 84–5
  and agricultural policy, 244–5
  and multiple exchange rates, 203
income effects, 87
inflation, 33
  and exchange rates, 199–201
  and real wages, 102
informal economy, see unofficial economy
information, 8–10, 20, 46, 49, 51–4, 72
  asymmetric, 45
  in the labour market, 90–1, 97
insurance, 10–11
integration of firms
  backward, 69
  forward, 69
  horizontal, 67–9
  lateral, 70
  vertical, 69–70, 72
interest rates
  and bank lending, 133–4
  Bank of England's influence, 131–43
  and consumption, 34
  and the cost of capital, 78
  and demand for bonds, 154–60

and demand for money, 121, 133
and Eurodollars, 217
and exchange rates, 204, 205, 209–10, 214
international commodity agreements, 241–2
international liquidity, 191
International Monetary Fund, 200, 213, 215
International Tin Council, collapse of, 242–4

J-curve, 198

Keynes, J. M., 120–1, 133, 181

labour
  contracts, 80, 102–3
  demand for, 78–86
  supply of, 86–90, 92
labour force, 94–5
labour markets,
  distinctive features of, 93–103
  and housing markets, 96
  internal, 80, 103
  primary, 80, 104
  secondary, 80, 104
  segmented, 104
Leibenstein, Harvey, 41
'lemons', 45, 105
liability management, 133
loan stock, 151

marginal cost, 20, 58, 66
marginal revenue, 58, 66
market clearing, 16, 19
market-makers, 161, 184, 187–8, 207
mergers and takeovers, 62, 63, 66, 67–70, 73–6
merit and demerit goods, 46
Minimum Lending Rate, 144, 162

money, 106–9
  bank lending and supply of, 125–9
  defined, 107
  demand for, 118–21, 133
  market equilibrium, 121–2
  measures of, 108–9
  stocks and flows, 113, 124, 125–9
  supply of, 112–18
  targets and outturns, 124
monetary base, 117, 123
Monopolies and Mergers Commission, 76
monopoly, 57
  bilateral, 101
monopsony, 58

Non-tariff barriers to trade, 53, 71, 238–9

oligopoly, 57
open positions in foreign exchange, 207–8
opportunity cost, 8, 12, 28, 86
OPEC, 240–1

penetration pricing, 59
price adjusting markets, see flex price markets
price discrimination, 23
profits
  normal, 53–6, 72
  supernormal, 56, 58, 59, 74
property rights, 4, 6–7, 46–7
PSBR, 151–2, 155, 157
public goods, 4–5

quantity adjusting markets, see fix price markets
quotes and import licences, 238–9

regulation, 4, 7, 8
  of financial markets, 176, 185–7
  of labour markets, 101–2
  of product markets, 45–53, 73–6
reservation wage, 90, 104
resource allocation, 20–2

self-regulation of markets, 49–50
snob effects, 41, 42, 44
social costs and benefits, 5–6, 46–8
  in agriculture, 230–1
social taboos, 41, 42, 44
speculation
  in commodities markets, 247–9
  in foreign exchange markets, 207, 210, 212
'striking price', 163
subsidies, 48, 71, 73, 231–2
  on exports, 236–8
substitution effects, 87
supply of money, 112–18

tariffs, 71, 73, 81, 82
  fixed and variable, 234–6
technological change
  and the demand for labour, 82–5
term structure of interest rates, 158–60
time lags
  in foreign exchange markets, 197–8
  in commodities markets, 224–6
time yield curve, 158
trade unions, 79, 80, 81, 82–5, 98–101

unemployment, 77,
  frictional, 90
  involuntary, 104–5
  and labour market search, 90–1
  problems in measurement of, 94–5
  stocks and flows of, 95–6
  and technological change, 82–6
  voluntary, 89
unofficial economy, 93, 96

Veblen, Thorstein, 41–2
Veblen effects, 42
voluntary export restrictions, 239

wage differentials, 77
  and net advantages, 91–2, 97
  and non-competing groups, 92, 98
  in a quantity adjusting market, 104

X-inefficiency, 74